Anonymous

A Memorial of the American Patriots who Fell at the Battle of

Bunker Hill, June 17, 1775

Anonymous

A Memorial of the American Patriots who Fell at the Battle of Bunker Hill, June 17, 1775

ISBN/EAN: 9783337306557

Printed in Europe, USA, Canada, Australia, Japan

Cover: Foto ©ninafisch / pixelio.de

More available books at **www.hansebooks.com**

A MEMORIAL

OF THE

AMERICAN PATRIOTS

WHO FELL AT THE

BATTLE OF BUNKER HILL,

JUNE 17, 1775.

WITH AN ACCOUNT OF THE DEDICATION

OF THE

MEMORIAL TABLETS

ON WINTHROP SQUARE, CHARLESTOWN,

JUNE 17, 1889,

AND

AN APPENDIX CONTAINING ILLUSTRATIVE PAPERS.

FOURTH EDITION.

BOSTON:
PRINTED BY ORDER OF THE CITY COUNCIL.
1896.

CITY OF BOSTON.

IN COMMON COUNCIL, June 20, 1889.

Ordered, That the Joint Special Committee on the Bunker-Hill Tablets be authorized and directed to have prepared and distributed a Memorial volume to contain the proceedings at the dedication, together with such accompanying documents as they deem appropriate; the edition to consist of twenty-five hundred copies, and the expense to be charged to the appropriation for Printing.

Passed.
Sent up for concurrence, June 24, 1889.
Concurred in Board of Aldermen.
Approved by the Mayor, June 26, 1889.
A true copy.
              Attest: EDWIN U. CURTIS,
                                                                 City Clerk.

IN COMMON COUNCIL, Dec. 19, 1889.

Ordered, That the Superintendent of Printing be directed to have printed and published an edition of two thousand (2,000) copies of the Bunker-Hill Tablets Memorial Volume, with any suitable additions or corrections, the expense to be charged to the Contingent Fund of the Common Council; whereof twenty-five (25) copies shall be delivered to each member of the present Common Council.

Passed in Common Council, Dec. 19, 1889.
Approved by the Mayor, Dec. 24, 1889.
A true copy.
              Attest: JOSEPH O'KANE,
                                          Clerk of the Common Council.

IN COMMON COUNCIL, Jan. 16, 1890.

Ordered, That the Superintendent of Printing be directed to have printed and published an edition of 2,000 copies of the Bunker-Hill Tablets Memorial Volume, with any suitable additions or corrections, the expense to be charged to the Contingent Fund of the Common Council; and the City Messenger is directed to furnish 25 copies to each member of the Common Council.

Passed in Common Council, Jan. 16, 1890.
Approved by the Mayor, Jan. 18, 1890.
A true copy.
              Attest: JOSEPH O'KANE,
                                          Clerk of the Common Council.

IN COMMON COUNCIL, Dec. 19, 1895.

Ordered, That the City Registrar be hereby authorized to prepare and have printed an extra edition of one thousand copies of the Memorial to the American Patriots who fell at the Battle of Bunker Hill, with necessary additions, the said edition to be distributed by the City Registrar; the expense to be charged to the appropriation for Registry Department.

Passed. Sent up for concurrence. In Board of Aldermen, December 23, concurred. The foregoing order was presented to the Mayor Dec. 24, 1895, and was not returned by him within ten days thereafter.
              Attest: JOHN T. PRIEST,
                                          Assistant City Clerk.

CONTENTS.

	PAGE
PREFACE	5
ACTION OF THE CITY GOVERNMENT	14
DEDICATION OF THE BUNKER HILL TABLETS	17
Prayer by Rev. Philo W. Sprague	17
Ode by Dr. Thomas W. Parsons	20
Remarks by Mayor Thomas N. Hart	24
Oration by Hon. John R. Murphy	29
ANNIVERSARY SERMON BY REV. EDWARD M. TAYLOR	41

LIST OF APPENDICES: —

		PAGE
A.	Sketch of the Battle	73
B.	Americans killed at Bunker Hill	85
C.	English Opinion of Colonial Troops	139
D.	History of the Monument	166
E.	Webster Oration at Laying of Corner Stone, 1825	197
	Webster Oration on Completion of Monument, 1843	218
F.	Grandmother Story of Bunker Hill Battle	245
G.	Revolutionary Army Regulations	251

LIST OF ILLUSTRATIONS.

View of Tablets, looking North	Facing Title.
View of Tablets, looking South	11
Trumbull's View of Charlestown	39
Plan of Action, drawn by Lieut. Page	73
View of the Attack	81
Statue of Col. Prescott	84
Views of the Country round Boston, taken from Beacon Hill in 1775	88
View of Boston from Breed's Hill	102
Views of the Bronze Tablets erected by the City of Boston	127–134
Boston and Vicinity in 1775	139
View of the Monument as designed, from the Certificates of 1834	166
First stage of the Monument, 1830	174
Second stage, 1837	176
View of Monument as proposed, 1836	185
Whig Procession of 1840	186
Interior section of Monument	196
Plan of Foundation stones	217
Greenough's design for base of Monument	244
Manual of English Foot-Guards	252–259
Continental Manual, by Steuben	262

PREFACE.

It is a gratifying fact that in the six years following the first issue of this roll of patriots, so few errors or omissions have been discovered. The names of two officers and one private have been found to be entitled to places on the list, and the fate of a few of the prisoners captured by the British has been traced a little more distinctly. The evidence is hereto subjoined, or will be found on p. 123.

The two officers were Lieutenant Benjamin West of Salem, and Captain William Meacham, of New Salem. The private was John Meads, enlisted from Ashby in Capt. Abishai Brown's company, Nixon's regiment.

The Evidence.

In 1889 the venerable Caleb Foote of Salem, then aged some eighty-six years, called attention to the case of his grand-uncle, Capt. Benjamin West, as given in Felt's Annals of Salem in 1849; verified by family traditions heard by Mr. Foote in 1807: and corroborated by contemporaneous records. The full text of a communication to the City Council of Boston will be found in City Document No. 54, of 1890.

In our third edition, p. 87, the case of Lieut. West was given, and his name was added on the tablet printed on p. 133. Afterwards the name was repeated in its proper place among the officers, on the tablet given on p. 136. The difficulty of amending a bronze tablet made this the best course to adopt.

In the case of Capt. William Meacham, the evidence was most ample and of an official nature. It is found at the State House in Boston after the publication of the first edition of this book. The entries are:

"*Massachusetts Archives*, vol. 138, page 375.

"December ye 15th 1775 This may certify that I William Stacy & I William Smith & I Ben'n Haskall were well-knowing to the guns of Capt Wm Meacham and that of John Ganson, the sd Capt were killed the sd John were wounded in the action on Bunkers hill ye 17 of June last we therefore have Prized the sd Capt. gun at £3 00ˢ 00ᵈ the Bayonet and Belt at £0 09ˢ 08ᵈ and the sd Jno. gun at £2 14ˢ 00ᵈ the sd capt. gun was a compleat fuze [fuzee, probably], the other a New french Regular gun

"William Stacy   Maj'ʳ
"William Smith   Lt
"Benj'ⁿ Hascal   Sergt."

And again, in Mass. Rolls, vol. 15, p. 61, we find one entitled, "A muster-roll of the Company under the command of Captain John King in Colonel Woodbridge's Regiment to the first of August, 1775."

The first line is in substance as follows:

"William Meacham, town, New Salem; rank, Captain; killed June 17; time of enlistment, May ye 11th; travel, 90 miles; amount, 1ᵈ a mile 7/6; time of service, 1 month 9 days; whole amount, £8 05ˢ 11ᵈ 1ᵠ; guns 1, bayonet 1, himself lost June 17, and so on."

On receipt of these facts, by authority of the Mayor, these two names were inscribed upon the proper tablet in Charlestown. In April, 1895, E. S. Willcox, of Peoria, Ill., a great-grandson of Capt. Meacham, published an article in the New England

Historical and Genealogical Register, reciting these facts and adding some genealogical notes, together with the roll of Capt· Meacham's company, dated August 1, 1775. This article was reprinted in Boston City Document No. 147, of 1895.

The third addition, that of private John Meads of Ashby, is made pursuant to the following document, the original of which is owned by the well-known antiquary, Walter K. Watkins of Chelsea, Mass. :

"CAMP ATT WINTER HILL, Sep^t 17th 1775 them Receeed of Lt Silus Man of Capt Abishai Brown Companey the clotheing of John Meeds of Ashby and belonging to said Companey how Died the 17 of June Last to such and one Pare of Gray yarn Stoxings one tump line and snapsack Isa R^d P^r Mc

DAVID LOCKE"

Mr. Watkins also states that the roll of Capt. Abishai Brown's company, of Col. Nixon's regiment, dated 1 August, 1775 (Mass. Rev. Rolls, vol. 14, p. 24), gives the name of John Meads, enlisted from Ashby, 25 April, 1775, who served one month, twenty-six days. In the roll for 30 Sept., 1775 (Rolls, vol. 56, p. 24), of the same company, John Meads is marked deceased.

No doubt exists that his name belongs on the roll of glory, and it has been also added on the bronze tablet, and printed on p. 136.

It must be remembered that the object of these tablets and this memorial has been to furnish the names of those who were *killed or mortally wounded* at Bunker Hill. The credit of fighting there, and surviving, has been claimed for many soldiers, but the proofs are mainly traditional.

One piece of evidence of the highest value remains, in the list of those survivors who attended the laying of the corner stone of the Monument, June 17th, 1825. It is not a complete list of the combatants, but it is certain that these men were all in the battle.

It was printed in Boston City Document No. 147, of 1895, and is as follows:

THE SURVIVORS OF BUNKER HILL IN 1825.

The following list of officers and soldiers who were in the Battle of Bunker Hill, and who reported themselves to the acting quartermaster-general, June 17, 1825, on the occasion of laying the corner-stone of the Bunker Hill monument, is taken from the original rolls in the office of the adjutant-general. The rolls were made up in pursuance of the following resolve respecting Revolutionary soldiers, passed by the General Court, June 16, 1825:

"*Resolved*, That there be allowed and paid out of the treasury of the Commonwealth to such of the officers and soldiers who were in the Battle of Bunker Hill, on the 17th of June, A.D. 1775, and who may be present in the town of Charlestown or city of Boston on the approaching anniversary of that event, the sum of three dollars each, and also the sum of one dollar for every twenty miles of travel to or from said town or city.

"*Resolved*, That the acting quartermaster-general be directed to prepare a roll of all such officers and soldiers as may report themselves to him for the procession aforesaid, and that His Excellency the Governor with the advice of the Council be requested to draw his warrant on the treasury for the amount in favor of each person who may be on said roll."

A resolve, extending the time for the surviving officers and soldiers of the Battle of Bunker Hill to obtain the sum allowed them for their attendance at the celebration of that event on the 17th of June, 1825, was passed by the General Court, January 26, 1826.

These pay-rolls (three in number) were signed by each officer and soldier or his representative, giving the name and residence, miles from Boston, amount of travel, and total amount.

The rolls were first printed in the "Boston Journal," August 5, 1894. In the 1894 year book of the Massachusetts Society of the Sons of the American Revolution the names are classified by regiments.

ROLL No. 1.

Josiah Pierce	Buckland.
John Holden	Leicester.
Isaac Livermore	"

Obadiah Perry . . . . Westford.
Daniel Jackson . . . . Newton.
John Hart . . . . So. Reading.
Thomas Emerson . . . . "   "
Tilly Mead . . . . Barre.
Abel Parmenter . . . . Sudbury.
Amos Foster . . . . Tewksbury.
James Dalrymple . . . . Marlboro'.
James Frost . . . . Cambridge.
Isaac Goodenow . . . . Lincoln.
Samuel Lawrence . . . . Groton.
Holland Wood . . . . Walpole.
Jonathan Clark . . . . Abington.
John Pushee . . . . Westford.
Abraham Childs . . . . Groton.
Aaron Noyes . . . . Andover.
Neverson Hastings . . . . Brookfield.
Thomas Bixby . . . . Francistown, N.H.
William Campbell . . . . "   "
Jonah Howe . . . . Shrewsbury.
Job Spofford . . . . Berlin.
Nathan Johnson . . . . "
Joseph Greeley . . . . W. Nottingham, N.H.
Elijah Simmons . . . . Chaplin, Conn.
Jonas French . . . . Dunstable.
William French . . . . "
Elisha Parker . . . . Hopkinton.
David Parker . . . . Reading.
Daniel Nutting . . . . Westford.
Aaron Haynes . . . . Princeton.
Caleb Abbott . . . . Andover.
Elnathan Sawtell . . . . Groton.
Samuel Jones . . . . Sudbury.
John Brett . . . . Newburyport.
Samuel Bassett . . . . Keene, N.H.
Simeon Tyler . . . . Camden, Me.
Theodore Gridley . . . . Paris, N.Y.
Ebenezer Peabody . . . . Boxford.
Nathaniel Rice . . . . E. Sudbury.
William Davis . . . . Haverhill.
Sampson Wood . . . . Groton.
John Hoppin . . . . Templeton.

Moses Blood . . . . Pepperell.
Moses Richardson . . . . Concord.
Samuel Wheeler . . . . "
Daniel Lake . . . . Rindge, N.H.
John Goodridge . . . . Leominster.
Stephen Emory . . . . Winchendon.
Enos Lake . . . . Rindge, N.H.
Abram Hagar . . . . Princeton.
Jonathan Stevens . . . . Andover.
Isaac Wright . . . . Dunstable.
Nehemiah Wright . . . . Nelson, N.H.
Moses Bennett . . . . New Gloucester, Me.
John Barker . . . . Andover.
Russell Dewey . . . . Westfield.
Josiah Seward . . . . Sullivan, N.H.
Samuel Seward . . . . " "
Ivory Hovey . . . . Boxford.
Ephraim Robbins . . . . Lancaster.
Henry Gates . . . . Hubbardstown.
William Cary . . . . Oxford.
Ezekiel Wardwell . . . . Andover.
Abraham Perkins . . . . Ipswich.
William Low . . . . Gloucester.
John Burnham . . . . Londonderry, N.H.
John Coolidge . . . . Natick.
John Cook . . . . Newburyport.
Benjamin Gould . . . . "
Joshua Yeomans . . . . Norwich, Conn.
Daniel Somerby . . . . Newburyport.
Isaac H. Ely . . . . Charlestown, N.H.
Enos Reynolds . . . . Boxford.
William Warren . . . . Worcester.
Jesse Smith . . . . Salem.
William Marden . . . . Portsmouth, N.H.

Roll No. 2.

Daniel Ingersoll . . . . Keene, N.H.
Nathaniel Thwing . . . . Brookfield.
Daniel Brown . . . . Moultonboro', N.H.
Isaac Andrews . . . . Hillsboro', N.H.
Solomon Twist . . . . Boston.

VIEW OF MEMORIAL TABLETS FROM ADAMS STREET, LOOKING SOUTH.

Richard Gilchrist	Dublin, N.H.
Josiah Cleveland	Oswego, N.Y.
John Ware	Deerfield.
James Clark	Lebanon, Conn.
John Wright	Billerica.
Timothy Gordon	Newbury.
Francis Mitchell	New Ipswich, N.H.
Samuel R. Trevett	Boston.
William Harris	Marblehead.
Henry Hanson	"
Elias Bacon	Boston.
Nehemiah Abbott	Lincoln.
Samuel Ivers	Boston.
Joseph Dane	Andover.
Jeduthan Wellington	W. Cambridge.
Benjamin Webber	Gloucester.
John Stevens	Greenwich.
Uriah Wright	Beverly.
Azariah Dickinson	Boston.
Jacob Frost	Norway, Me.
Benjamin Butman	Dixmont, Me.
Benjamin Bullard	Hopkinton.
Joseph Powars	Charlestown.
Nathan Maynard	Jaffrey, N.H.
George Leach	Salem.
Joshua Danforth	Saugus.
William Thorning	Lexington.
Ebenezer Parker	South Reading.
Nathan Fisher	Westboro'.
Nathaniel Wade	Ipswich.
Joseph Hodgkins	"
Jabez Farley	"
Elias Pike	Salisbury.
Philip Bagley	Newburyport.
Amos Pearson	"
Jonathan Woodman	"
Lemuel Coffin	"
Abijah Wool	Westminster.
Jonas Pierce	Hopkinton.
Edmund Rice	E. Sudbury.
Robert Steel	Dedham.
Enoch Baldwin	Milton.

PREFACE.

Baruch Leland	Sherburn.
William Clark	"
Abijah Fox	Dracut.
James Varnum	"
Joseph Nichols	Grafton.
Henry Flint	Carlisle.
Simon Wardwell	Andover.
Stephen Long	"
David Brewer	Framingham.
Isaac Smith	Holliston.
Theophilus Frye	Andover.
Nathan Craig	Spencer.
Thomas Sprague	"
Benjamin Mann	Troy, N.Y.
John Trowbridge	Framingham.

ROLL NO. 3.

Ephraim Squires	Ashford, Conn.
Simeon Noyes	Salem.
Edward Harrington	Concord.
Moses Greenwood	Hopkinton.
Josiah Haskell	Boston.
Samuel Temple	Acton.
Aaron Merrill	Hampton Falls, N.H.
John Towne	Boxford.
Jacob B. Currier	Amesbury.
Joseph Trask	Billerica.
John Tucker	Gloucester.
Leonard Parks	Cambridgeport.
Richard Loring	Newburyport.
Jonathan Weston	So. Reading.
Gershom Hyde	Newton.
Amos Farnsworth	Groton.
Hezekiah Thorndike	Chelmsford.
Joseph Boutelle	Reading.
Benjamin Farnum	Andover.
Jonas Varnum	Dracut.
Jonathan Minot	Westminster.
Caleb Barton	Leicester.
Benjamin Butterfield	Chelmsford.
Onesimus Newell	New Ipswich, N.H.
Solomon Smith	Acton.

PREFACE. 13

Thomas Thorp . . . . Acton.
Francis Davidson . . . . Londonderry, N.H.
William Dickson . . . . Charlestown.
Thaddeus Munroe . . . . Hillsboro', N.H.
Jonathan Wheelock . . . . Concord.
Zibeon Hooker . . . . Newton.
Caleb Stark . . . . Dunbarton, N.H.
Calvin Stevens . . . . Mt. Vernon, N.H.
Jonathan Maynard . . . . Framingham.
Thomas Davis . . . . Holden.
Jonathan Beard . . . . Harvard.
John Edmons . . . . Malden.
Reuben Baker . . . . Lunenburg.
Jacob Peirce . . . . Jaffrey, N.H.

The variations in this edition from previous ones are, the Preface, pp. 5-13, and on pages 96, 101, 113, 123, 133, 136.

Four of the heliotype views have been taken anew, as the tablets have been altered since they were first erected.

WILLIAM H. WHITMORE.

BOSTON, January, 1896.

BUNKER-HILL TABLETS.

In the year 1888 the suggestion was made that tablets be provided, giving a list of the soldiers who fell at the battle of Bunker Hill, and the following order was introduced in the Common Council, March 29, by Mr. KEENAN, of Ward 8, and unanimously adopted: —

Ordered, That the Joint Special Committee on the Seventeenth of June Celebration consider the expediency of providing suitable tablets, to be placed on Bunker Hill Monument, said tablets to bear the names of the American patriots who fell in the battle of June 17, 1775, and that said committee be requested to report at the next meeting of the Common Council.

The committee, however, failed to make a report upon the subject, although at a subsequent meeting of the Common Council Mr. REILLY, a member of the committee, stated that they had made inquiries in regard to the matter, and had learned that an incomplete but reliable list could be obtained at the State House. Nothing further was done, as the committee were unable to procure the lists before the close of the year.

On the 24th of January, 1889, the subject was revived by Mr. KEENAN, of Ward 8, who submitted another order regarding the matter, as follows: —

Ordered, That a special committee of five members of the Common Council, with such as the Board of Aldermen may join, be appointed to arrange and prepare four bronze tablets to bear the names of the American patriots killed or fatally injured at Bunker Hill, June 17, 1775; said tablets to embrace the requisite list of names now in the hands of the Record Commissioners, with such other names that belong in the list; said tablets to be completed in season for erection on the occasion of the coming celebration of the anniversary of the battle of Bunker Hill, June 17, 1889; said tablets to be placed in such position as the committee may determine in connection with the site of the battle, and the expense of the tablets to be charged to the appropriation for Incidentals for the fiscal year of 1889 and 1890.

The order was discussed somewhat in the two branches, but was passed unanimously and approved by His Honor the Mayor, February 6, and the committee was constituted as follows: —

Aldermen: BENJAMIN F. STACEY, ALBERT A. FOLSOM, HOMER ROGERS; Councilmen, THOMAS F. KEENAN, WILLIAM H. OAKES, FRANK E. BAGLEY, ISRAEL F. PIERCE, and WILLIAM J. DOHERTY.

The committee lost no time in entering upon the work assigned them, and in their labors they were ably assisted by WILLIAM H. WHITMORE, Chairman of the Board of Record Commissioners, and an antiquarian of established reputation. The work performed by the committee, and the difficulties encountered by them, are fully set forth in their reports to the City Council, which are printed as city documents,[1] and are incorporated in the appendix to this volume. It is, therefore, only necessary to state that the

---

[1] City Documents of 1889, Nos. 73 and 111.

lists were completed as satisfactorily as possible, and the contract for casting the bronze tablets that should contain the names was awarded to C. T. ROBINSON & Co., of this city.

As objections were made to locating the tablets upon the Monument grounds it was decided to place them upon Winthrop square, a small plot of ground belonging to the city, adjacent to the Monument grounds, and formerly known as the "Training Field," and arrangements were made accordingly. A design for mounting the tablets was prepared by CHARLES J. BATEMAN, City Architect, and a position assigned for them, and a new entrance made at the northwest corner of the square. The arrangements for the dedication, which was to take place June 17, having been completed, invitations to attend the exercises were issued to His Honor the Mayor and the members of the City Council, His Excellency the Governor and staff; also to the governors of New Hampshire and Connecticut, the committee securing the services of Hon. JOHN R. MURPHY as orator and Dr. THOMAS W. PARSONS as poet upon the occasion.

DEDICATION OF THE BUNKER-HILL TABLETS.

The 17th of June dawned unpropitiously for the celebration of the day; the elements were threatening and the skies lowering and forbidding. At 9 o'clock A.M., the hour fixed for the dedicatory exercises, the committee and a goodly number of invited guests assembled at Winthrop square. A stand had been provided for those who were to participate in the ceremonies, and was well filled with an interested group of spectators, composed chiefly of city officials. The Germania Band, stationed near the fountain in the centre of the square, enlivened the occasion, at appropriate intervals, with patriotic airs, and around the square were collected a large number of people to witness the ceremonies of the dedication.

As the hour arrived His Honor Mayor HART arose and invited the attention of the audience while prayer was offered by Rev. PHILO W. SPRAGUE, of St. John's Episcopal Church, as follows: —

PRAYER.

Our Father who art in heaven; hallowed be Thy name. Thy kingdom come. Thy will be done on earth, as it is in heaven. Give us this day our daily bread. And forgive us our trespasses as we forgive those who trespass against us. And lead us not into temptation; but deliver us from evil: For Thine is the kingdom, and the power, and the glory, for ever and ever. Amen.

Heavenly Father, we come into Thy presence with grateful hearts this day. We would acknowledge Thee as the giver of every good and perfect gift. We bless Thee. We praise and magnify Thy glorious name.

We thank Thee for all Thy mercies to us as a nation. Thy hand has been over us from the first even unto this day. Our fathers believed in Thee and were holpen. They trusted in Thee and were not ashamed.

We recognize Thee, our Heavenly Father, as the source of all that is highest and noblest in us. The desire for liberty and for light, the love of truth and of righteousness come to us from Thee. We have them because we are Thy children.

We thank Thee for the good example of those whom we commemorate to-day. They were strong and brave because Thou didst enable them. When men are heroes, when they give their lives, as these men did, for freedom and for righteousness,—it is of Thee; and the glory of what they did is Thine.

Heavenly Father, we pray Thee to be with us as Thou hast been with those who have been before us. Bless this nation in the future as Thou hast blessed her in the past. Bless this city and this Commonwealth. Give us the love of truth and righteousness. Help us to reverence Thy laws. Help us to accomplish Thy purposes for us as a nation. Bless the homes throughout this land. Adorn them with purity, with sobriety, and goodness. Bless our schools and churches, and every instrumentality that labors for the common good. Give to us all a love for this land Thou hast so signally blessed. Fill us with true patriotism, banishing from our hearts all sectional spirit; and may all citizens of this land, from whatever part of the world they may come, whatever their color or their creed, unite in love and devotion to their fatherland.

Bless, we beseech Thee, the work in which we are now engaged. May the memorials of the fathers excite the emulation of the children. As we think of the brave deeds done by the men of whom we think to-day, may it lead us to be brave and true in whatsoever work Thou shalt give us to do. Let no thought of the past be in vain, but may it stimulate us to nobler action and to higher life.

Direct us, O Lord, we beseech Thee, in all our doings with Thy most gracious favor, and further us with Thy continual help, that in all our works begun, continued, and ended in Thee, we may glorify Thy holy name, and finally by Thy mercy obtain everlasting life, through Jesus Christ our Lord. Amen.

At the close of the prayer the Mayor introduced Master JOHN S. KEATING, who read in a creditable manner the following ode, composed for the occasion by Dr. THOMAS W. PARSONS.

ODE FOR THE DEDICATION OF THE BUNKER-HILL TABLETS.

I.

Under the golden dome where laws are made,
The stones yet stand that once around the base
Rose, of the ancient column in that place;
    And on those graven tablets is displayed
    A record of the mighty train
      Of great events that, following fast
Through seven long years of watchings and fears,
    Throes, and unutterable strain,
    In God's ripe season led at last
Our land to glory through that vale of tears.

II.

    And this, moreover, the stones have said:
While from this eminence you survey
    Scenes of luxury, gardens of wealth,
    Homes of laborious industry and health,
Tilth and orchard, uplands, plain,
And clovered meadows reaching far away,
With halls of learning hid in elmy bowers
    Your supereminent domain!
Whate'er of republics may have been
Spoken aforetime, the imputed sin
Of thanklessness must not be ours.

III.

From the golden dome where laws are made
There went a mandate forth:
On yonder hallowed mount to the north

Let the best men in building skilled
A tower of rocks to the high heavens build,
To stand at once a monument and shrine,
A pillar, in everlasting sign,
Like that which Hercules of yore
Set on the Gaditanian shore,
Crying to tyrants, Come no more!
And the fire in the cresset that flamed of old,
Beaconing the mariners up Boston bay,
Shall burn forever from this new tower,
Like a ruling star of benignant ray
    For every people to behold, —
A watch-fire in the purpled west,
Steadfast and strong for all the oppressed
    To fly to from tyrannic power.

IV.

  New England's air was never tainted long
With any tyranny; the prairie-winds
Breathed from the illimitable West
Into those English hearts and minds
    A new-born sense of space that made more strong
A vigour chafed for centuries by the sea,
And for high ventures nerved each daring breast.
    Our Fathers always had been free.
  Those men who Freedom's battle fought,
    Holding all kings but One in scorn,
  Though with a mighty price they bought
    Your freedom, were free born;
And Carolina's and Virginia's blood
Tempered to like disdain of shackled thought,
Beat with one pulse, when Liberty's glad morn
Alike to North and South broke o'er the Atlantic flood.

V.

Why should the Muse on dreadful details dwell,
   To make a calendar of her lyre?
Is it a story of no renown —
The redoubt, the frigates, the blazing town,
   Fronting the Falcon's fire;
How the regulars rushed and the yeomen fell,
Butts and bayonets plying as well;
   Rolled and trod in the crimson mire
Of the dust and blood beneath?
   Close quarters then! for a captain cries, —
As the troops marched up, — " Let them come nigher!
Hold till you mark the whites of their eyes,
And the gleam of their British teeth."
   Ah! many felt, as the bullets flew,
   We fight for Englishmen in fighting you.

VI.

On from that dread to this triumphal June,
And now while natures are all in tune,
That children hereafter may come to spell
Prescott and Warren and all who fell,
Hard by on that bitter afternoon,
Bearing on History's page so proud a part,
We hang these bronzes on our country's heart.
   Not for the splendour of the fight,
   Not for the number of the slain,
   Not for the day's defeat and flight,
   But for the final crowning of the right,
   And mankind's measureless gain.
   This other commonwealth of kings,
   Born here on Bunker's height,
     Have fluttered their flag of stars,
   Like a labarum of light,

Beyond the Tiber, by Peter's throne,
  Beyond the hill of Mars,
As those elder freemen, through every zone
Carried their eagles on outspread wings,
  And blazoned S. P. Q. Rs.

VII.

Say then, O poet! when sages
  Shall anew the tale relate,
Not for a thousand ages
  Was a little battle so great;
Yea, write, besides, on your pages,
  With an adamantine pen,
Not for a million ages
  May such battle be fought again.

VIII.

Remembering what our statesman said,
"*That the blood of your fathers may not have been shed
  For humankind in vain,*"[1]
Up with your tablets to grace the dead!
And while you hang them, let great London hear
  Little Boston's exultations,
  Let all nations far and near;
  Let sacred Italy and Spain,
  Norway, Denmark, and the men
  We love in Germany and France
  Rejoice at this day's doings. Then
  "*Advance, ye future generations,*"[1]
  And lead the world's advance!

---

[1] Words of Webster.

At the close of the reading of the poem, Mayor HART read a letter from His Excellency Governor AMES, regretting his inability to be present on account of sickness, and he then delivered the following address: —

REMARKS OF MAYOR THOMAS N. HART.

FELLOW-CITIZENS: — We are met to dedicate and consecrate the tablets commemorating the names of the patriots who fought and fell that we might be a great nation. This is filial and right. It proves once more that cities and republics are not ungrateful, and that we know how to honor the plain yeoman, as well as the captain and commander. But more important and far nobler than to dedicate bronze tablets is it to dedicate and consecrate ourselves and all that we have and hope to the cause for which the patriots contended. I hold the 19th day of April, 1775, to be the true birthday of this nation. The Battle of Bunker Hill, fought less than sixty days after Lexington, showed that the infant nation had a sturdy being of its own, which even the mother from whom we sprung was bound to recognize and to respect. The patriots were defeated at Bunker Hill, the first great battle of our Revolution; but the defeat proved only that a child is not in all respects as strong as is a full-grown man. In a few years the child attained manhood. The bloody battle of Bunker Hill convinced America, Great Britain, and all the world that we had ceased forever to be a colony and dependent. In 1775 we had no national flag or national constitution; but we had that which is greater, — a nation with all the attributes of independence and true sovereignty. At Lexington we proclaimed with joy that a new nation was born; on Bunker Hill we declared, convincingly and from deep conviction, that the new-born nation was not disposed to succumb to the power of another. We have now the oldest flag and the oldest written constitution of all the great nations. The child has become a man. And may we be as strong in purity and justice, in the reign of equality and true righteousness, as we are in material magnitude.

Mayor HART then introduced the orator of the occasion, Hon. JOHN R. MURPHY, of Charlestown. His address was a fine effort, fully in accord with the spirit and sentiment of the occasion, and it was heartily approved and applauded by the audience.

ORATION
BY
HON. JOHN R MURPHY.

THE ORATION.

We are assembled here to dedicate a memorial, in the form of bronze tablets, inscribed with the names of one hundred and forty men who died in defence of liberty and human rights at the battle of Bunker Hill, June 17, 1775. To-day, the one hundred and fourteenth anniversary of that battle, is a fit and appropriate day for such a ceremony. It is never too late to repair an oversight, or to pay a debt of honor. These tablets are erected by the city of Boston to perpetuate the memory of the common soldiers, as well as that of the leaders, who fought and died in that famous fight. It is a tribute from a representative government of the people to the men of the people. The ground where the tablets are placed is appropriate. Above us, on yonder eminence, stands the Bunker Hill monument, commemorative of the battle, a plain, granite shaft, yet how grand and majestic in its simplicity! The eloquence of Webster, that illustrious son of New England, was at its foundation and completion. It speaks in silent eloquence of the patriots who fought and the brave men who died on that eventful day in June, 1775. Upon the slope of Bunker Hill you place the tablets in the old training field, where the citizens of years gone by were trained in the use of arms under the shadow of yonder modern soldiers' monument, which a grateful municipality erected to perpetuate the patriotism of the soldiers of the war of the rebellion. What more fitting spot than this? You honor here in bronze the men who died in giving birth to our nation, who helped to light the torch of liberty's fires. In the granite of our old New England hills yonder you perpetuate the fame of the worthy successor of the soldier of the Revolution, the soldier of the rebellion, who died to keep the Union whole and preserve for his children the heritage of freedom which came to him pure and unsullied from his revolutionary sires. Tributes of honor to the first and the last American soldier down to our day can find no more fitting ground than this to rest upon.

It has been left for our country to recognize and respect the individual citizen and the individual soldier. We are a government of the people, and a man who makes a sacrifice for his fatherland, be he never so lowly, his name should be forever written in the history of the nation. In the lands beyond the seas, where kings and emperors rule by so-called right divine, when men die in battle, their bones lie buried in a common trench, and over their nameless grave is raised perhaps a common monument. The officers and men of birth alone are known by name to posterity. In our free land they honor every man who dies for fatherland; on the roll of fame you'll find his name, be he rich or poor, black or white. In our national cemeteries, " fame's eternal camping-ground," lie the nation's dead of the war of the rebellion, not nameless and unknown, but marshalled rank on rank, and file on file, as once they proudly stood on parade. Underneath the green sod every man still keeps his recognized place, and there he will remain forever, each man's name chiselled in stone upon his grave, that future generations may know that he died for his country. It has been said, "It is sweet to die for one's country." It is sweeter still to die, and to know that, if we die, a grateful people treasures our name and fame, and that we are not forgotten. The memories of our soldiers are the nation's heritage, to be kept forever fresh and green, to be forgotten only when this government of the people perishes from off the earth.

Honor has been given in the past to the leaders who died at Bunker Hill; their names and fame are perpetuated. To-day we give to the world, on tablets of everlasting bronze, the names of the men who stood in the ranks, who fought valiantly, and died nobly,— the common soldiers, who gave all that man could give (their lives) to plant the seed that gave free government of the people. It is appropriate that Boston should raise these tablets, for then, as now, she was ever foremost in championing the rights of man. Well has it been sung —

> "Boston, as long as she shall stand,
> As long as her tides shall rise and fall,
> Shall sit on her ancient throne,
> And plead for the rights of all."

Her citizens were leaders in all popular movements against the aggression of the British government. In Faneuil Hall were heard the voices of her sons demanding justice for the people. On our streets oecurred the Boston massacre, the first blood shed for liberty. In our harbor the tea was thrown overboard, an act which set at defiance the British crown. From the steeple of our Old North Church was hung the light that caused the firing of the shot at Lexington "heard around the world." From the roofs and hills of our city, on that morn in June when the British marched up the hill to the attack, the wives and daughters of Boston were anxious watchers, and they prayed for victory for their countrymen. Almost every act of opposition to the crown, — every step taken toward liberty, — saw its beginning in this town and neighborhood. As we were the principal aggressors, so were we the ones to receive the first attacks of the crown. The port of Boston was closed, and by every possible means the crown sought to coerce our city, but without avail. The English government of that day likened the agitation to a snake, each part representing a section of the country. Boston was the head. Crush that, and you stamp out the agitation forever. Without Boston there would have been no Bunker Hill, and without Bunker Hill the torch of liberty would not have burned so brightly on our shores. There was no necessity to have fought the battle of Bunker Hill. With the whole country behind them, the Americans could have easily spared the hill to the British. It was more a desire to test the comparative fighting capacity of the American and British soldiers that led to the contest than any immediate material gain that was to be obtained by either side. The Americans burned with an ardent desire to meet their enemy in open field, while the English, confident of their superiority, were equally anxious to wipe out the disgrace of Lexington, and crush at one blow the rebellion. At that time an idea prevailed among Englishmen that the American, as a race, had run to seed, had deteriorated from the high standard of the people whence he sprung. Lexington, they said, was but a skirmish, where their troops were shot down from ambush behind fences and trees. Let but the Americans meet them in battle, and another story would have to be told. We can form an idea of the estimate in which we were held from the statement of the English colonel who said that he would march from one end of the country to the other with only one regiment. They forgot the fact that the American colonies were practically a nursery for soldiers from the earliest settlement, in 1620, down to the days almost of the Revolution.

In 1645 the colonists fought the Narragansett Indians; in 1675 the second generation fought the bloodiest of wars with the Indians under King Philip. Ten years later the Indians of Maine were fought, and the colonists dared to depose Governor Andros and array themselves in arms against England. Later on they conquered Port Royal, attempted the capture of Canada, and in 1745, five thousand Provincials under Pepperell captured Louisburg, the Gibraltar of America, spreading the fame of their arms throughout Europe. Up to within twelve years before the breaking out of the Revolution the colonists were continually engaged in war with the French and Indians, the rifle and the powderhorn their daily companions. If the English had paused to think, they would have realized that they were to meet men, many of whom had been trained for war by practical experience in war, officered by veterans of many a hard-fought field.

I shall not tell the story of the battle of Bunker Hill. It is written in the hearts of all true and loyal Americans. We know that the Americans occupied the heights of Bunker Hill the night before the battle, and that the English came over the river from Boston and sought to dislodge them. After a bloody conflict, lasting one and one-half hours, the powder of the Americans being exhausted, they retreated in good order, and left the hill in the hands of the English. It is in our hands now,— a fact that speaks for itself. The Americans lost in killed 140, and in wounded 271, captured 30,— in all, 441. The English loss was 226 killed, 828 wounded,— total, 1,054. The result was a victory in every sense of the word for the Americans, and was so considered by the British, as shown in General Burgoyne's letters to the English government. This was the General Burgoyne who afterward surrendered to General Gates, at Saratoga. The importance of the battle can hardly be realized. It gave renewed confidence to the revolutionists. The steadiness and bravery shown by them when opposed to the veteran troops of England, was a cause of pride and joy to the whole country. It fired the hearts of all with patriotism. Before the battle there might have been some chance for a peaceful settlement of the existing difficulties, but after the battle the voice of all was for war, and a government independent of England. The battle of Bunker Hill was the beginning of the end of English domination on our western hemisphere. An example was set the world. The desire for liberty spread from the example set on our shores. On this side of the ocean, the Spanish colonies of Mexico, Central America, and of South America, one after the other, revolted and threw off their allegiance to monarchy, and established the republican form of government, until in the New World, with the exception of Brazil, a few islands, and our northern neighbor, Canada, the people, instead of being subjects of a monarchy, governed everywhere. The flame of liberty spread beyond the seas to France, and all over Europe. There was not a country where liberal concessions were not made to the people, and where the power of the ruling kings was not curtailed. The human race was the gainer to an extent inestimable, by the battle of Bunker Hill and the events that went to make up the American Revolution.

One hundred and fourteen years ago occurred the battle the memory of which we here revere. It is within the memory of many here assembled when men who fought at Bunker Hill walked and lived among us. In the countries governed by monarchies for a hundred years, that length of time speaks for very little; but in our land what a picture of progress do we behold under the free government which Bunker Hill and the Revolution gave to us! At the end of the Revolution, when England acknowledged our independence, we had thirteen colonies, weak and frail, stretching a narrow fringe of land along the Atlantic seaboard, with a population of less than three millions, — a farming community with little or no commerce or manufacturing. To-day our number consists of forty-two sovereign States, continental in extent, bounded only by the Atlantic ocean and the Pacific ocean on the east and west, and stretching on the north from the Great Lakes to the Gulf of Mexico and the Rio Grande on the south. The land that in the days of our fathers was a trackless wilderness, peopled only by savage men, now in our time, from end to end, is covered with populous cities, and everywhere the busy hum of the advancing march of man. Three millions have grown to nigh on to seventy millions of people. We have the richest, the safest, the most progressive, and the freest land on the earth. On our domain the sun never ceases to shine. We have fought great wars and conquered. We have indulged in the greatest of intestinal quarrels, when the North was arraigned against the South, brother against brother, in the war of the rebellion. By its result the one blot on the flag of our country was effaced. Slavery of the black man was abolished forever. In peace we have had our victory, as well as in war. The world has never seen such magnanimity as was shown by the victor to the vanquished, when the North welcomed back their erring brothers of the South, when the war of the rebellion was at an end. It takes a great and noble people, and a free and grand system of government, to heal the breach made by a fratricidal strife, so as to present, in less than one generation, the picture our land makes to-day, with her free government and institutions stronger than ever; peace, loyalty, contentment, and prosperity from one end of the land to the other. "Our country, our whole country, and nothing but our country," is the watchword of all her citizens, black or white, be they from the North, the South, the East, or the West.

> "Chief of our own blest land
> To whom turned long oppressed mankind,
> A sacred refuge here to find.
> Of every race the pride and boast,
> From wild Atlantic's stormy coast
> To far Pacific's strand.
> Millions on millions here maintain
> Your generous aims with steady will,
> And make our vast imperial reign
> The world's asylum still."

The world's asylum we are for those who hate oppression and love liberty. On these bronze tablets of Bunker Hill heroes we find the names of men of all nationalities; but they were none the less Americans. Then, as now, the people were originally from many lands. At Bunker Hill fought and died the Saxon from England, the Celt from Ireland and from Scotland, and the black man from Africa. They responded promptly in the hour of the country's peril, forgetful of all else but the freedom and the wrongs of the land of their adoption. What truer American can there be than the man who, although his eyes may have first seen the light upon a foreign shore, under an alien flag, yet closes his eyes in death upon the battle-field in defence of American institutions, and in helping to perpetuate the freedom of his adopted country.

Our fathers, after the successful terminus of the revolutionary war, founded a government based on the equality of man, — a government of the people, for the people, and by the people. The oppressed of all climes were invited to come to free America, and here make a home. They came, and the nation has been the gainer. Ours is to-day a wonderful land, and in the future it promises to be still more wonderful. Seventy millions of people, composed of different races and creeds, are here living harmoniously, working out the future destiny of a future homogeneous nation, such as has never been seen since the world first began. The lines that in the past have divided men of different races and creeds are disappearing, and to-day a man stands for what he really is as a man; in his own keeping lies his future and his destiny. No longer class prejudice prevents patriotism and genius from coming to the front. The questions to be asked are: "Is he honest?" "Is he capable?" "Is he true?" The possession of these qualities is the test of true Americanism. The past half-century has seen wonderful progress in the amalgamation of races here on our shores. Yet the future will be still more wondrous. Their past in other lands is but a memory: the future is here, where their homes are, where they live and their children are to live after them. The day is not far distant when, like the sectional feeling which formerly existed here, the small remnants of those Old World prejudices of race and creed which we find, will be banished, like disease, and Americanism, founded on individual worth, love of country, and pure patriotism, shall reign from one end of our free land to the other.

VIEW OF CHARLESTOWN IN 1775. BY TRUMBULL.

ANNIVERSARY SERMON
BY
REV. EDWARD M. TAYLOR.

PREFATORY NOTE.

The celebration of the Seventeenth of June, 1889, was begun in reality on Sunday, the 16th. The members of Trinity Methodist Episcopal Church, on High street, Charlestown, of which Rev. E. M. Taylor was pastor, decided to hold commemorative services. The committee in charge of the affair were Messrs. B. F. Hatch, G. H. Stetson, and G. H. Gammans, of the church, and Maj. W. H. Oakes, of the congregation. Invitations were sent to the Mayor and the City Council of Boston; A. Lincoln Post, No. 11, and G. L. Stearns Post, No. 149, G.A.R., and the Ladies' Relief Corps of both posts; the Union Veterans' Union; the U.S. Marine Corps; the Sons of Veterans' Corps; the High School Cadets of Charlestown; and the officers of the Bunker Hill Seventeenth of June Association. The Charlestown Cadets, the Charlestown City Guards, and the Charlestown Artillery represented the military of the State. These guests, with citizens, filled the spacious church, which was appropriately decorated with bunting and plants.

The services were commenced at 10.30 o'clock, A.M. The organ prelude, played by J. D. Jones, was Raff's march, "Leonora." The solo and chorus of Keller's "American Hymn" was effectively rendered. Miss Lizzie S. Fox sang Tours' "Gate of Heaven," a violin obligatory by Frank O. Mason adding to its beauty and power. The pastor's prayer was a fervent and impressive one, and was followed by the anthem "To Thee, O Country," by Eichberg.

The eloquent sermon which followed is given in full in this volume.

The chorus "Triumphal March," by Costa, followed the address. The congregation united in singing "America," and the exercises closed with the benediction.

The excellent arrangements of the committee were thoroughly executed, and this unique service was universally recognized as a fitting prelude to the public exercises on the following day. Charlestown has for years given much time and care to the proper celebration of this anniversary. but none has been more appropriate than this, nor more fully appreciated by the citizens.

ANNIVERSARY SERMON,

PREACHED JUNE 16, 1889,

IN THE TRINITY METHODIST EPISCOPAL CHURCH,

ON HIGH STREET, CHARLESTOWN.

BY

REV. EDWARD M. TAYLOR.

"Then Samuel took a stone, and set it between Mizpeh and Shen, and called the name of it Ebenezer, saying, Hitherto hath the Lord helped us."—1 Sam. vii. 12.

Universal humanity loves to commemorate the great crises in its history. Every nation has its holidays, every religion its festal days.

The very pages of secular and religious history owe their existence to this fact, that man will not permit the great doings of the past to be swept into oblivion by the tides of time.

National birthdays are celebrated by orations and patriotic pageants. No inspiration guides the eye of the sculptor like that which puts in marble form the hero of some great cause.

No colors are mixed in such lasting hues as those of the artist's soul when commissioned to put upon the canvas some great historic scene where God and man have met to arbitrate in the crisis scenes of the race.

Few traits of human nature are more beautiful than that sentiment of gratitude and thanksgiving that accompanies the intellectual appreciation of great historic events, where the men of the past have measured up to duty, and left, as the results of their courage and sacrifice, choice blessings for posterity; turning-points in history are always places for profound meditation.

In our text we have our attention called to one of these memorable scenes.

The children of Israel had won, by valor in arms, a great victory over the Philistines, and Samuel, wishing to manifest his thanksgiving and transmit the fact to posterity, celebrates the occasion by raising a stone monument on the plains of Mizpeh, and carving thereon the devout acknowledgment of the text, "Hitherto hath the Lord helped us." Let us take these words as the suggestive basis of a few thoughts appropriate to the occasion of our gathering together this morning.

What is the significance of this hour? What has called this vast audience together this morning in this sacred edifice? What sentiment is it that places me before these civic and military representatives of this great municipality? One hundred and fourteen years ago to-morrow the yeomanry of New England gathered on this hill to measure swords with the soldiers of the greatest military power then on earth. Here was opened the contest between British tyranny and American liberty. Within the sound of my voice, twelve decades ago, American patriotism knew not the fear of death, when "bonds were to be broken and liberty won."

To one who is a novice in American affairs there is a tinge of absurdity when they view our Bunker Hill monument lifting its graceful form in commemoration of a battle that was a victory for English tyranny, and a defeat to American patriots.

I remember sailing up Boston harbor, a few years ago, with an English tourist, whose attention was called to the granite shaft on Bunker Hill as it was catching the last rays of the setting sun.

He quickly replied in these words, "To an Englishman it appears as a gross inconsistency, that Americans should erect a monument commemorative of an English victory and a Yankee defeat. As I read history," said he, "General Gage drove Colonel Prescott from his intrenchments and took possession of the hill."—"Yes," said a genuine Yankee, in reply; "that is true, but I have read that in ancient Germany, when two farmers wished to fix the line that divided their farms, each took his eldest son and led him to the dividing line, and there gave him a severe flogging, in order to impress upon the mind of each boy the position in which they stood when they received the chastisement; that ever afterward they would remember the dividing line." So we remember Bunker Hill as the spot on which we were whipped in battle; but that marks forever the line where British tyranny ended and American liberty began.

Even in the sense of a mere dividing line, we are on ground made classic by the struggle for American liberty. This spot is rich in those sentiments that stir the patriotic heart. Here American patriotism lighted the torch of liberty, and carried forward that light, through scenes of conflict and discouragement, till its rays touch every face in a Republic numbering more than sixty million human beings. We are on an eminence whose heroic memories focus the light of freedom. The celebration in which we are to engage to-morrow is not a wild burst of ignorant fanaticism. It is a memorial of the patriotism of our fathers. The event here chronicled vitally affects our personal fortunes as a nation, and is the tap-root of the independence of our national existence. The courage, the patriotism, the sacrifice of the men who aimed the muskets over yonder redoubt, more than one hundred years ago, were the constructive agencies of that peace, prosperity, and happiness that broods over every American fireside to-day. The heroic deeds of Colonel Prescott's men, in 1775, have given stamina and grit to every contest in which our nation has engaged during the long and eventful years intervening between their day and ours. And whatever are to be the contingencies of the future, amid the temptations of statesmanship, or the selfishness of partisanship, the spirit of freedom, crystallized by the heroes of Bunker Hill, will be a talisman against baseness and the betrayal of national trust to generations yet unborn. This hill will be the pilgrimage and Mecca of patriotic Americans till time's last hour. In appreciation of this thought, it is becoming that our Mayor and City Government should place before the eyes of the American people, on fixed memorial tablets, the names of the valiant men who bared their bosoms to the leaden storm, and went down amid the wild, tempestuous burst of battle-flame that illuminated Bunker Hill when American liberty was on trial for its life.

Astronomers tell us that there is doubtless magnetic contact between every planet of our solar system, and that, if an alphabet of telegraphic signals could be arranged, we would be able to communicate with our sidereal neighbors. However visionary this scheme may appear, let it be asserted as a fact that all the developments of the American Republic are vitally connected, through the medium of patriotism, with the glorious scenes of devotion and sacrifice for liberty, the light of which irradiated the brow of Bunker Hill one hundred and fourteen years ago. On this spot the yeomanry of New England asserted the principles of "Freedom's great experiment." Here, amid the terrible scenes of battle, was the young Republic cradled, and here was the infant principle defended from the strangling clutch of kingly tyranny. Here the living form of classic Freedom rose from the wrecked hopes of the past; defying her enemies and setting firm foot upon this virgin soil, with her faith in one hand, and her sword in the other, commenced the conflict that unfurled her starry banner of freedom over a permanent Republic among the nations of the world.

As our immortal Webster says: "The great event in the history of this continent, the prodigy of modern times, and the blessing of the world, is the American Revolution."

At the present hour we are so accustomed to the civil and religious blessings of this free country, that we find it difficult to conceive of a state of affairs otherwise than they now exist.

We read the Declaration of Independence, and never dream of the contradiction of those sentiments by any rational mind. But when those sentiments were put forth in the actions of our fathers in 1776, when those immortal names were added to that sacred document, it was *treason* and *rebellion;* and these were unpardonable crimes in the views of the proud and unscrupulous monarch with whom they had to deal.

Fellow-citizens: Have you ever tried to imagine yourselves members of that army that Prescott brought from Cambridge to fortify this hill on the night of June 16, 1775? There was at that time no banner under which they could march as the palladium of liberty. Working with pick and shovel to throw up their intrenchments, and during the long night hearing the cry from the sentry on the English man-of-war: "All's well! All's well!" and yet feeling in the depth of the heart that on the morrow it would be very far from "*well*" with many of them. What forebodings must have filled their minds as they challenged the mother-country to arms! If the difficulty must be settled by the dread arbitrament of war, how could a skeleton of insignificant colonies, stretching from Maine to Georgia, raise and support an army to contend with the foremost military nation on the globe?

The men who entered upon such a course of action knew not but that they were signing their own death-warrants. It was a grim pun, but there was truth enough in it to make it terrible, when one of the signers of the Declaration of Independence remarked, as he wrote his name, "Unless we all hang together, we shall all hang separately."

There were some terrible examples of the failure of such work in the past. The bloody scenes of the Jacobite rebellion, from 1715 to 1744, were still fresh in the English mind; and the memory of Culloden field, where the courageous Highlanders were defeated and butchered by the regulars of the British army, was a threatening prophecy of what English regulars might do in these struggling colonies, and begin the work on Bunker Hill. It was personal risk, home risk, business risk, risking everything but *self-respect*. But the conscious self-approval of a just cause led them to count life itself as nothing in comparison with the great boon of freedom for which they were contending.

> "One self-approving hour whole worlds outweighs
> Of stupid starers and of loud huzzas,
> And more true joy Marcellus, exiled, feels
> Than Cæsar with a senate at his heels."

It was simply impossible to enslave the inhabitants of these colonies through a sense of fear, or to intimidate them by the presence of well-trained English soldiers. History describes no set of men less fitted by character, habits, and traditions to endure oppression than the early settlers of the American Republic. Schooled in their pioneer life to hardship and endurance, they were just the material to successfully oppose the oppressions of kingship.

The reverberating echoes of the axe and the cowbell through the leafy depths of the primeval forest opened their whole life to the idea of freedom. Innocent of literature, they learned the Bible by heart, and steeped their souls in the rich melody of those hymns that had been the consolation and inspiration of the sleeping centuries.

Ignorant of astronomy, they sat in their cabin doors counting the stars, and dreaming of the spirit shores beyond their golden sands. To such men and women "Dulce et decorum est pro patria mori."

There is another thought connected with our celebration to-morrow claiming our attention, and that is the potency of educated leaders in our revolutionary crisis.

The valor and heroism of the men who stood in battle line on this hill more than a century ago crushed forever the hopes that England had entertained of easy triumph by her trained and disciplined soldiers over the hastily collected bands from the farms and workshops of New England. It, moreover, created a confidence in the minds of the Continental troops of their ability to cope successfully with British regulars on equal terms.

The English had possession of Bunker Hill; but they were shut within their lines about Boston more closely than ever. When the English officer called the roll, after the din of battle had ceased, more than one thousand men were found missing; for the number of soldiers engaged, England never sustained such a loss on her bloodiest battle-fields in the Old World! Yet there was wanting at this time the chief feature that was to secure the success of the American cause, namely, the unification of the American forces in the struggle for liberty. As yet the conflict was simply a New England quarrel. The thirteen colonies at this time were not a unit in their desire for independence. When Sam Adams, Cushing, Paine, and John Adams were sent as delegates to the first Congress at Philadelphia, a party of Philadelphia "Sons of Liberty" came out to meet the Massachusetts delegation, and warned them that they had been represented as "four desperate adventurers, John Adams and Paine being lawyers of no great talents, reputation, or weight, who were seeking to raise themselves into consequence by courting popularity;" moreover, that "they were suspected of having independence in view."

In this state of affairs something more than valor on the battle-field was required. The union of the disintegrating forces of the thirteen colonies must be secured; the quarrel to the bitter end must be shared by all. Unless this stake could be won, all would be lost. In this alone, at this critical time, was the salvation of the cause of freedom. Far-seeing statesmanship was required now. Intelligent judgment must steer the craft of American liberty into a safe harbor; and in John Adams, of Braintree, the need found the man. At the second session of Congress John Adams arose and moved that the Congress should adopt the army before Boston, and appoint Colonel George Washington, of Virginia, the commander-in-chief.

Many wise heads expressed their doubts of the propriety of putting a Southern man at the head of an army in New England, composed of New England men, and commanded by New England officers. John Hancock, the President of that Congress, could not conceal his mortification, for he had his own aspirations in that direction. Pendleton, Washington's associate from Virginia, opposed it; and Sherman, of Connecticut, was against it.

In the face of such opposition it was a bold assumption of responsibility.

However, within a fortnight after the battle of Bunker Hill, Washington took command of the American forces, under the classic elm of Cambridge. The result was the salvation of the cause of freedom. The matchless character and wonderful organizing skill of Washington consolidated the former disintegrating forces in the colonies, presenting united hearts and a solid front to the enemy.

By this act John Adams shows what an educated mind and well-poised judgment did for the cause of freedom in a critical hour. Truly says the historian, that "this Puritan statesman assumed one of the greatest political risks recorded in the world's history."

This incident leads us to the contemplation of a thought that frequently is overlooked on the occasions of our national celebrations, and that is the leadership of educated men in the critical period of our national history. There is an idea abroad in our land to-day, that any man is fit for office, provided he may secure the requisite number of votes. In our political contests, *availability* is frequently the requisite of official position, rather than intelligent *ability*.

In this judgment we are flying in the face of all the annals of the past. All history shows that the unresting pressure of a body of able, intellectual men, resolutely striving for a definite end, furnishes a motive-power that the reluctant masses cannot resist.

While we never weary of the encomiums pronounced over the heroes of the Revolution, who made up the rank and file of that army, the leadership of educated and well-developed men in those days affords a very profitable field of study. The successful weaving of the principles of liberty into the fabric of this great Republic was accomplished by educated statesmanship, as well as indomitable soldier courage.

The development of this majestic, consolidated nation of to-day, from the imperfect league of thirteen jealous colonies, is a triumph to be laid at the feet of educated citizenship as truly as it belongs to the prowess of the citizen-soldier. American scholarship paved the way for the union of the States.

Our national life did not begin with ignorant and savage men. The foundation-stones of our nation were laid by skilful hands and educated minds. Roger Williams was banished because Massachusetts said, "He had broached and divulged new and dangerous opinions against the authority of magistrates." One hundred years later that thought was the life-blood of the American Revolution. The great work of preparing the thirteen colonies for the Revolutionary war, for the reception of the Declaration of Independence, for the adoption of the Constitution, originated in the minds of men who were giants in intellectual accomplishments, and proverbial for moral character. These men were the intellectual peers of any of the great statesmen who adorned the monarchies of the Old World.

It was a Harvard College boy, delivering his master oration in 1743, — Sam Adams by name, — who argued that it was lawful to resist the supreme magistrate if the State could maintain its life no other way. The sentiment of that oration led to the ratification of the same on Bunker Hill.

In 1750, the chief pulpit orator of New England, Jonathan Mayhew, preached in Boston the famous sermon called the "morning gun" of the Revolution, applying the principle of rebellion against the tyrannical authority of the magistrate. The New England pulpit generally took up the note, and spread the idea in every hamlet and village, and twenty-five years later it broke forth in the roar of battle on Bunker Hill.

It was a son of Harvard College, James Otis, who, listening to a sermon from the text, "Ye are many members in one body," conceived the idea of the American Congress.

It was a son of Yale College, John Morin Scott, who declared that if taxation without representation were to be enforced, the colonies ought to separate from England.

It was a New England scholar, John Adams, of whom Jefferson said, "He was a colossus of debate," and of whom Stockton said, he was the "altar of independence," and of whom Rufus Choate, in later days, said, "He was the distinctive and comprehensive orator of the Revolution." It was the Puritan scholar who, in the Continental Congress, forged arguments with the power of a thunderbolt, "touching every spot of passion, pride, tenderness, interest, conscience, and lofty indignation up swept his country into a chariot of fire, and soared to independence."

In these statements we do not overlook the heroic sacrifice and service, laid on the altar of liberty, from the farm and workshop. Nathaniel Green and his deserted blacksmith-shop; Esek Hopkins, with his plough left in the furrow, — these and their like will ever be classic incidents in the story of our country.

But we do emphasize the fact, that in the preparatory work of constructing and perpetuating this Republic it was educated men who, from the pulpit and platform, conducted the great discussions that made possible such an event as the Revolutionary war, and that created our sacred document, the Constitution of the United States.

Let us look in upon that Constitutional Convention for a few moments. There were fifty members in that august body of nation-makers. Bancroft calls them the "goodliest fellowship of lawgivers whereof this world holds record." And of their work, our National Constitution, Mr. Gladstone declares that it is "the most wonderful work ever struck off at a given time, by the brain and purpose of man."

These fifty-five men were all of them respected for family and for personal qualities. Twenty-nine of the members of that convention were university men: graduates of "Harvard," "Yale," "Columbia," "Princeton," "William and Mary," "Oxford," "Glasgow," and "Edinburgh." And the eight leaders of the great debate were all college men.

It was Alexander Hamilton, a son of Columbia College, who drew New York into the Union from under the strong hand of George Clinton. It was a son of "Princeton," James Madison, who in the very face of the fiery eloquence of Patrick Henry brought Virginia into the compact, and our union of States under our Constitution was complete.

I am not reviewing these facts with any derogatory purpose of reflecting on the great and good men who were active spirits in those days, through their self-made efforts, supreme intelligence, and consummate tact. Let my audience be the judges, if I have not done justice to the herculean efforts and martyrs' sacrifices of the other heroes who, with brawn and brain, helped launch our Republic on the ocean of national life.

I am only trying to show you that this great nation was not the product of the pique and treason of ignorant and disgruntled foreigners, and that the principle of civil and religious liberty that could find no home among the monarchies of the Old World required for their adjustment and establishment on these shores, not only the heroism and soldier courage of Bunker Hill and Yorktown, but the far-reaching intelligence and deep-toned judgments of statesmanship, — such as these men brought to their great task.

There is another thought that presses upon the devout student of American affairs and claims a place in the thoughtful consideration of our national development, namely, the manifest hand of Divine Providence in the founding and perpetuation of our great Republic. There was the working of an unseen hand in the events which resulted in the planting of this Republic in her geographical position, and also in the selection of the emigrants who should be instrumental in laying the foundation-stones of civil and religious liberty upon which our national structure has been built.

Let us look at some of the facts of history in this connection. France, the land of refinement and culture, made five unsuccessful attempts to colonize America. Spain, heroic and covetous of empire, whose munificent patronage made possible, through

Columbus, the discovery of the New World, whose Queen Isabella declared that the ideas of Columbus should be carried out "Even if I pawn the crown jewels;" but neither Columbus nor his Spanish successors could make America a Spanish province. The valiant Ponce de Leon, from his discovery of Florida in 1513, dazzled with the charms of wealth and power, struggled, with unparalleled energy, for eight years, to effect a permanent settlement; but an Indian arrow sent him to Cuba to die. After this, three heroic attempts were made by Spain to colonize America, yet they all failed.

Then the sturdy descendants of the Saxon began the work of building America into a nation, upon the basis of civil and religious liberty. Two grand representative colonies appear on this continent, both having noble spirits as their leaders. The one begins the work of nation-building at Jamestown, Virginia; the other, with Puritanic grit, strikes the New World at Plymouth, Massachusetts. The tap-roots of the American Republic strike firmly into our soil from these two settlements, — from the one came our Washington; from the other, our Adams.

Again, there is a peculiar significance in the section of country over which these two colonies asserted their sway. What is the meaning of the press of emigration that even in these early times selected the coast line between Maine and Florida as their destination? "I know of no way of judging of the future but by the past," is a classic sentence of one of our early statesmen; and applying that sentiment to the colonization in the early days of American history, this thought suggests itself, — that around this globe is a narrow belt stretching between the 30th and 60th parallels of north latitude, within which have been enacted the greatest dramas in the development of the human race. St. Petersburg is on its northern boundary, in Europe, and Jerusalem is on its southern boundary, in Asia. Within this narrow belt have lived and acted the nations that have given direction to the thought of mankind. The peoples living within these bounds have created the philosophy of the race. All the ancient peoples that have given law, history, oratory, poetry, art, science, and government to mankind have lived within this belt. Examine the map of the world! There, within this zone, is the Mediterranean Sea, on whose islands and shores have been enacted the greatest events of the ancient world. There lies Italy, the throne of the once mighty empire of Rome; and Roman jurisprudence, as formulated in the code of Justinian, is the basis of all English law to-day. Within this border lies Greece, the nation of culture, that gave a language to the world in which was set the words of Jesus, the Saviour of the world. Within this belt lies Palestine, the land that gave a Christ and his wonderful teachings to the darkened souls of men. Here lies the Germany of Luther, and the France of the Huguenots, and England, with her mighty sceptre of Protestant political power. And within this magic belt, my hearers, lies our national home. There is something very significant in the fact that, in the providence of God, the American Republic was founded in just this quarter of the world. Blessed with such national resources, and crowned with a continental position from which has come the world's greatest blessings, we seem to have been selected by God for the enactment of the last and greatest achievement in the history of the world's governments. The problems of our civilization to-day are being solved by inspirations imported from the religion preached at Jacob's well in Palestine, and the culture and philosophy given to the world from the region of the Grecian archipelago.

Again, the providential direction in the development of our Republic is seen in the readjustment of our boundary lines since the time we became a nation. British America was England's possession on the north. Florida, on the south, was a Spanish possession; and the great Louisiana tract, on the west, was the property of the Spanish king. According to these boundaries, if civil difficulties ever should arise in the future, our nation would be at the mercy of foreign neighbors. The great artery of commerce, the Mississippi river, could not be used by us. Yet in due time, by a treaty that statesmanship could not have foreseen, Florida was ceded to the United States by Spain, and the great Louisiana tract, including most of our country west of the Mississippi river, was by secret treaty deeded to France. At that critical time Napoleon was threatening England with his world-conquering policy. Bonaparte, fearing that England would take possession of Louisiana, and desiring to turn his foreign territory into money for war supplies, gave the United States of America the privilege of purchasing the Louisiana territory for fifteen millions of dollars. Consequently Robert R. Livingston, the American Minister at Paris, commenced negotiations, the result of which was the purchase of the Louisiana territory. This purchase extended our national domain from ocean to ocean, and from the lake chain on the north to the gulf coast on the south. The significance of this, as a providential contingency in the future progress of our nation, must not be overlooked. It was not the wisdom of statesmanship that suggested the purchase. It was not the result of any far-seeing diplomacy. It was the result of a complicated state of European affairs that made it necessary for France to sell, and offered the privilege of buying to the United States of America.

Bonaparte feared that when it became known that Louisiana was French territory, the overpowering fleet of Great Britain would seize and occupy the mouth of the Mississippi. To avoid this danger he was willing to sell; and our government, already staggering under a crushing debt, found courage enough to buy.

The agreement between the French and the United States was scarcely closed before six British men-of war were on their way to take possession of the territory of Louisiana; but on hearing that it was United States territory they returned to British waters. All that saved us, as a nation, from contact with an immense British Empire on our western border was the providential opportunity of buying Louisiana. I need not state to this audience the difficulties and embarrassments we escaped, as a nation, by that act of purchase. Suffice it to say, that when the sale was completed Bonaparte is said to have exclaimed: "This accession of territory strengthens forever the power of the United States. I have just given to England a maritime rival that will sooner or later humble her pride."

Again, note the manner in which a Divine Providence interposed to strengthen the arm of our nation in the dark days of our Civil war. Our country was lying bleeding and sore by the roadside of nations. The union of States was assailed by a haughty slave oligarchy, whose buttresses were social caste and moneyed selfishness. In this hour of our national trial the mother-country, and even France, who was our godmother when we were christened as a nation, played the part of the priest and Levite, and passed by on the other side. As Charles Sumner said: "At a great epoch of history, no less momentous than that of the French Revolution, or that of the Reformation, when civilization was fighting a last battle with slavery, England gave her influence, her material resources, to the wicked cause, and flung a sword into the scale with slavery."

France, with her former friendship turned into the treason of a Judas, attempted to establish a monarchy in Mexico, with the hope that the American Republic would be destroyed, and she share in the division of the loaves and fishes. It was plainly seen that the

Union cause had very little sympathy in Europe. As Mr. Blaine says: "There was a spirit of arrogance manifested towards the United States by some foreign prime ministers which they would not have dared to manifest had our country not been lying wounded in the house of her friends."

It is worthy of note that just at this time a providential communication strengthened the heart of our government, and made somewhat timid the seeming hostility of other foreign powers; and, strange as it may seem, this word of sympathy came from the most autocratic government on the globe to-day. "We desire above all things the maintenance of the American Union as one indivisible nation," was the kindly and ever-to-be-remembered greeting that came to us from the Emperor of Russia. Shortly after this, to use the words of Gen. N. P. Banks, in the House of Representatives, in 1868: "In the darkest hour of our peril during the rebellion, when we were enacting a history which no man yet thoroughly comprehends, when France and England were contemplating the recognition of the Southern Confederacy, the whole world was thrilled by the appearance in San Francisco of a fleet of Russian war-vessels; and nearly at the same time, whether by accident or design, a second Russian fleet appeared in the harbor of New York. From that hour France on the one hand, and England on the other, receded, and the American government regained its position and its power."

With your consent I will close this review of the

providence of God in our national history by reference to one scene more in our national life. At a critical period in our Civil war the rebel ram known as the "Merrimac" began devastating our naval forces with tremendous power. This mysterious monster became a source of great dread to the Union fleet around the Lower Chesapeake and Hampton Roads. Sometime before her devastations on the Union men-of-war, Captain John Ericsson presented, before a conference of naval officers, his plan of the "Monitor." They laughed at his idea, and told him that he could take it home and worship it without violating any of God's commandments, for it resembled "nothing in the heavens above nor in the earth beneath."

Meanwhile the "Monitor" was being built, — a unique iron-clad, destined to revolutionize naval warfare. We are all familiar with the disastrous fight between the "Merrimac" and the Union fleet, — resulting in what seemed to be the annihilation of the Federal fleet. Just after the "Merrimac" had finished her destruction, a singular-looking craft appeared in the offing. It was the Ericsson invention, — the "Monitor." She reported for duty, and took her position for battle. It was on a Sunday morning when the "Merrimac" came out to engage the "little cheese-box on a raft," as they called it. But the fight resulted in the defeat of the "Merrimac" and victory for the "Monitor."

On that Sabbath ended the most influential naval duel that ever occurred, and made the Union navy master of all sea engagements.

Under the providence of God, the Philistine Goliath met defeat at the hands of little David from the sheepfolds of Bethlehem. I have not the time, and perhaps this is not the place, to draw lessons of duty for the present hour. But I will venture this much: that no danger can ever seriously affect this nation if the proper use of our educational facilities are applied to political affairs by the rising generation as faithfully as they were applied by the fathers who launched this great Republic on its great voyage. If the patriotic addresses of our annual commencements take practical form and character in the lives of the men of the future; if the admiration of our students for the orations of Demosthenes and Cicero is transmuted into the manhood of the coming citizen, and made effective in condemning the political and unscrupulous boss, and ridding both legislature and lobby of the viper pest of boodlers; if we could depend upon every college diploma as not only a testimonial of a curriculum mastered, but a promissory note to discharge the duties of the higher citizenship; if the Argus-eyed press, with its educated editors and reporters, will keep a clear political conscience, — these will stand as Gibraltar fortresses against all dangers that threaten the life of our nation.

Socialism may threaten, nihilism may plot, and the foreign prejudices of emigration may complicate the problem here and there; but once turn the light of intelligent American citizenship upon them, and the dull, lustreless carbon of these decaying isms will be crystallized into diamonds of beauty worthy of the diadem of American liberty.

What is to be the end? is the question that every thoughtful man asks himself as he faces the great problem of American civilization. Can any good come out of this chaos of uncongenial elements which compose our nation? Can the people assimilate these hordes of immigrant men and women, educated and ignorant, civilized and barbarous; or is the government to disappear under the modern Goths and Vandals, as years ago proud Rome fell under the ancient invaders?

Let me quote the words of one who, in the ancient manner, was both bard and seer, whose words on all subjects are carefully treasured, who looked at the present by the clear light of the past. This man has made a most beautiful prophecy of the future of our country.

"In that memorable hour," wrote Dean Stanley, not long before his death, "memorable in the life of every man, memorable as when he sees the first view of the pyramids, or of the snow-clad ranges of the Alps, — in the hour when for the first time I stood before the cataracts of Niagara, I seemed to see a vision of the fears and hopes of America. It was midnight; the moon was full, and I saw from the suspension bridge the ceaseless contortion, confusion, whirl and chaos, which burst forth in clouds of foam from the immense central chasm which divides the American from the British dominion; but as I looked on that ever-changing movement, and listened to that everlasting roar, I saw an emblem of the devouring activity, and ceaseless, restless, beating whirlpool of existence in the United States. But into the moonlight sky there rose a cloud of spray twice as high as the falls themselves, silent, majestic, immovable. In that silver column, glittering in the moonlight, I saw an image of the future of the American destiny, of the pillar of light which should emerge from the distractions of the present, a likeness of the buoyancy and hopefulness which characterize the Americans, both as individuals and as a nation."

I have heard of a poor idiot boy on one of the hill farms of New England, who, — when the curtains of evening hung around the form of dying day and the stars, one after another, would come out to diadem the brow of night, — the ignorant boy would mount the ox-cart in the farm-yard, and, with club in hand, would strike at the moon and stars, crying with each stroke, "Go back, or I will knock you down! Go back, or I will knock you down!" Nevertheless, the moon rode serenely through the mighty camp of the constellations, and the stars only shone the brighter in the sword-belt of Orion as the deeper shades of night came on, and the little idiot, exhausted by his fruitless efforts, sank into helpless slumber.

So I have imagined with this galaxy of States known as the American Republic, rising with a continuous unfolding of beauty and strength as one after another the harsh voice of threatening danger falls into the slumber of oblivion. In spite of all opposition, we shall flourish in full orbit splendor when the feebleness and folly of all opposition shall have sunk into the quiet of eternal slumber.

What splendid progress! What heroic achievements mark the period between the America of Bunker Hill and the America in which we live!

As a people we stand upon the threshold of a mighty future, — a future in which all the events of the past have a constructive influence.

All that this future contains must be the result of the creative work done by the men who, more than a century ago, determined that this vast territory should be dominated by a powerful federal nation instead of being parcelled out to forty or fifty small communities like the States of ancient Greece, or the smaller nations of Europe to-day.

The men who fought and died on Bunker Hill in 1775 are as vitally connected with what we are and what we are to be, as the men who shouldered the musket in 1861 and 1864. The men of 1775 made *possible* a federal union; the men of 1864 made *impossible* forever, may we trust, the dissolution of that union.

Our mission is to make it a grander nation than that of which Romulus dreamed, and Jove guided to universal empire. We have the religion of Jesus, the culture of Greece, the laws of Rome, and the language of Shakespeare and Bacon. Before us are the limitless latent possibilities of development. Great problems confront us; great destinies await us. Here, on these shores, is yet to be enacted the sublimest scenes of free government ever consummated in the history of man. Each year makes real, grander possibilities: the assimilation of heterogeneous races into a homogeneous people of a great Republic.

The protection of poverty and weakness from the avarice and tyranny of the wealthy and mighty; the extension of our suffrage, either in part or in whole, to the mothers and wives of the nation; the dissemination of intelligence, by our public-school system, over every square foot of our vast domain, until it is a proverb, that in America to be ignorant is to be criminal, — all these great possibilities are before us. And, fellow-citizens, the outstretching aurora of a day of such blessings is already upon us. At no period of the past was this nation better than it is to-day. The new era is dawning.

"The hours are growing shorter for the millions who are toiling,
And the homes are growing better for the millions yet to be;
The poor shall learn the lesson how that sin and wrong are spoiling
The fairest and the finest of a grand humanity.

"It is coming, it is coming; for men's hearts are growing deeper;
They are giving of their millions as they never gave before;
They are learning the new gospel: man must be his brother's keeper,
And *right* not *might* shall triumph, and the selfish rule no more."

I leave this subject with you, my hearers, by reference to a vision of the future of America that I have somewhere read or heard.

This union of States under one federal head is represented by a great organ, with many banks of keys, and having an infinite diversity of stops.

Columbia one day invited her subjects to an organ recital that she would give in honor of them all. They assembled, representing all lands and climes. The Goddess of Liberty mounted the organ stool and opened the concert. She touched the deep diapason notes, and there came forth the majestic march of the Saxon, and some of her fair-haired children kept sturdy time by the beating of their feet upon the floor.

Then she changed the theme, and brought in some refining strains of the Norman conquests, and in the audience some well-formed faces looked up with delight.

Then came sunny themes from Italy, and there were tears in a few eyes as they thought of vineyards and cottages over the deep blue sea.

Then came a solemn sonata from a German composer, breaking into the martial strain of the "Watch on the Rhine," and the sturdy Germans turned to look at each other with looks and words of approval.

Then came the rippling strains of Irish melodies, and the enthusiasm of Patrick could stand it no longer, and some arose, crying, "Hurrah for the shamrock and Erin!"

Then Columbia opened the full organ and touched the deep pedal keys, and there came forth a strain that united every heart, the whole audience rising and singing to the accompaniment,—

> "My country, 'tis of thee,
>   Sweet land of liberty,
>   Of thee I sing.
>   Land where my fathers died!
>   Land of the Pilgrim's pride!
>   From every mountain side
>   Let freedom ring!"

And in the grand chorus not even the listening angels could discern the national accents in the hymn. The lands beyond the sea were forgotten in the jubilant outburst of liberty's song.

ILLUSTRATIVE PAPERS

PREPARED BY

WILLIAM H. WHITMORE.

APPENDIX A. SKETCH OF THE BATTLE.
B. AMERICANS KILLED AT BUNKER HILL.
C. ENGLISH OPINION OF COLONIAL TROOPS.
D. HISTORY OF THE BUNKER-HILL MONUMENT.
E. WEBSTER'S ORATIONS AT THE LAYING OF THE CORNER-STONE AND AT THE DEDICATION OF THE MONUMENT.
F. GRANDMOTHER'S STORY; A POEM BY DR. OLIVER WENDELL HOLMES.
G. MANUAL OF ARMS AND ARMY REGULATIONS IN 1776.

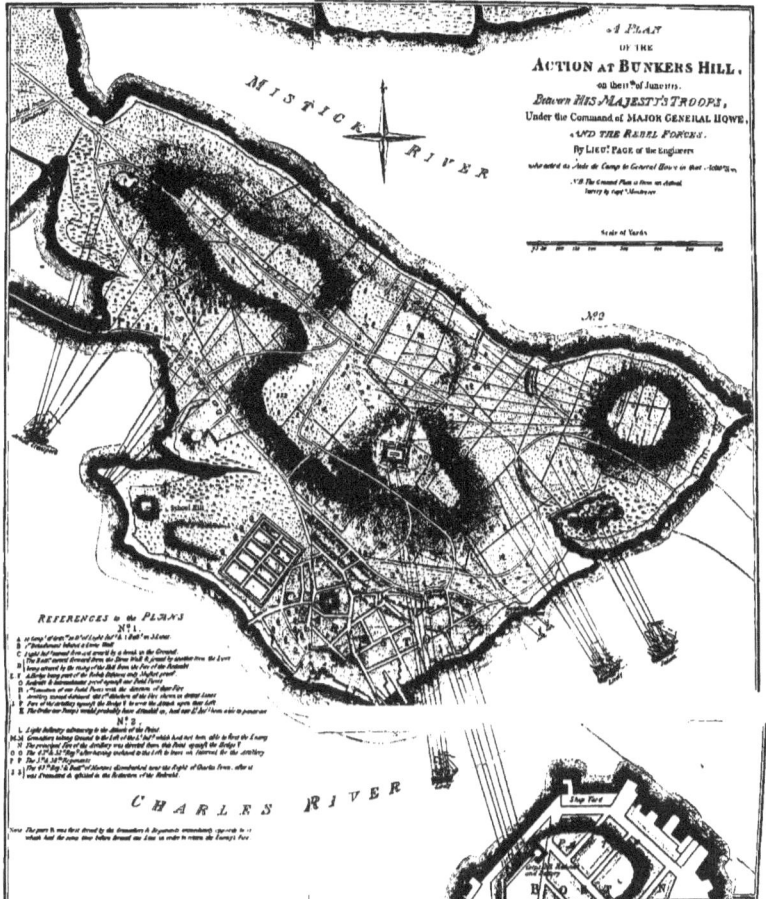

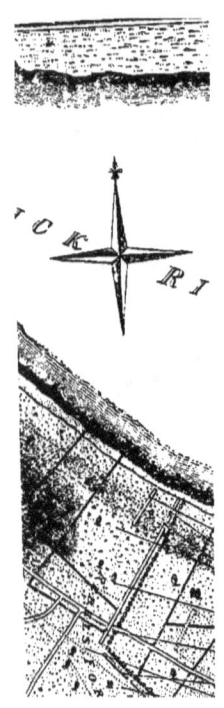

APPENDIX A.

BATTLE OF BUNKER HILL.

THE object of this volume being the recognition of the valor of the American troops in the battle of June 17th, 1775, it seems impossible to avoid some slight sketch of the engagement. The story however has been fully told by Frothingham in his History, and again repeated in Gen. Devens's Oration in 1875 (Bunker Hill Memorial), and Dr. Ellis's Oration in 1876 (The Evacuation of Boston), both of which were delivered at the request of the City Government of Boston, and published at its expense.

Assuming that the reader will refer to these admirable works for the more detailed narration, it will be sufficient to state the position of affairs in and around Boston in the month of June 1775.

Gov. Thomas Gage arrived at Boston May 13, 1774, and on June 1st, the Boston Port Bill, the first of the repressive acts of the British government against the discontented but not yet rebellious colonists, went into effect. In August 1774 Gage received the later laws, which provided that the Council should henceforth be appointed by the King, and that town-meetings, except the annual ones in March and May, and all other public meetings, should be held only by permission of the governor.

The colonists regarded a legislature thus chosen, as entirely contrary to their charter rights, and as some new form of government was indispensable, they decided to call a Provincial Congress. Gage issued writs for a meeting of the General Court at Salem, Oct. 5th, 1774, but dissolved it by a proclamation dated Sept. 28th. The members elected however met at Salem Oct. 7th, and resolved themselves into the First Provincial Congress.[1] It adjourned the same day and met at Concord Oct. 11, where it sat three days and then removed to Cambridge. Here its sessions were Oct. 17th to 29th, and Nov. 23 to Dec. 10. John Hancock was president of this body.

The Second Provincial Congress, John Hancock, president, sat at Cambridge Feb. 1st to 16th, 1775, and again from March 22 to April 15th. It met April 22 at Concord and adjourned to Watertown, where it continued till May 29, 1775.

The Third Continental Congress met at Watertown May 31st, 1775, and dissolved July 19, 1775. Joseph Warren was president, and after his death, James Warren of Plymouth was chosen. This Congress had provided for a resumption of the Provincial government, though no Governor could be recognized, and accordingly the Representatives met at Watertown July 19th, 1775, and chose eighteen Councillors, thus making a Legislature of two branches.[2]

The winter of 1774 had been a period of suspense for both parties. Gage began the concentration of troops immediately after his arrival, and by the middle of November he had eleven regiments and the artillery. The harbor was of course controlled by the British fleet, and supplies were freely brought in. In September, Gage sent a little expedition to Cambridge, and took away the stock of powder belonging to the province. In January, 1775, he sent a detachment to Marshfield, to protect the local loyalists. February 26th, 1775, Col. Leslie was sent to Salem to seize some guns, and was obliged to return unsatisfied, having escaped, by a prudent compromise, an actual resort to arms. Boston, estimated to contain 17,000 inhabitants, was, during this season, in a state of suppressed excitement, but had received no material injury.

On the outside of the town matters were assuming a threatening

[1] See Journals of these Congresses, etc., printed by the State in 1838, edited by William Lincoln.

[2] We see that the Legislature was thus continuous, except for the period from Oct., 1774, to July, 1775. The Laws published by the State under the charge of Abner C. Goodell, Jr., are continuous to 1780, except for the few months herein noted. The sessions of this new Legislature were four as usual, and a regular election being held, a new Legislature met at Watertown May 29, 1776. Boston was evacuated by the British March 17, 1776, but the Legislature did not move in from Watertown till November 12, 1776, when the old State House was ready for its occupancy. W. H. W.

form, but no distinct plan of action had been evolved. The Charter government was forever broken and lost. The Governor and his newly created Council were on one side, the House of Representatives no longer able to continue the exact forms and traditions of the past century, was in session as a Provincial Congress. Fortunately the Massachusetts system of town governments was such that little harm could result from the dissolution of the central authority. These little, self-governed communities had for a century and a half exercised all the powers necessary to preserve order, and a Congress was needed only to provide for the emergencies of war.

In April 1775, Gen. Gage, whose forces had increased to some four thousand men, determined to make an attempt to overawe the provincials, as he had a firm belief that a successful display of British power would end all attempts at resistance to the plans of King George and his obsequious ministers. On the 8th of April, 1775, the Provincial Congress resolved to take measures to raise an army, and to obtain the assistance of Rhode Island, Connecticut and New Hampshire. On the 15th of April it adjourned, leaving the work to be continued by its Committees of Safety and Supplies. On the night of April 18th, a force of 800 men, under Lt.-col. Smith started from the foot of Boston Common, under orders to proceed to Concord, to seize there the supplies which had been collected by the provincial authorities.

No American is ignorant of the events of that day. Smith sent forward from Cambridge six companies of light infantry, under the command of Major Pitcairn, to secure the bridges at Concord. About 4½ or 5 o'clock in the morning, these troops reached Lexington, were there confronted by the militia of the town, and after a straggling encounter, most probably begun by the regulars, the Americans were dispersed with the loss of eight killed and ten wounded. Col. Smith, with the remainder of the troops, soon joined Pitcairn, and proceeded to Concord without further interruption; arriving there at seven o'clock. The ostensible object of the expedition was a failure, as but a small portion of the stores could be found, and the damage done was trifling. For two hours however, the British troops were employed in this farcical manner, while the alarm spread from town to town. Concord's troop had prudently drawn out of the town early; it was joined by companies from Carlisle, Chelmsford, Westford, Littleton, and Acton. By 10 o'clock, some four hundred Americans were in arms on the west side of the river.

The approaches to the town from the westward were two, the north and south roads crossing the river, then joining at the centre of Concord and running east to Lexington. Col. Smith remaining at the centre, had sent Capt. Parsons with a force to destroy stores at the North Bridge, and Capt. Pole for a similar purpose to the South Bridge. The Americans opened fire at last on the troops at the North Bridge, and drove them back upon the main body. Two Acton men fell, and the British lost one man with several wounded. Col. Smith called in his troops, obtained conveyances for his wounded, and started on his return to Boston at twelve. From that moment the rout began. Troops arrived from all the neighboring towns, Reading, Billerica, Lincoln, Woburn and Lexington, and an incessant contest raged until Lexington was reached about $2\frac{1}{2}$ o'clock. Here the exhausted British troops received a welcome reinforcement of three regiments of infantry, two divisions of marines and two field-pieces, under the command of Lord Percy, who had been despatched at 9 o'clock from Boston. This force of 1,800 veterans was able only to fight its way on that bloody afternoon through Lexington and West Cambridge to Charlestown, where it was safe under the guns of the fleet. The Americans lost 49 killed, 39 wounded, 5 missing; the British had 73 killed, 174 wounded, and 26 missing.

Thus began the war of the Revolution, and the position of affairs was changed in a day. The Provincial Congress was now forced to assume authority, to create an army, and to prepare for the inevitable struggle with the whole power of the British nation. Every town in the colony was urged to send forward its quota, and the other New England colonies were invited to afford assistance. The plan of organization was to raise 13,600 troops in Massachusetts, in regiments of ten companies, fifty-nine men to a company; and Artemas Ward was appointed commander-in-chief. For nearly two months preceding the battle of Bunker Hill, the work of collecting troops and munitions

APPENDIX A.   77

of war went on, but in that time order was not fully established. "The official returns of the army, until the arrival of General Washington, are so defective and inaccurate, that it is impossible to ascertain with precision its numbers." Thus wrote the diligent Frothingham in 1851, and though many valuable documents have since been secured for the State archives, the record is still imperfect. That Massachusetts is still so far behind her sister states in publishing the records of her glorious past, is one of the mysteries of state-craft.

Frothingham cites a Return of the Army at Cambridge, June 9th, 1775, as follows: —

Whitcomb's reg't,	470 men.	Frye's re'gt,	493 men.
Brewer "	318 "	Scammon "	396 "
Nixon "	224 "	Prescott "	456 "
Little "	400 "	Gerrish "	421 "
Mansfield "	345 "	Woodbridge "	242 "
Gridley "	370 "	Ward "	449 "
Bridge "	315 "	Gardner "	425 "
Doolittle "	308 "	Patterson "	422 "
			6,063
		Drummers, &c.,	1,581
			7,644

The New Hampshire troops at Medford, April 26, voted to enlist in the Massachusetts service; but May 20, the New Hampshire Congress voted to raise 2,000 men and adopt those. Two regiments under Colonels John Stark and James Reed were ready before June 17th, and were under the orders of Gen. Ward. Connecticut sent Gen. Joseph Spencer with one regiment, another under Gen. Israel Putnam, and a third under Col. Samuel H. Parsons; but these troops were subject to a Committee of War. Rhode Island sent three regiments under Colonels Varnum, Hitchcock and Church, all commanded by Gen. Nathaniel Greene. This latter force also was not subject to Gen. Ward, except by voluntary submission.

Both sides immediately after the battle of Lexington began to fortify their lines. The British had only to close in Boston Neck to be secure, since their navy was sufficient to control the water-front, though unable to defend the islands, which were stripped of supplies by expeditions from the American side. The American forces were ranged around Boston, from Somerville and Cambridge to Dorchester. Occasional skirmishes took place, but the British showed no desire to sally forth, while the Americans naturally were reluctant to take any steps which might lead to the destruction of their much-loved capital. At length Gage decided to assume the offensive and to occupy Dorchester Heights, now South Boston, on the night of June 18th. Information of this plan being received by the Americans, the Committee of Safety, on the 15th of June, passed the following resolve[1]: —

"Whereas, it appears of importance to the safety of this colony, that possession of the hill called Bunker's Hill in Charlestown, be securely kept and defended ; and also some one hill or hills on Dorchester Neck be likewise secured; therefore resolved, unanimously, that it be recommended to the council of war, that the above mentioned Bunker's Hill be maintained by sufficient forces posted there, and as the particular situation of Dorchester neck is unknown to this committee, they desire that the council of war take and pursue such steps respecting the same, as to them shall appear to be for the security of this colony."

"On Friday, June 16th., the commanders of the army, in accordance with the recommendation of the committee of safety, took measures to fortify Bunker Hill. Orders were issued for Prescott's, Frye's and Bridge's regiments, and a fatigue party of 200 Connecticut troops to parade at 6 o'clock in the evening with all the intrenching tools in the Cambridge camp." "Also, Capt. Samuel Gridley's company of artillery, of 49 men and two field pieces was ordered to parade." The Connecticut men were under Capt. Thomas Knowlton.

---

[1] Journals of the Provincial Congress of Massachusetts, edited by Wm. Lincoln, and published by the State, 1838, p. 500.

"The detachment was placed under the command of Col. William Prescott, of Pepperell, who had orders in writing from Gen. Ward, to proceed that evening to Bunker Hill, build fortifications to be planned by Col. Richard Gridley, the chief engineer, and defend them until he should be relieved." "The number of troops may be fairly estimated at 1,200." (Frothingham.)

About 9 o'clock in the evening the troops started, Col. Prescott leading, and at Charlestown Neck they were joined by Gen. Putnam and Maj. Brooks. A delay was caused by a discussion upon the order to fortify Bunker's Hill, as Breed's Hill to the southward was evidently more fit. "Bunker's Hill begins at the isthmus and rises gradually for about 300 yards, forming a round, smooth hill, sloping on two sides towards the water, and connected by a ridge of ground on the south with the heights now known as Breed's Hill." (Frothingham.) Bunker Hill was well-known; Breed's Hill was a name purely local and hardly in use. Luckily common sense prevailed over forms, and the southern eminence, regardless of its exact name, was fixed upon for the works. It was midnight before the engineer had traced the lines of the proposed redoubt. "It was a bright starlight night of midsummer, when the long hours of the day almost deny an interval to the darkness, and we expect almost momentarily after twilight in the west to behold the gray of morning in the east. There was a remnant of a waning moon just before midnight. . . . The narrow space between the shores was wider than the distance between these midnight delvers and their enemies. At least five armed vessels then floated in the middle of the stream . . . These ships were most aptly moored for the purposes of the enemy, and it seems almost impossible that the sentries could have been wakeful at their posts and not have heard the operations of nearly a thousand men upon the Hill and near it." (Ellis.) Twice during the night Prescott went down to the beach, unable to believe in the truth of this marvellous blindness.

At the first light of the morning of the 17th, however, the entrenchments, already some six feet high, were seen from the ships, and the "Lively," of 20 guns, lying where the Navy Yard is, opened fire. Admiral Graves ordered the firing to cease, but it was soon renewed from a battery of six guns and howitzers at Copp's Hill, and from the shipping. No interruption to the work was caused, although one man was killed.[1]

The English commanders were at first in doubt as to their plan of attack. Generals Grant and Clinton, and a majority of the council of war, called by Gage, were in favor of embarking a force at Boston Common, and landing in the rear of the American force, at Charlestown Neck. Gage fortunately over-ruled this and decided to attack the redoubt from the front.

Between 12 and 1 o'clock, a large body of English troops was safely landed at Moulton's Point in Charlestown. These were the ten oldest companies of grenadiers and light infantry (exclusive of two regiments, the 35th and 49th, just arrived), the 5th, 38th, 43d, and 52d regiments. After landing, reinforcements were required, and the 47th regiment, the first battalion of marines, and several companies of grenadiers and light infantry were sent over.

The American lines were really of slight importance. The redoubt occupied the top of Breed's Hill and controlled the two lower roads and the town. Here Prescott commanded the Massachusetts troops. About 600 feet to the rear, on the side towards the Mystic River, Col. Knowlton with the Connecticut troops was posted behind a double rail-fence which was filled in with newly cut grass from the meadows. Before the battle, Col. Stark arrived with his New Hampshire regiment and took most of them with him to the rail-fence, which was extended to the river.

The Massachusetts men in the redoubt were those of the three regiments, Prescott's, Bridge's, and Frye's, which had been at work, joined just before the battle, by portions of Brewer's, Nixon's, Woodbridge's, Little's, and Doolittle's. The artillery was posted at the exposed point between the redoubt and the rail-fence; and the latter line was held by the New Hampshire and Connecticut troops.

About 3 o'clock the British advance was ordered, their troops marching in two wings. The right under Gen. Howe aimed at the

---

[1] This is said to have been Asa Pollard of Stickney's company, Bridge's regiment. Swett's History seems to be the authority for it. But on the Muster Rolls it is said that Aaron Barr of Meryfield (now Rowe), who was of Nutting's company in Prescott's regiment, was the first man killed. It seems impossible to reconcile these statements. — W. H. W.

View of The ATTACK on BUNKER's HILL, with the Burning of CHARLES TOWN, June 17, 1775.

APPENDIX A. 81

American left at the rail-fence. Their left under Gen. Pigot, consisting of the 5th, 38th, 43d, 47th, 52d regiments and the marines, attacked the redoubt. No phrase is more familiar to us than the watch-word of Putnam to his men, "Wait till you see the white of their eyes!" The fire of the American troops, delivered at short range, was so overwhelming, that Pigot was forced to order a retreat. The same fate attended Howe's attack on the left, where the same tactics were pursued by the Americans, with like success.

A second attack and repulse followed, and a second reinforcement of some 400 British marines was landed, and Gen. Clinton hastened over as a volunteer. Charlestown was set on fire, partly by shells thrown from Copp's Hill, and partly by the torches of a party of marines from the "Somerset." The British vessels maintained a constant fire not only on Breed's Hill, but on Bunker's Hill, where some attempts at fortification had been made. Especially, from boats in the Charles River cannonading was kept up at the low land of Charlestown Neck, preventing the Americans from pushing forward reinforcements or supplies of ammunition.

Howe now massed his troops for a third assault, concentrating his attack upon the redoubt. He ordered his men to lay aside their knapsacks, to move forward in column, to reserve their fire, to rely on the bayonet, and to push the artillery forward. The ammunition of the Americans was now well-nigh spent, and after a desperate defence Prescott was forced to order a retreat. At this time Warren fell, and the loss of the Americans was greater than at any other period of the action. Fighting to the last, the American troops were forced backward over the crest of Bunker Hill, and were joined by their brethren from the rail-fence, whose position had likewise become untenable. The whole body retired over the Neck while the British about 5 o'clock took possession of the heights.

I have thus endeavored to give in the briefest form a mere outline of the events, preparatory to a more full account of the brave men who fell on the American side. The British loss as officially reported was 35 officers and 191 soldiers killed, 122 officers and 706 soldiers wounded. These belonged to the Artillery, to the Marines, and to the

View of The ATTACK on BUNKER's HILL, with the Burning of CHARLES TOWN, June 17, 1775.

following regiments of foot: the 4th, 5th, 10th, 18th, 22nd, 23rd, 35th, 38th, 43rd, 47th, 52nd, 59th, 63rd, and 65th.

The American loss is difficult to be ascertained, as so little organization had been secured at that time. Frothingham estimates it at 140 killed, 271 wounded, and 30 captured. This matter will however be discussed in Appendix B.

In one aspect this battle was entirely unnecessary. Daniel Webster has summed up the matter in the shortest form.

"I suppose it would be difficult, in a military point of view, to ascribe to the leaders on either side any just motive for the engagement which followed. On the one hand, it could not have been very important to the Americans to attempt to hem the British within the town, by advancing one single post a quarter of a mile; while on the other hand, if the British found it essential to dislodge the American troops, they had it in their power, at no expense of life. By moving up their ships and batteries, they could have completely cut off all communication with the main land over the neck, and the forces in the redoubt would have been reduced to a state of famine in forty-eight hours.

"But that was not the day for any such considerations, on either side. Both parties were anxious to try the strength of their arms. The pride of England would not permit the rebels, as she termed them, to defy her to the teeth; and without for a moment calculating the cost, the British general determined to destroy the fort immediately. On the other side, Prescott and his gallant followers longed and thirsted for a decisive trial of strength and of courage. They wished a battle, and wished it at once. And this is the true secret of the movements on this hill."

It has always been felt that the victory remained with the Americans, although the British held possession of the hill. As a recent writer (see the Appendix to Boston City Document, No. 73, of 1889) has shown that a contrary idea obtains among a small section of our inhabitants, I will again invoke the testimony of Webster.

"The consequences of the battle of Bunker Hill are greater than those of any ordinary conflict, although between armies of far greater force, and terminating with more immediate advantage, on the one side or the other. It was the first great battle of the Revolution; and not only the first blow, but the blow which determined the contest. It did not, indeed, put an end to the war, but in the then existing hostile state of feeling, the difficulties could only be referred to the arbitration of the sword. And one thing is certain: that after the New England troops had shown themselves able to face and repulse the regulars, it was decided that peace could never be established but upon the basis of the independence of the colonies. When the sun of that day went down, the event of independence was no longer doubtful. In a few days Washington heard of the battle, and he inquired if the militia had stood the fire of the regulars. And when told that they had not only stood that fire, but reserved their own till the enemy was within eight rods, and then poured it in with tremendous effect, — 'Then,' exclaimed he, 'the liberties of the country are safe."

Many years after the battle, a foolish controversy arose as to who was the commander of the Americans at the battle. It was a question incapable of exact reply, because there was no regular body of forces, no thorough military organization, and no general in supreme control. The sober judgment of all recent writers seems to point to the following conclusions: The Massachusetts Committee of Safety ordered Gen. Ward to occupy Charlestown. He directed Col. Prescott to perform this duty, and the command of the Massachusetts troops, by far the most numerous part of the allied forces, was solely in Prescott's hands. The redoubt was the centre of the position, the visible object of the British attack, and the other fighting both in attack and defence, was subsidiary to the possession of this earth-work. Here Prescott was supreme, and Gen. Warren, his nominal superior, expressly disclaimed any idea of interference. The New Hampshire troops seemed to have obeyed Prescott's orders, both in standing with him and in occupying the rail-fence. The Connecticut troops probably looked more to Gen. Putnam for orders, but that gallant officer seems to have displayed less generalship than valor.

But above all, the American troops were lacking in exact discipline, and regimental formations even seemed to have been largely disregarded. Many men doubtless rushed forward to the fight without orders, and some doubtless straggled away into safety who ought to have remained by their colors. Hence the folly of attempting to measure out the exact precedence among the many brave men who gained the first decisive victory for the American arms.

The statue of Prescott stands to-day on Bunker Hill, and no voice is raised to object to this recognition of his merit. In the future we may hope for similar monuments to other heroes, also deserving of our gratitude and respect.

STATUE OF COL. PRESCOTT, MONUMENT GROUNDS.

APPENDIX B.

LIST OF THE AMERICANS KILLED AT BUNKER HILL.

As the object of the memorial described in this volume is to honor the soldiers who lost their lives on the American side at the battle of Bunker Hill, a full statement is given of the authority for the list of names so commemorated. Prior to the establishment of a Joint Committee of the Boston City Council on this subject, no information had been put in print in regard to the names of the soldiers, at least in any general and connected form. In some local histories due importance had been given to the soldiers of particular towns, but such books are not easily obtainable. Frothingham in his exhaustive account of the battle has the names of only one or two privates. Most of the officers who fell were well known, but no steps had been taken apparently by any parties to prepare a list of the rank and file who were killed or mortally wounded on that glorious day. Even the exact number of these victims is a matter of doubt, as no official report was ever made. July 7, 1775, the Provincial Congress ordered (Journal, p. 463), that the Committee of Safety "draw up and transmit to Great Britain, a fair and impartial account of the late battle at Charlestown as soon as possible." This was promptly done, and the following paragraph gives all the details on this point: —

"The loss of the New England army amounted according to an exact return, to 145 killed and missing and 304 wounded; thirty of the first were wounded and taken prisoners by the enemy." (Frothingham, 384.) Undoubtedly this return, whatever it may have been, was the basis of the following record in Gen. Ward's orderly book,

— the only reference to the battle it contains, — of the loss of the Americans.

"'June 17. The battle of Charlestown was fought this day. Killed, one hundred and fifteen, wounded, three hundred and five, captured, thirty. Total, four hundred and fifty.'" (Frothingham, 192.)

Frothingham (History, p. 193) has the following table, prepared from various sources: —

AMERICAN LOSS AT BUNKER HILL.

	Regiment.	Killed.	Wounded.		Regiment.	Killed.	Wounded.
I.	Prescott	42	28	X.	Gridley	0	4
II.	Bridge	15	29	XI.	Ward	1	6
III.	Frye	15	31	XII.	Scammans	0	2
IV.	Brewer	7	11	XIII.	Gerrish	3	2
V.	Little	7	23	XIV.	Whitcomb	5	8
VI.	Gardner	6	7	XV.	Stark	15	45
VII.	Nixon	3	10	XVI.	Reed	5	21
VIII.	Woodbridge	1	5		Putnam & Coit's Co.	11	26
IX.	Doolittle	0	9		Chester's Co.	4	4

Total: killed, 140; wounded, 271; captured, 30.

Colonel Swett, in his account of the battle, agrees with these figures, except that he makes Bridge's loss in killed 16, and omits Reed's, 5. His total is 136. I am inclined to think that the estimate of 140 killed is rather high, and that the lists subjoined, including the mortally wounded, will cover nearly all of those who fell.

As will be seen, we have recovered the names of 141 of the rank and file, and it must be conceded that this is a most satisfactory approximation to the 140 mentioned in the official summary.

The names given are those found on the muster-roll of the nearest date, and are marked thereon, at the time, as being those of men who were killed. These rolls are contained in Massachusetts Revolutionary Rolls, vol. 56 and vol. 14 in the Secretary's office. They have been examined most thoroughly, and it is thought that this source of information is exhausted. The detail of the entries is given later. A careful examination was also made of what are called the Coat Rolls of the same period. I have also incorporated the facts stated in a contemporary list of the prisoners taken by the British, as reprinted in the New England Historical and Genealogical Register for April, 1888. For the list of New Hampshire soldiers killed, recourse was had to a most thorough list prepared by George C. Gilmore, Esq., of Manchester, N.H. The names of the Connecticut men were kindly furnished by Col. White of the Adjutant-General's office at Hartford, and the list is as complete as could be prepared from the records there.

The following summary of the evidence was submitted by the Committee on June 20th. A careful revision of the rolls has revealed no errors therein; but by some error Joseph Hibbard of Dracut, in Frye's regiment, is recorded on the tablet in the wrong company. He served under Capt. Davis, not Capt. Sawyer.

I have since then received very satisfactory evidence[1] that to the list should be added

    Lt. Benjamin West of Salem. (Not numbered but put on Officers' Roll.)

138. Corp. Philip Fowler of Tewksbury.
139. Corp. Samuel Hill of Billerica.
140. Samuel Bailey jr. of Andover.
141. Darius Stevens of Connecticut.

---

[1] Lt. Benjamin West is said by Felt, (Annals of Salem, p. 520) to have fallen there. My attention was called to the fact by the venerable Caleb Foote of Salem, father of the late Rev. Henry W. Foote of Boston. Mr. Foote writes that his grandmother was the sister of Lieut. West, and that he lived with her from the age of 5 to 12 (1808 to 1815) and often heard the story from her lips. Mr. Foote also has the portrait of his great-uncle, painted by himself, in his uniform. Such evidence must be conclusive. He belonged to Mansfield's regiment, of whom Frothingham says (p. 189) that Col. John Mansfield's regiment was ordered to Charlestown, but marched to Cobble Hill, to protect the detachment of artillery. Col. M. was tried and cashiered for remissness in his duty, but Col. Swett says he was only guilty of an error arising from inexperience.

As to Darius Stevens, the evidence is to be found in a sermon preached at Stoneham in 1831, by Rev. W. C. Whitcomb, on the death of Rev. John H. Stevens. Mr. Stevens was born at Canterbury, Conn., Sept. 20th, 1766, and died Aug. 9, 1851, aged 85. In this sermon (p. 31) it is said of him, that one of his brothers served with Gen. Washington, and another, named Darius, fell at the Battle of Bunker Hill, aged only 19 years. Here the evidence seems to be unquestionable also, but confirmation can be had only from the Connecticut records.

The evidence as to Corp. Philip Fowler, Corp. Samuel Hill, and Samuel Bailey, jr., is set forth, *post*, pp. 92, 93.

While I deeply regret that these five names were not received in time to put them on the Bronze Tablets before the dedication, I do not feel that any mistake was made in erecting the monument. During the present month, by direction of the Committee, these five names have been placed on the Tablet which records the "Soldiers Unassigned," and the names are duly entered in our Index and consecutive numberings. We may yet recover two or three more names, but surely it was better to do honor to the 137 men who were then known, than to postpone such public recognition indefinitely in hopes of a well-nigh impossible completeness. The neglect of over a century has at last been repaired, and if more heroes are discovered our successors will extend to them similar recognition and honors.

DETAILED LIST OF MEN KILLED OR MORTALLY WOUNDED.

Officers Killed or Mortally Wounded.

1. Maj.-Gen. Joseph Warren.
2. Col. Thomas Gardner.
3. Lt.-Col. Moses Parker, of Bridge's regiment.
4. Major William Moore, of Doolittle's regiment.
5. Major Andrew McClary, of Stark's regiment.
6. Capt. Isaac Baldwin, of Stark's regiment.
7. Capt. Benjamin Walker, of Bridge's regiment.
8. Lieut. Amaziah Fausett, of Prescott's regiment.
9. Lieut. Joseph Spaulding, of Prescott's regiment.
10. [Lieut. Benjamin West, of Mansfield's regiment.]

Rank and File.

I. PRESCOTT'S REGIMENT.

Prescott's regiment, commanded by Col. William Prescott, claims precedence, both for its losses and the prominence of its chief. It was raised in Middlesex, but it is uncertain how many of its companies

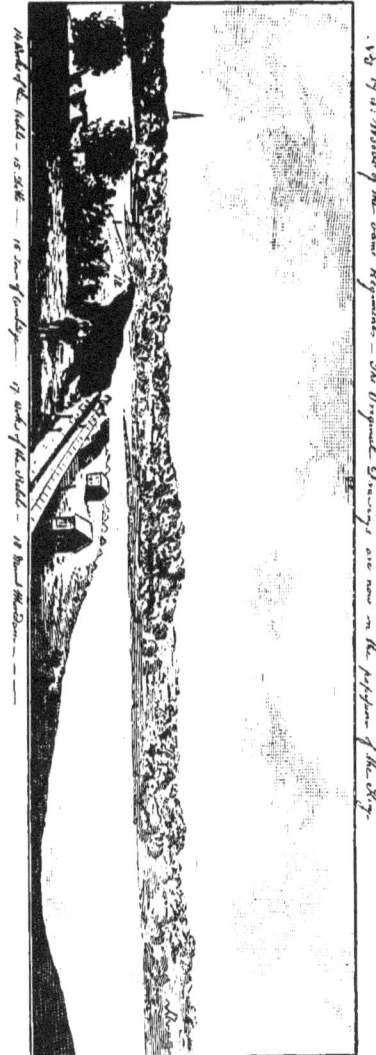

were in the fight. The adjutant, William Green, Captains Maxwell and Farwell, and Lieutenant Brown, were wounded. Frothingham says that Lieutenant Prescott, a nephew of the colonel, and probably serving in this regiment, was killed. It is certain, however, that he means (my number, 78) Benjamin Prescott, who was sergeant in Dows' company in this regiment. Lieut. Amaziah Fassett, of Groton, was mortally wounded, captured, and died in Boston.

The evidence is very strong that Lieutenant Joseph Spaulding, of Groton, was also killed. Vol. 56, p. 61, of Rolls, has his name, with five others, as killed or taken. Vol. 15, p. 55, has a full list of Lawrence's company. 1st Lieut. Joseph Spaulding, of Pepperell, is entered as enlisted April 30th, 1775, and credited with forty-nine days' pay, while most of the others have ninety-eight days' pay. This would take him just to June 17th, and confirms the other entry.

The evidence here given recovers for us the names of thirty-six of the rank and file of this regiment killed, or mortally wounded. To Aaron Barr, of Meryfield (? now Rowe), of Capt. Hugh Maxwell's company in this regiment, these rolls give the honor of being "the first man killed June 17." [*]

Captain Dow's and Captain Moor's companies include some New Hampshire men who served in this regiment.

Killed.

1.	Peter Whitcomb,	Littleton,	Capt. Samuel Gilbert.
2.	Benjamin Dole,	Littleton,	do
3.	John Lawrence,	Littleton,	do
4.	James Whitemore,	Littleton,	do

Died from Wounds.

5.	Isaac Whitcomb,	unknown,	do
6.	Archibald McIntosh,	Brookline, N.H.,	do
7.	James Coneck,	Brookline, N.H.,	do

---

[*] See, however, Bridge's regiment, *post*.

Killed.

8.	Chambers Corey,	Groton,	Capt. Ephraim Corey.

Died from Wounds.

9.	Daniel McGrath,	Amherst,	do

Killed.

10.	John Gibson,	Fitchburg,	Capt. Abijah Wyman.
11.	Cesar Bason,**	Westford,	do

Died from Wounds.

12.	Amos Wheeler,	unknown,	do
13.	Oliver Stevens,	Townsend,	do

Killed.

14.	Nathaniel Parker,	Pepperell,	Capt. John Nutting.
15.	William Warrin,	Pepperell,	do
16.	Edmund Peers,	Pepperell,	do
17.	Wainwright Fisk,	Pepperell,	do
18.	Ebenezer Laughton,	Pepperell,	do
19.	Jeremiah Shattuck,	Pepperell,	do
20.	Jesse Corless,	Deerfield,	Capt. Hugh Maxwell.
21.	Eben Faills,	Charlemont,	do
22.	Aaron Barr, " first man killed," Meryfield (Rowe),		do
23.	Jonathan Bate,	Winchendon,	Capt. Samuel Patch.
24.	Jonas Looker,	Sudbury,	do
25.	Joseph Minott,	Westford,	Capt. Joshua Parker.
26.	Jonathan Hadley,	Westford,	do
27.	Peter Fisk,	Groton,	do
28.	Jonathan Jenkins,	Groton,	Capt. Henry Farwell.
29.	James Dodge,	Groton,	Capt. Asa Lawrence.
30.	Stephen Foster,	Groton,	do
31.	Abraham Blood,	Groton,	do
32.	Benjamin Wood,	Groton,	do
33.	Simon Hobart,	Groton,	do
34.	Robert Parker,	Groton,	do

** Presumably a colored man, as several were in the fight.

APPENDIX B. 91

These last-named six men are entered on Captain Lawrence's roll as killed or taken. Dodge and Foster died in captivity in Boston, and the evidence is reasonably strong that the other four died. As to Robert Parker, he is entered at the corner of Lawrence's Coat Roll; but Vol. 56, p. 64, gives Robert Parker, and Robert Parker, jr., in Capt. Ephraim Cory's company, and adds that Robert Parker died Sept. 30th, at Cambridge. I presume that these two entries on the two rolls mean the same man, and that it is a fair inference that the Groton man died of wounds received at Bunker Hill.

Died from Wounds.

35. John Gordon,	Stow.	Capt. Asa Lawrence.
36. David Kemp,*	Groton,	do

II. BRIDGE'S REGIMENT.

Commanded by Col. Ebenezer Bridge; was represented, probably, by only a part of its companies. Lieut.-Col. Moses Parker, of Chelmsford, was mortally wounded, captured, and died in Boston, as did also Capt. Benjamin Walker, of Chelmsford.

There is no doubt that Corp. Philip Fowler, of Tewksbury, who was also in Walker's company, was killed in the fight.

In Vol. 56, roll 178, it is noted,

Captain Benjamin Walker	of Chelmsford,	Dead.
Reuben Beacon	" Bedford,	Dead.
Jacob Crosby	" Billerica,	Dead.
Jacob Frost	" Boston,	Prisoner.
Corp. Philip Fowler	" Tewksbury,	Missing.

In Volume 16, p. 57, is a careful pay-roll made up to August 1, but unfortunately defective, many names being missing at the bottom, and undoubtedly among them were those of Beacon and Crosby, which are not found on the portion of the list which is intact. Frost has 3 mos. 11 days' pay, from April 19th, and we know he was

---

* Kemp died at Boston, in captivity, Sept. 10th.

a prisoner in Boston and alive Sept. 14th. Philip Fowler has 1 mo. 23 days from April 19th. The Coat Rolls, Vol. 57, hereinafter cited, show that he never was found after the fight.

I cannot positively affirm that Reuben Beacon and Jacob Crosby also fell at Bunker Hill. As I cannot determine the date of their death, I deem it most probable, and urge inquiry into these cases. But, so far, we have placed no names on the Tablets, except on official evidence.

The Coat Rolls furnish us with another name, that of Samuel Bailey, jr., of Andover, certified to by Capt. Charles Furbush, who succeeded to the command of Jacob Tyler's company.

In Capt. Jonathan Stickney's roll, Vol. 56, no. 180, I find at the bottom:

Corp. Samuel Hill
Asa Pollard
Benjamin Easty } Dead.
Timothy Toothaker

Jere^m Read
Isaac G^r. White
Joel Walker } Listed in the Train, 24 May.
John Wilson

There is a duplicate roll in Vol. 16, and the last seven names though torn are evidently these. It reads:

Asa Pollard,	Billerica,	enlisted May	8,	served	1 mo.	13 days.		
. . . .	do	"	do	22,	"		26	"
. . . . . ker . .	do	"	do	8,	"	1	"	
. . . . . . d. . .	do	"	April 25,		"	1	"	1	"
. . . . . White	do		do			1	"	1	"
. . . . Walker	do		do			1	"	1	"
. ohn Willson	do		do			1	"	1	"

There is no doubt that the Corp. Samuel Hill who enlisted April 25 and served 1 mo. 26 days must have died June 20th. Asa Pollard is paid to June 21, Benjamin Easty to June 17th; but Timothy Toothaker is paid only to June 8th, and evidently died in camp before the fight. I have no doubt that Corp. Samuel Hill is entitled to the credit of being mortally wounded on the 17th, and dying three days later.

I therefore enter as additional

138	Corp. Philip Fowler	of Tewksbury,	Capt. Benj. Walker.
139	Corp. Samuel Hill	" Billerica,	Capt. Jona. Stickney.
140	Samuel Bailey, jr.	" Andover,	Capt. Jacob Tyler.

Frothingham (p. 126) says that early on June 17 a private was killed by a cannon-ball, and that it was (38) Asa Pollard, of Billerica, of Captain Stickney's company in this regiment. Swett's history seems to be the authority for this anecdote. See, however, *ante*, Aaron Barr, of Prescott's regiment, No. 22.

Our rolls give —

Killed.

37.	Benjamin Eastey,	Billerica,	Capt. Jona. Stickney.
38.	Asa Pollard,	Billerica,	do
39.	John Thessill,	Dracut,	Capt. Peter Coburn.
40.	Joseph Kemp,	Dunstable.	Capt. Eben Bancroft.
41.	Francis Pool,*	Gloucester,	Capt. John Rowe.
42.	Josiah Brooks,	Gloucester,	do
43.	William Parsons,	Gloucester,	do

NOTE. — Seven men killed in Dow's company, three killed and two mortally wounded in Moore's company, all serving under Prescott, and recorded in the New Hampshire list later on. This makes a total of forty-eight killed under Prescott, besides the three officers.

* Babson's "History of Gloucester" states that Pool and Brooks were killed at the rail-fence, and Parsons at the redoubt. They are recorded as killed in Rolls vol. 16, p. 11.

III. Frye's Regiment.

Col. James Frye's regiment, from Essex, was commissioned May 20. The loss as recorded was: —

Killed.

44.	David Huntington,	Amesbury,	Capt. John Currier.
45.	John Eaton,	Haverhill,	Capt. James Sawyer.
46.	Simeon Pike,	Haverhill,	do

Died of Wounds.

47.	Joseph Hibbard,	Dracut,	Capt. John Davis.

Killed.

48.	Ebenezer Herrick,	Methuen,	do

Killed.

49.	Samuel Russell	(not stated),	Capt. Jonas Richardson.
50.	Daniel Evens	(not stated),	do
51.	James Milliken**	(not stated),	do
52.	John Blyth	(not stated),	do
53.	Ichabod March,	Amesbury,	Capt. Wm. H. Ballard.
54.	Joseph Simmons,	Boxford,	Capt. Wm. Perley.

Died of Wounds.

55.	James Boynton,	Boxford,	do

Killed.

56.	Philip Abbot,	Andover,	Capt. Benj. Ames.
57.	William Haggitt,	Andover,	do
58.	Joseph Chandler,	Andover,	do

Died of Wounds.

59.	Jesse Holt,	Andover,	do

** Milliken *seems* to have been of Cambridge. See Coat Rolls, later on.

IV. Brewer's Regiment.

Col. Jonathan Brewer's regiment, from Worcester and Middlesex, consisted, June 15, of 397 men. It seems that only about one-half of the regiment was in the fight, and they were stationed mostly on the diagonal line between the breastwork and rail-fence. The colonel and the lieutenant-colonel (William Buckminster) were both wounded, and the regiment evidently made a brilliant record.

Killed.

60.	Josiah Bacon,	Hutchinson (Barré),	Capt. John Black.
61.	John Barrett,	Hutchinson (Barré),	do
62.	Ebenezer Childs, jr.,	Hutchinson (Barré),	do

Died of Wounds.

63.	Lucas Green,	Winchendon,	do

Killed.

64.	Comeing Fairbank,	Framingham,	Capt. Aaron Haynes.
65.	Joshua Haynes,	Sudbury,	do
66.	Lebbeus Jennings,	Deerfield,	Cap. Thad. Russell.

Died of Wounds.

67.	Jonas Barnard,	Watertown,	Capt. Isaac Gray.
68.	Timothy Evins,	Ware,	Capt. Jona. Bardwell.
69.	Stephen Ayres,	Belchertown,	do

V. Little's Regiment.

Col. Moses Little's regiment, from Essex, was not commissioned till June 26. Three companies were led on by Colonel Little, and distinguished themselves.

Killed.

70.	Daniel Callahan,	Gloucester,	Capt. Nath'l Warner.
71.	Benjamin Smith,	Gloucester,	do
72.	Moses Pigeon,	Newburyport,	Capt. Benj. Perkins.
73.	Samuel Nelson,	Newburyport,	do
74.	Jesse Story,	Ipswich,	Capt. Abraham Dodge.

VI. Gardner's Regiment.

Col. Thomas Gardner's regiment was from Middlesex. He was mortally wounded, and died July 3, 1775. Our rolls contain no names from this regiment, though Swett makes their loss six killed and seven wounded. The Charlestown company especially distinguished itself.

VII. Nixon's Regiment.

"Col. John Nixon's regiment, from Middlesex and Worcester, was neither full nor commissioned, and both the returns and the details of it are very meagre." (Frothingham.) Col. Nixon was badly wounded, and Swett credits the regiment with 3 killed and 10 wounded. Our lists have no names from this regiment.

[But see the preface to this edition. W. H. W.]

VIII. Woodbridge's Regiment.

"Col. Benjamin R. Woodbridge's regiment, of Hampshire, also was not commissioned, and there are few details of it, or of its officers, in the accounts of the battle." (Frothingham.) Swett estimates one killed and five wounded, but none are on our rolls.

IX. Doolittle's Regiment.

"Col. Ephraim Doolittle's regiment was commissioned June 12th, when a return names only seven companies. The colonel and lieutenant-colonel were absent on the day of battle, and Major Willard Moore led on, it is stated, three hundred of its men." (Frothingham.)

Major Moore was mortally wounded and died on the field. Our roll give three soldiers also as

Killed.

75. Joshua Whitcomb,	Templeton,	Capt. Joel Fletcher.
76. Jeduthan Alexander,	Marlboro',	Capt. Jona. Holman.
77. Benjamin Reed,	Rutland,	Capt. Adam Wheeler.

X. Gridley's Regiment.

Col. Richard Gridley commanded the artillery, of which three companies were in the fight, though of little service. He was a veteran of the French wars, planned the works at Breed's Hill, and was wounded in the battle.

XI. Ward's Regiment.

Gen. Artemas Ward's regiment, from Worcester, was commissioned May 23, 1775. It was not ordered to Charlestown till late in the day, and only a few companies were engaged.*

Our lists give as

Killed.

78. Samuel Heards,	Grafton,	Capt. Luke Drury.

XII. Scammans's Regiment.

"James Scammans's regiment, from Maine, did not advance nearer the battle than Bunker Hill; and its colonel was tried for disobedience of orders, but acquitted." (Frothingham.) Swett notes two soldiers as wounded, but none as killed.

XIII. Gerrish's Regiment.

Samuel Gerrish commanded this regiment, but only a part went into battle, under command of the adjutant, Christian Febiger. Swett credits it with three killed.

Our Rolls give as

Killed.

79. Thomas Doyl,	a deserter from the King's troops,	Capt. Wm. Rogers.

---

*Sergt. John Brown of Leicester, and Corp. Kerley Ward of Oakham, in Capt. Washburn's company are returned as wounded, but they evidently lived till August.

XIV. WHITCOMB'S REGIMENT.

Col. Asa Whitcomb's regiment, of Worcester, had probably two companies in the battle, and Swett records that five men were killed and eight wounded.

Our Rolls give as

Killed.

80.	David Robbins,	Lancaster,	Capt. Andrew Haskell.
81.	Sergt. Robert Phelps,	Lancaster,	do.
	(died a prisoner).		

GLOVER'S REGIMENT.

Under Col. John Glover, our rolls give one man.

Killed.

82.	Thomas Allen,	Marblehead,	Capt. Joel Smith.

THE NEW HAMPSHIRE CONTINGENT.

We have now to consider New Hampshire men. Our rolls give from those serving under Colonel Prescott: —

Killed.

83.	Sergt. Nathan Blood,	Hollis,	Capt. Reuben Dows.
84.	Phineas Nevens,	Hollis,	do.
85.	Thomas Wheat, jr.,	Hollis,	do.
86.	Peter Poor,	Hollis,	do.
	[Caleb Eastman*],	Hollis,	do.
87.	Isaac Hobart,	Hollis,	do.
88.	Jacob Boynton,	Hollis,	do.
89.	Sergt. Benj. Prescott,**	Groton,	Capt. Joseph Moors.
90.	Ebenezer Youngman,	Hollis,	do.
91.	Thomas Colbourn,	Dunstable,	do.

---

* Killed June 19 by the bursting of his gun.   ** A Massachusetts man.

XV. Stark's Regiment, N.H.

Col. John Stark's regiment was large and well filled. The major, Andrew McClary, was killed on the 17th, after the British had occupied Bunker Hill. Capt. Isaac Baldwin, of Hillsborough, also fell. The New Hampshire records, according to Mr. Gilmore's list printed in full, later on, give the following persons as

Killed.

92.	Paul Caldwell,***	Londonderry,	Capt. Scott.
93.	William French,***	Nelson,	do.
94.	Jonas Howe,***	Marlborough,	do.
95.	Joseph Taylor,	Peterborough,	do.
96.	Thomas Collins,	Windham,	Capt. Woodbury.
97.	Moses Poor,	———,	do.
98.	Caleb Dalton,	———,	Capt. Richards.
99.	William Mitchell,	Concord,	Capt. Abbot.
100.	John Manuel,	Bow,	Capt. Kinsman.
101.	Sergt. Asahel Nims,***	Keene,	Capt. Stiles.
102.	George Shannon,	Canterbury,	Capt. G. Hutchins.

Mortally Wounded.

103.	William McCrillis,	Nottingham,	Capt. Dearborn.
104.	Joseph Broderick,	———,	Capt. Moore.

*** These four men are on the Mass. Cont Rolls as commanded by Col. Paul Dudley Sargent.

XVI. REED'S REGIMENT, N.H.

This regiment was commanded by Col. James Reed, and consisted, June 14, of 486 rank and file.

The New Hampshire records (Gilmore's list) give as

Killed.

105.	Isaac Adams,	Rindge,	Capt. Thomas.
106.	George Carlton,	Rindge,	do.
107.	Jonathan Lovejoy,	Rindge,	do.
108.	Joseph Blood,	Mason,	Capt. Mann.
109.	Ebenezer Blood, jr.,	Mason,	do.
110.	David Carleton,	Lyndeborough,	Capt. Spaulding
111.	John Cole,	Amherst,	Capt. Crosby.
112.	James Hutchinson,	Amherst,	do.
113.	John Davis,	Chesterfield,	Capt. Hinds.
114.	Joseph Farwell,	Charlestown,	Capt. Marcy.
115.	James Patten,	———,	do.
116.	John Melvin,	———,	do.
117.	Benjamin Chamberlain,	———,	do.
118.	Parker Hills,	Candia,	Capt. H. Hutchins.
119.	David Scott,	Peterborough,	Capt. E. Townes.

The same records also give as

Mortally Wounded.

120.	Paul Clogston,	Nashua,	Capt. Walker.
121.	Asa Cram,	Wilton,	do.
122.	Jonathan Gray,	Wilton,	do.
123.	Jason Russell,	Nashua,	do.
124.	Oliver Wood,	Nashua,	do.

APPENDIX B.

THE CONNECTICUT TROOPS.

"The conduct of the Connecticut troops is mentioned in terms of high commendation in the private letters and the journals of the time. Major Durkee; Captains Knowlton, Chester, Coit; Lieutenants Dana, Hide, Grosvenor, Webb, Bingham, and Keyes, are especially named as deserving of credit." (Frothingham.) Col. White, of the Adjutant-General's office, Hartford, has kindly furnished the following list of

Killed.

125. Roger Fox.
126. William Cheeney.   ⎫
127. Asahel Lyon.   ⎬ All three of Ashford, Conn., in Capt. Thomas Knowlton's company.
128. Benjamin Ross, (or Russ). ⎭
129. Samuel Ashbo.
130. Gershom Smith.
131. Matthew Cummings.
132. Daniel Memory.
133. Wilson Rowlandson.

SOLDIERS UNASSIGNED.

134. Amasa Fisk,   Pepperell.
135. William Robinson,
136. John Dillon,   Jersey, Eng.
137. John Lord.

Additional List.

138. Corp. Philip Fowler,   See *ante*, p. 93.
139. Corp. Samuel Hill,   do   p. 93.
140. Samuel Bailey, jr.,   do   p. 93.
141. Darius Stevens, of Conn., do   p. 87.

INDEX OF NAMES OF THE SOLDIERS KILLED OR MORTALLY WOUNDED, JUNE 17, 1775.

(The numbers are the continuous ones prefixed to the names.)

Abbot, Philip	56	Corey, Chambers	8
Adams, Isaac	105	Corless, Jesse	20
Alexander, Jeduthan	76	Cram, Asa	121
Allen, Thomas	82	Cummings, Matthew	131
Ashbo, Samuel	129	Davis, John	113
Ayres, Stephen	69	Dalton, Caleb	98
		Dillon, John	136
Bacon, Josiah	60	Dodge, James	29
Bailey, Samuel, jr.	140	Dole, Benjamin	2
Barnard, Jonas	67	Doyl, Thomas	79
Barr, Aaron	22		
Barrett, John	61	Eastey, Benjamin	37
Bason, Cæsar	11	Eaton, John	45
Bate, Jonathan	23	Evens, Daniel	50
Blood, Abraham	31	Evins, Timothy	68
Blood, Ebenezer, jr.	109		
Blood, Joseph	108	Faills, Eben	21
Blood, Nathan	83	Fairbank, Coming	64
Blyth, John	52	Farwell, Joseph	114
Boynton, James	55	Fisk, Amasa	134
Boynton, Jacob	88	Fisk, Peter	27
Broderick, Joseph	104	Fisk, Wainwright	17
Brooks, Josiah	42	Foster, Stephen	30
		Fowler, Philip	138
Caldwell, Paul	92	Fox, Roger	125
Callahan, Daniel	70	French, William	93
Carleton, David	110		
Carlton, George	106	Gibson, John	10
Chamberlin, Benjamin	117	Gordon, John	35
Chandler, Joseph	58	Gray, Jonathan	122
Cheeucy, William	126	Green, Lucas	63
Childs, Ebenezer, jr.	62		
Clogston, Paul	120	Hadley, Jonathan	26
Colburn, Thomas	91	Haggitt, William	57
Cole, John	111	Haynes, Joshua	65
Collins, Thomas	96	Heards, Samuel	78
Coneck, James	7	Herrick, Ebenezer	48

View of the Town of BOSTON from Breeds Hill in CHARLESTOWN.

APPENDIX B.

Hibbard, Joseph 47
Hill, Samuel 139
Hills, Parker 118
Hobart, Isaac 87
Hobart, Simon 33
Holt, Jesse 59
Howe, Jonas 94
Huntington, David 44
Hutchinson, James 112

Jenkins, Jonathan 28
Jennings, Lebbeus 66

Kemp, David 36
Kemp, Joseph 40

Laughton, Ebenezer 18
Lawrence, John 3
Looker, Jonas 24
Lord, John 137
Lovejoy, Jonathan 107
Lyon, Asahel 127

McCrillis, William 103
McGrath, Daniel 9
McIntosh, Archibald 6
Manuel, John 100
March, Ichabod 53
Melvin, John 116
Memory, Daniel 132
Milliken, James 51
Minott, Joseph 25
Mitchell, William 99

Nelson, Samuel 73
Nevens, Phineas 84
Nims, Asahel 101

Parker, Nathaniel 14
Parker, Robert 34
Parsons, William 43
Patton, James 115

Peers, Edmund 16
Phelps, Robert 81
Pigeon, Moses 72
Pike, Simeon 46
Pollard, Asa 38
Pool, Francis 41
Poor, Moses 97
Poor, Peter 86
Prescott, Benjamin 89

Reed, Benjamin 77
Robbins, David 80
Robinson, William 135
Ross, Benjamin 128
Rowlandson, Wilson 133
Russell, Jason 123
Russell, Samuel 49

Scott, David 119
Shannon, George 102
Shattuck, Jeremiah 19
Simmons, Joseph 54
Smith, Benjamin 71
Smith, Gershom 130
Stevens, Darius 141
Stevens, Oliver 13
Story, Jesse 74

Taylor, Joseph 95
Thessill, John 39

Warrin, William 15
Wheat, Thomas 85
Wheeler, Amos 12
Whitcomb, Isaac 5
Whitcomb, Joshua 75
Whitcomb, Peter 1
Whitemore, James 4
Wood, Benjamin 32
Wood, Oliver 124

Youngman, Ebenezer 90

THE COAT ROLLS.

Besides the regimental muster rolls, another class of documents has thrown light upon the question of the soldiers killed at Bunker Hill. These papers are known as Coat Rolls, and are in Vol. 57 of the Massachusetts Archives.

July 5th, 1775 (Journal Prov. Congress, p. 456), it was "*Resolved*, that thirteen thousand coats be provided, as soon as may be, and one thereof given to each non-commissioned officer and soldier in the Massachusetts forces, agreeably to the resolve of Congress, on the 23rd day of April last." This resolve (*Ib.* p. 148) was,—"*Resolved*, unanimously, that it is necessary for the defence of the colony, that an army of 30,000 men be immediately raised and established. *Resolved*, That 13,600 men be raised immediately by this province."

The various towns, according to a schedule printed, were to have the coats made up, being paid 4 shillings for making, and also for the cloth at the rate of 5 shillings 4 pence for cloth ⅞ of a yard wide. Moreover, the soldiers from each town were to be clothed in the coats made in such town so far as possible.

The result was, that this coat was quite an item in the soldier's pay, and was demanded by the heirs of those who died. A great mass of receipts has fortunately been preserved, and is arranged in Vol. 57. Naturally, the series is not complete, especially in regard to the orders and receipts for men deceased, but the information contained is very interesting. This volume has been repeatedly examined for the purpose of noting all mention of the soldiers killed at Bunker Hill, and it is hoped that no such entry has escaped notice.

It is from this source that I have obtained a certainty that Corp. Philip Fowler and Samuel Bailey, jr., belong upon our list.

The following abstracts of these certificates show the nature of the evidence. I prefix a list of the names, giving to each the number by which he is designated in the preceding pages.

APPENDIX B.

SOLDIERS NAMED IN THE COAT ROLLS.

Ichabod March	53	Simon Hobart	33
James Millikin	51	Robert Parker	34
John Eaton	45	Jeremiah Shattuck	19
Simeon Pike	46	Nathaniel Parker	14
Joseph Simmons	54	Ebenezer Laughton	18
Joseph Chandler	58	Archibald McIntosh	6
Ebenezer Herrick	48	Peter Poor	86
Joseph Hibberd	47	Oliver Stevens	13
Joshua Haynes	65	Cæsar Bason	11
Jonas Barnard, jr.	67	Ebenezer Youngman	90
Josiah Bacon	60	Joseph Minott	25
John Barrett	61	Amos Wheeler	12
Ebenezer Chuid, jr.	62	Benjamin Dole	2
Lucas Green	63	Isaac Whitcomb	5
Jacob Boynton	88	Chambers Corey	8
Phineas Nevens	84	Benjamin Smith	71
Isaac Hobart	87	Daniel Callahan	70
Nathan Blood	83	Samuel Nelson	73
Thomas Wheat	85	Thomas Allen	82
John Gibson	10	Philip Fowler	138
James Dodge	29	Samuel Bailey, jr.	140
Stephen Foster	30	Benjamin Easty	37
Abraham Blood	31	John Thessill	39
Benjamin Wood	32	Asahel Nims	101

ABSTRACT OF CERTIFICATES, ETC.

Ichabod March killed in Battle at Charlestown June 17, signed W^m. Hudson Ballard Capt. Also a certificate that the men mentioned in this roll belonged to Col. Frye's Reg^t.

Cambridge. January 1, 1775. To the Committee of Supplys at Watertown. Gentlemen Please to Pay unto David Vallet the sum of twenty-five shillings lawful money in the lieu of a coat which his brother *James Milliken*, has due, killed in Battle at Bunker Hill on the 17th of June last, belong to my Company in Col. Frye's Reg. Jonas Richardson Capt.

Haverhill. March 20, 1776. To the Committee for Clothing. Please to pay to Jonathan Webster one pound and five shillings, it being for a coat allowed to my son *John Eaton* as bounty by the province, he having never received it; he being killed in the fight at bunker hill signed, John Eaton of Capt James Sawyers Company of Col. Frye's Reg also a certificate that he was a soldier, and was killed signed John Eaton and three selectmen of Haverhill.

Haverhill. March 1, 1776. To the Committee of Clothing. Please to pay to Jonathan Webster Esq. twenty five shillings which was allowed in the room of a Bounty Coat to my late husband *Simeon Pike* killed in the fight at Bunker Hill and you will oblige yours to serve Mary Pike also certified to by the selectmen of Haverhill.

Boxford. March 19, 1776, To the Committee of Supplies. Gentlemen, Whereas my late husband *Joseph Simmons* was a soldier in Capt William Perleys Company, in Col. Frye's Comp. and was lost in Battle on Bunker Hill on ye 17th June last, Gent. these are to desire you to deliver to ye above s^d Capt Perley a coat as voted by Congress Jerusha Simmons.

Andover. Feb 6, 1776, To the Committee of Clothing. Gentlemen, Please to pay Saml Phillips Junr. the amount of a Coat, which was promised to the soldiers who enlisted after the nineteenth of April, 1775, that was due *Joseph Chandler* a private in Capt Ames' Comp. Col. Frye's Reg. said Chandler was an indented servant of me, the subscriber, and was slain in the Battle at Bunker Hill. Jonathan Cummings Jr.

Methuen. April 2, 1776, To the Committee of Clothing. Gentlemen, this may certify that *Ebenezer Herrick* of Methuen enlisted into my company in Col Frye's Reg^t and served from the 19th of April to the 17th of June, and then was killed in Battle on Bunker Hill, and was entitled to a coat and blanket which he has not had — John Davis Capt.

APPENDIX B.

Methuen. Feb 2nd, 1776, To the Committee of Supplies this may certify that *Joseph Hebberd*, the son of Joseph of Dracutt, enlisted into my Company in Col James Frye's Reg^t. and served from the 19th of April till the Battle at Bunker Hill, and was then wounded, of which wound he died, and was entitled to a Coat, which he has not rec^d. John Dewey Capt.

Camp at Roxbury. March 14, 1776, This may certify that *Joshua Haynes*, son to Mr. Joshua Haynes, was a solder in my company till the 17th of June last, when he was killed in the Battle of that day. he never received a coat as was promised by this Colony. Aaron Haynes Capt

---

This may certify that *Jonas Barnard* Junr. of Watertown enlisted himself agreeable to the Provincial Congress, to serve under me as his captain in the Continental Army, and received the post of a sergeant and continued in the Service of the United Colonies two months and five days, and died without receiving any pay   Isaac Grey Capt.

Hutchinson. Sept 23rd, 1776, This may certify that *Josiah Bacon, John Barrett* and *Ebenezer Child, Junr*, were soldiers in Capt. John Black's Company, in Col, Jon. Brewers Reg^t, and were slain in the Battle on Bunker Hill, on the 17th Day of June 1775, John Black Capt.

Prospect Hill. Jan 1. 1776, This may certify that *Lucas Green*, a soldier in the company lately commanded by Capt John Black in Col. Brewers Reg^t. who has not received a coat or pay for it, and was wounded in the action on ye 17 of June and since deceased.   John Patrick Lieut.

Hollis. Feb 10, 1776. A certificate that John Boynton, William Nevens, Shubaell Hobart, Enoch Noyes, Amos Eastman, Abigail Wheet and Sarah Fisk, are the proper heirs of the money due to Jacob Boynton, Phineas Nevens, Isaac Hobart, Nathan Blood, Caleb Eastman, Thomas Wheet and James Fisk, all of Capt. Dows company, and all are dead.* Signed by five selectmen of Hollis.

Fitchburg. April 23rd, 1776, To the Committee of Clothing for the Massachusetts bay Gentlemen this may certify to you that *John Gibson* who was supposed to be killed in the Battle at Bunker Hill had his last place of residence at Fitchburg, and belonged to Capt Abijah Wyman's Comp. in Col. Prescotts Reg., and has not drawn coat, or money in lieu thereof, therefore we desire you would pay one of the subscribers, the sum of twenty-five shillings, for the benefit of the heirs signed by three selectmen of Fitchburg.

Cambridge. Oct 30th 1775, To the Committee of Supplies an order to deliver to Capt Asa Lawrence, a coat for each of the subscribers signed by 35 men, killed, or taken *James Dogg, Stephen Foster, Abraham Blood Benj^a Wood, Simon Hobart, Robert Parker.*

Pepperell. Sept 16 1776, We hereby certify that *Jeremiah Shattuck* that was slain in the Battle of Bunker Hill the 17th of June 1775, was ye son of Jeremiah Shattuck Junr of Pepperell, and then a single man and under 21 years of age, signed by three selectmen of Pepperell.

---

* Of these seven men, five are on the New Hampshire roll as killed at Bunker Hill. But Caleb Eastman was killed June 19th by the bursting of his gun, and James Fisk is noted on his company list (Roll 63) as having died May 29th, at the same date as one Jeremiah Shattuck, of Hollis, not to be confounded with Jeremiah Shattuck, of Pepperell (my No. 19) of Roll 67, Capt. Nutting's company.

Pepperell. Oct 4, 1776, We hereby certify that Mrs Ruth Parker Widow was wife to *Nathaniel Parker* late of Pepperell who was a sergeant in Capt John Nuttings company in Col. Prescotts Reg^t in the army at Cambridge and was slain in the Battle at Charlestown on the 17th of June 1775, and therefore has an undisputed right to receive what belongs to him she being the heir   signed by two selectmen of Pepperell.

Pepperell. Sept 30 1776, To the Gentlemen upon the Committee of Clothing sitting at Watertown Please to pay to Capt. Edm^d Bancroft the money for a uniform coat that my son was entitled to who was a soldier in the year 1775 and lost his life in the Battle at Bunker Hill, and you will oblige your hum^l serv^t Jeremiah Shattuck.

Pepperell. Oct 9 1776, To the Gentlemen Committee of Clothing Be pleased to pay to Capt Edm^d Bancroft the money allowed for a uniform coat which *Ebenezer Laughton* my late husband deces^d who was slain in the Battle at Bunker Hill was entitled signed Abigail Laughton.

Camp at Cambridge. Nov 30 1775, This may certify that *Archibald McIntosh*, a soldier in my comp^y in Col. Prescotts Reg^t was taken or slain in battle at Bunker Hill, and never rec^d a coat, nor have I drawn any pay for the same, or for the heirs   signed Samuel Gilbert Capt.

Hollis. Feb 10 1776, We do hereby certify that Capt Reuben Dow is the only proper person to receive the Clothing, that is due to *Peter Poor* a transient person who enlisted in his company, and last resided in this town and went away in debt   said Poor was lost in Bunker Hill fight   signed by 5 selectmen of Hollis.

Townsend. Nov 14 1775, To the honorable the paymaster general, for the Colony of the Massachusetts bay we hereby inform that the Widow Margaret Stevens is the proper person, to draw the money or the coat belonging to *Oliver Stevens* of Capt Abijah Wyman's Comp^y in Col Prescotts Reg^t who was taken captive at Charlestown fight and is since dead   signed by 4 selectmen of Townsend.

Feb. 16 1776, This may certify that *Cesor Bason* was a soldier in my company in Col Prescotts Reg^t. who was slain in Battle at Bunker Hill and has not rec^d his coat & blanket as bounty granted him by Congress signed Abijah Wyman Capt.

Feb. 22, 1776, To the Committee of Clothing in Watertown   Gentlemen, this may certify M^r. Nicholas Youngman's son *Eben^r Youngman*, was a soldier in Capt Moor Comp^y, in Col. Prescotts Reg^t. and was killed in the Battle at Bunker Hill and desire you would pay the s^d Youngman the money or his coat, voted to him by Congress   Zach. Walker Lieut.

Pepperell. Oct 6 1776, This certifies that Abigail Laughton Widow was wife to *Ebenezer Laughton* of Pepperell who was slain in the Battle at Charlestown June 17th, 1775, then a private in Capt John Nutting's Comp^y in Col. Prescotts Reg^t. of the army at Cambridge she is therefore the proper person to receive the pay or wages due deceased signed by 4 selectmen of Pepperell

---

Westford. March 12, 1776, To the Committee of Clothing, This certifies that *Joseph Minott* was a soldier in my company in Col. Prescott's Reg^t. and was killed in Battle, the 17th of June last on Bunker Hill and did not receive his bounty coat nor money for it   Joshua Parker Capt.

APPENDIX B.   111

Ashby. Feb 20 1776, This may certify that *Amos Wheeler* was a soldier in my company, in Col. Prescotts Reg^t. and was wounded in Battle at Bunker Hill on the 17th of June and died the 21st and hath not drawn his coat & blanket as bounty granted by Congress Abijah Wyman Capt.

Cambridge. January 5, 1776, To the Committee of Supplies for clothing, This may certify that *Benjamin Dole* of my company in Col. Wm Prescotts Reg^t was killed the 17 of June last in the Battle on Bunker Hill and has not rec^d any Coat or money in lieu of it Samuel Gilbert Capt

Camp Sewal's Point. March 27, 1776, I the subscriber hereby certify that *Isaac Whetcomb* a soldier in my company in Col. Wm. Prescott's Reg^t. died of a wound that he received at a battle at Charlestown on the seventeenth of June 1775, it being before there was any coats or money for the same received, which was due to the soldiers in said company and by reason of his being killed I have not received coat or money for the s^d Whetcomb Saml Gilbert Capt

This may certify whom it may concern that *Chambres Corey* son to Samuel Corey never received his coat or money for it he was in my company and was killed at Bunker Hill Oliver Parker Capt.

Gloucester. July 8. 1776, This certifies that *Benjamin Smith* an indented servant of Capt Wm Ellery's was killed in the Battle on Bunker Hill and had no estate or relations in this country and said Ellery has the sole right to the coat he was to have signed by four selectmen of Gloucester, also a certificate that he was killed by a cannon ball signed by Wm Kingman Sergt in Warner's Company,

Sir Please to pay to Mr Saml Whitemore what is due me, for my servant *Benjn Smith*, who was killed, in Capt Warner's Comp, Col Little's Reg^t. and you will oblige your serv^t. William Ellery.

Gloucester. Aug. 27, 1776, This certifies that *Daniel Callahan*, who was killed at Bunker Hill Battle, was an indented servant to Mr Stephen Low, of this town, who has the sole right to s^d. Callahan's wages and anything that belonged to him he was in Warner's Company Col. Little's Reg^t.   signed by two selectmen of Gloucester.

Newburyport. June 17, 1776, Please to pay Tristam Dalton Esq the bounty of a coat which was due to *Saml Nelson*, a soldier in Capt Benjn Perkins Comp^y in ye 17 Reg^t of Foot, commanded by Col. Little, who lost his life in the Battle of Bunker Hill 17th June 1775, this will be a full discharge   Moses Hoyt administrator.

Marblehead. August 26, 1776, To the Committee of Clothing Please to pay to Azor Orne Esqr the bounty for the coat that is due to my servant *Thomas Allen*, who was killed in the fight at Bunker Hill June 1775, and there has been no bounty paid for said coat which he became entitled to by being a soldier in Capt Joel Smith's Company in Col. Glover's Reg^t. at the time he was killed   Mary Trefry.

Tewksbury. April 12 1776, This may certify that *Phillip Fowler* served as a soldier in the late Capt Benjamin Walker's Company in the 27th Reg^t comanded by Col. Eben^r Bridge and the said Phillip was taken or killed in the fight at Bunker Hill and has not rec^d the coat that was due him as stipulated by Congress   John Flint Lieut.

Andover. Aug. 8 1776, To the Hon, the Com^t of Clothing Sirs please to pay to Joshua Holt the sum due my late husband *Samuel Bailey Junr* deceased in lieu of a coat & blanket which he did not receive. Hannah Bailey admin^x.   This may certify that the above named Saml Bailey Junr was a soldier in my company and was killed at Bunker Hill Fight and never rec^d a coat or blanket.   Charles Furbush Capt.

APPENDIX B.

Billerica. Nov 9, 1775, These are to signify that Mary Easty hath a lawful right to draw the wages of *Benj. Easty* who was her husband lost on Bunker Hill in the Battle of the 17th of June, by order of the selectmen Joshua Abbott (a copy taken from the original).

Dracut. Nov 14, 1775, We, the subscribers do certify that Mr Richard Thissell is the sole right and proprietor of his son *John Thissell's* wages that was killed at Bunker Hill fight in June last. signed by two selectmen of Dracut.

Keene. November 3, 1775, These may certify those concerned that David Nims of Keene, we look upon to be the true heir to *Asahel Nims* estate who was killed at Bunker Hill and was under the Command of Capt. Jeremiah Stiles, signed by four selectmen of Keen.

[See item about John Meads, of Ashby, in the preface to this edition. W. H. W.]

RETURNS OF MEN KILLED JUNE 17, 1775.

From Massachusetts Revolutionary Rolls, Vol. 56.

COL. JAMES FRYE'S REGIMENT.

No. in preceding account.	No. of Roll.				
44..	1.	David Huntington	Amesbury	"Lost in battle, 17th June." Capt. John Currier.
45..	2.	John Eaton	Haverhill	"Killed 17 June." Capt. James Sawyer.
46..	2.	Simeon Pike	Haverhill	"Killed 17 June." Capt. James Sawyer.
47..	5.	Joseph Hibbard	Dracut	"Died June 20th." Capt. John Davis.
48..	5.	Ebenezer Herrick [1]	Methuen	"Died June 17th." Capt. John Davis.
49..	6.	Samuel Russel	Residence not stated.	"Killed June 17th." Capt. Jonas Richardson.
50..	6.	Daniel Evens	Residence not stated.	"Killed June 17th." Capt. Jonas Richardson.
51..	6.	James Millikin	Boston	"Killed June 17th." Capt. Jonas Richardson.
52..	6.	John Blyth	Residence not stated.	"Killed June 17th." Capt. Jonas Richardson.
53..	7.	Ichabod March	Amesbury	"Killed in battle, June 17th." Capt. William Hudson Ballard.
54..	9.	Joseph Simmons	Boxford	"Lost in battle, 17th June." Capt. William Perley.
55..	9.	James Boynton	Boxford	"Deceased 28th June." Capt. William Perley.
56..	10.	Philip Abbot	Andover	"Killed in battle, June 17th." Capt. Benjamin Ames.
58..	10.	Joseph Chandler	Andover	"Killed in battle, June 17th." Capt. Benjamin Ames.
57..	10.	William Haggit	Andover	"Killed in battle, June 17th." Capt. Benjamin Ames.
59..	10.	Jesse Holt	Andover	"Died June 21st." Capt. Benjamin Ames.

[1] James Ingals is entered on Roll 5 as dying July 8th, but I have no evidence to connect his death with the battle. Derbas Sessions of Andover is on Roll 4, Capt. Farnum, as taken captive 17 June at Bunker Hill; but he is reported alive in Boston in prison, Sept. 14th.

In this regiment also I find on Roll 12, in Capt. Carriel's company, Reuben Stockwell died July 13th. On Roll 17, in Capt. Curtis's company, Stephen Griffith died July 31st. No cause of death recorded.

APPENDIX B.

COL. JONATHAN BREWER'S REGIMENT.[1]

07..	35.	Serg. Jonas Barnard,	Watertown	"Died June 20th." Capt. Jesse Gray.
00..	36.	Josiah Bacon ...	Hutchinson (Barré),	"Killed 17th June." Capt. John Black.
01..	36.	John Barrett....	Hutchinson (Barré),	"Killed 17th June." Capt. John Black.
02..	36.	Ebenezer Childs, Jr.	Hutchinson (Barré),	"Killed 17th June." Capt. John Black.
03..	36.	Lucas Green	Winchendon	"Was wounded 17th June and died after." Capt. John Black.
04..	37.	Comeing Fairbank.	Framingham	"Killed 17th June." Capt. Aaron Haynes.
05..	37.	Joshua Haynes ...	Sudbury	"Killed 17th June." Capt. Aaron Haynes.
00..	39.	Lebbeus Jennings.	Deerfield	"Killed 17th June." Capt. Thad. Russell.

[1] On Roll 32, in Capt. Whiting's company, I find that Thomas Draper of Needham died August 10th, and John Stewart of Boston died August 29th.

COL. DAVID BREWER'S REGIMENT.[2]

08..	50.	Timothy Evins ...	Ware	"Deceased June 18th." Capt. Jonathan Bardwell.
00..	50.	Stephen Ayres ...	Belchertown	"Deceased June 18th." Capt. Jonathan Bardwell.

[2] In this regiment, in Capt. Bardwell's company, Roll 50, Asa Davis of Belchertown, died July 26th, and Jonathan Otis of Ware, died August 22nd. Isaac Hodgman of Brookfield, in Capt. King's company, Roll 53, died September 5th. In Capt. Danforth's company, Roll 55, Elias Rogers of Palmer died September 21st.

COL. WILLIAM PRESCOTT'S REGIMENT.

28	...60.	Jonathan Jenkins[4].	Groton	"Died 17th June at Charlestown." Capt. Henry Farwell.
34	.....	Robert Parker[5] ..	....	"Killed or taken 17 June." Capt. Asa Lawrence.
33	...61.	Simon Hobart ...	Groton	"Died July 28." Capt. Asa Lawrence.
29	...61.	James Dodge ...	Groton	"Killed in battle on 17 of June last or taken." Capt. Asa Lawrence.
30	...61.	Stephen Foster...	Groton	"Killed in battle on 17 of June last or taken." Capt. Asa Lawrence.
31	...61.	Abraham Blood ..	Groton	"Killed in battle on 17 June last or taken." Capt. Asa Lawrence.

COL. WILLIAM PRESCOTT'S REGIMENT. — *Continued.*

32	Cl.	Benj. Wood	Pepperell	"Killed in battle on 17 June last or taken." Capt. Asa Lawrence.
	61.	Lieut. Joseph Spaulding	Pepperell	"Killed in battle on 17 June last or taken." Capt. Asa Lawrence.
1.	62.	Peter Whitcomb	Littleton	"Killed June 17, 1775." Capt. Samuel Gilbert.
2.	62.	Benjamin Dole	Littleton	"Killed June 17, 1775." Capt. Samuel Gilbert.
3.	62.	John Lawrence	Littleton	"Killed June 17, 1775." Capt. Samuel Gilbert.
4.	62.	James Whitemore	Littleton	"Killed June 17, 1775." Capt. Samuel Gilbert.
5.	62.	Isaac Whitcombe	Littleton	"Died June 24, 1775." Capt. Samuel Gilbert.
6.	62.	Archibald McIntosh,[6]	Ruby	"Died August 10, 1775." Capt. Samuel Gilbert.
7.	62.	James Coneck	Ruby	"Died July 24, 1775." Capt. Samuel Gilbert.
83.	63.	Sergt. Nathan Blood,	Hollis	"Died June 17." Capt. Reuben Dows.
84.	63.	Phinehas Nevens	Hollis	"Died June 17." Capt. Reuben Dows.
85.	63.	Thomas Wheat	Hollis	"Died June 17." Capt. Reuben Dows.
86.	63.	Peter Poor	Hollis	"Died June 17." Capt. Reuben Dows.
	63.	*Caleb Eastman*	Hollis	"Died June 19." Capt. Reuben Dows.
87.	63.	Isaac Hobart	Hollis	"Died June 19." Capt. Reuben Dows.
88.	63.	Jacob Boynton	Hollis	"Died June 17." Capt. Reuben Dows.
8.	64.	Chambers Corey	Groton	"Killed June 17 on Bunker Hill." Capt. Ephraim Corey.
9.	64.	Daniel McGrath[7]	Amherst	"Taken captive June 17 on Bunker Hill." Capt. Ephraim Corey.
34.	64.	Robert Parker	Groton	"Died Sept. 30 at Cambridge." Capt. Ephraim Corey.
89.	65.	Sergt. Benj. Prescott,	Groton	"Killed June 17 at Bunker Hill." Capt. Joseph Moors.
90.	65.	Ebenezer Youngman,	Hollis	"Killed June 17 at Bunker Hill." Capt. Joseph Moors.
91.	65	Thomas Colbourn	Dunstable	"Killed June 17, Bunker Hill." Capt. Joseph Moors.
10.	66.	John Gibson	Fitchburg	"Died June 17." Capt. Abijah Wyman.
11.	66	Cesar Bason	Westford	"Died June 17." Capt. Abijah Wyman.

APPENDIX B.

COL. WILLIAM PRESCOTT'S REGIMENT. — *Continued.*

12	66	Amos Wheeler	Ashby	"Died June 21." Capt. Abijah Wyman.
13	66	Oliver Stevens [5]	Townsend	"Captivated June 17." Capt. Abijah Wyman.
14	67	Nathl. Parker	Pepperell	"Killed June 17." Capt. John Nutting.
15	67	Wm. Warrin	Pepperell	"Killed June 17." Capt. John Nutting.
16	67	Edmund Peers	Pepperell	"Killed June 17." Capt. John Nutting.
17	67	Wainwright Fisk	Pepperell	"Killed June 17." Capt. John Nutting.
18	67	Jeremiah Shattuck	Pepperell	"Killed June 17." Capt. John Nutting.
19	67	Ebenr. Laughton	Pepperell	"Killed June 17." Capt. John Nutting.
20	68	Jesse Corless	Deerfield	"Dead June 17." Capt. Hugh Maxwell.
21	68	Eben Foills	Charlemont	"Dead June 17." Capt. Hugh Maxwell.
22	68	Aaron Barr	Meryfield	"Dead June 18." Capt. Hugh Maxwell.
23	68	Jonathan Bato	Wlocheadoa	"Killed June 17." Capt. Samuel Patch.
24	69	Jonas Looker	Sadbury	"Killed June 17." Capt. Samuel Patch.
25	70	Jonas Mioott	Westford	"Killed in battle June 17." Capt. Joshua Parker.
26	70	Jonathan Hadley	Westford	"Killed in battle June 17." Capt. Joshua Parker.
27	70	Peter Fisk	Groton	"Killed in battle June 17." Capt. Joshua Parker.
	70	Lieut. Amaziah Fasset	Groton	"Taken captive June 17; died at Boston July ye 5." Capt. Joshua Parker.
36	70	David Kemp	Groton	"Taken captive; died at Boston Sept. 10." Capt. Joshua Parker.
35	70	John Gordon [9]	Stow	"Died in camp June 19." Capt. Joshua Parker.

[4] Oliver Warren of Townsend, in this company, died August 11th.

[5] Robert Parker's name is *not* on this roll, but is on the Coat Roll, cited later, with these other five men in Lawrence's company, as "killed or taken."

[6] Both McIntosh and Concek are claimed in the New Hampshire list as being resident there.

[7] I find that Daniel McGrath was dead in Boston before September 14. He is duly entered on Capt. Corey's Roll, and on the Coat Roll he and Chambers Corey are crossed off. The John McGrath, Wyman's company, Patterson's regiment, is elsewhere mentioned, and it is doubtful if that regiment was in the fight at all.

[8] Stevens died in captivity. Benjamin Bigelow of the same company was also taken prisoner, but was alive in Boston, Sept. 14th. See list later on.

[9] Abijah Mason of Westford, in Parker's company, died in camp July 30.

118 AMERICANS KILLED AT BUNKER HILL.

COL. MOSES LITTLE'S REGIMENT.

70..	82.	Daniel Callahan ...	Gloucester	"Killed June 17." Capt. Nathaniel Warner.
71..	82.	Benj. Smith	Gloucester	"Killed June 17." Capt. Nathaniel Warner.
74..	83.	Jesse Story	Ipswich	"Deceased June 17." Capt. Abraham Dodge.
72..	85.	Moses Pigeon[10] ...	Newburyport ...	Deceased June 17. Capt. Benjamin Perkins.

[10] Samuel Nelson, of Perkins's company, was killed June 17, according to the Coat Rolls, which see.

COL. JOHN GLOVER'S REGIMENT.

82..	131.	Thos. Allen	Marblehead	"Killed in battle." Capt. Joel Smith.

COL. ASA WHITCOMB'S REGIMENT.

80..	147.	David Robbins ...	Lancaster	"Killed on Bunker Hill June 17." Capt. Andrew Haskell.
81..	147.	Serg. Robert Phelps[11]	Lancaster	"Wounded and in captivity, June 17." Capt. Andrew Haskell.
	147.	Jeremiah Haskell ..	Lancaster	"Wounded and in captivity." Capt. Andrew Haskell.

[11] Sergt. Phelps died in prison in Boston. Haskell's name is not among the prisoners. Perhaps he escaped or was discharged before Sept. 14.

COL. EPHRAIM DOOLITTLE'S REGIMENT.

84..	155.	Phineas Nevers[12] .	Windsor	"Dead." Capt. Abel Wilder.
75..	156.	Joshua Whitcomb .	Templeton	"Slain June 17." Capt. Joel Fletcher.
76..	158.	Jeduthan Alexander,	Marlboro'	"Slain on Bunker Hill June 17." Capt. Jonathan Holman.
77..	161.	Benjamin Reed ...	Rutland	"Slain June 17." Capt. Adam Wheeler.
....	161.	Maj. Willard Moor .	Paxton	"Slain in battle on Bunker Hill June 17."

[12] Phineas Nevers's death is not given, but we know he died in captivity in Boston, before Sept. 14th. His name is frequently given as Nevens.

COL. JOHN PATTERSON'S REGIMENT.

....	176.	John McGrath[13] . .	Place unknown ...	"Wounded 17th of June and died 20th Sept." Capt. William Wyman.

[13] Undoubtedly a clerical error for my number 9, Daniel McGrath of Roll 64. Patterson's regiment was not in the fight.

APPENDIX B.

COL. EBENEZER BRIDGE'S REGIMENT.

	178 .	Jacob Frost [14] . . .	Tewksbury	"Prisoner." Capt. Benjamin Walker.
40 . .	185 .	Joseph Kemp . . .	Dunstable	"Killed in the fight at Charlestown, June the 17th." Capt. Ebenezer Bancroft.

[14] Frost was alive in Boston Sept. 14th. This Roll also notes Capt. Benjamin Walker as dead, Reuben Beacon of Bedford "dead," Jacob Crosby of Billerica, "dead," and corp. Philip Fowler of Tewksbury, missing. I think these names belong to the battle, but see *ante*, p. 85.

COL. PAUL DUDLEY SARGENT'S REGIMENT. [15]

101 .	189 .	Sergt. Asahel Nims,	Keene	"Died in battle 17 June." Capt. Jeremiah Stiles.
92	. . 194 .	Paul Caldwell . . .	Londonderry . . .	"Killed 17th June." Capt. William Scott.
93	. . 194 .	William French . .	Peckerfield	"Killed 17th June." Capt. William Scott.
94	. . 194 .	Jonas How	New Marlborough .	"Killed 17th June." Capt. William Scott.

[15] These names and also that of Joseph Taylor of Peterborough are all entered on the New Hampshire List.

COL. JONATHAN WARD'S REGIMENT. [16]

78	. . 227 .	Samuel Heards . . .	Grafton	"Died 17th day of June in battle." Capt. Luke Drury.

[16] Serg. John Brown and Corp. Kerby Ward, of Capt. Washburn's company (Roll 225), are both noted as wounded at Bunker Hill, but both survived.

COL. WILLIAM ROGERS'S REGIMENT.

70	. . 264 .	Thomas Doyl . . .	deserted from the king's troops . . .	"Died 17th June." Capt. William Rogers.

From Mass. Revolutionary Rolls, Vol. 16.

COL. EBENEZER BRIDGE'S REGIMENT.

41	. . . 11 .	Francis Pool	Gloucester	"Killed."
42	. . . 11 .	Josiah Brooks . . .	Gloucester	
43	. . . 11 .	William Parsons . .	Gloucester	Capt. John Rowe.

NEW HAMPSHIRE MEN KILLED OR MORTALLY WOUNDED AT BUNKER HILL, JUNE 17, 1775.

From a printed list kindly furnished by the Compiler.

Consecutive Numbering added by W. H. W.	No.	NAME.	RANK.	WHERE FROM.	REGIMENT.	COMPANY.	State Papers, Vol.	Page.	Swett's Notes, Page.
91	1	Adams, Isaac	P.	Rindge	Reed's	Thomas's	14	99	28
	2	Baldwin, Isaac	Capt.	Hillsborough	Stark's	Baldwin's	14	50	51
97	3	Blood, Joseph	P.	Mason	Reed's	Mann's	14	101	28
98	4	Blood, Ebenezer, Jr.	P.	Mason	Reed's	Mann's	14	101	29
73	5	Blood, Nathan [1]	Sergt.	Hollis	Prescott's	Dow's	15	743	
77	6	Boynton, Jacob [1]	P.	Hollis	Prescott's	Dow's	15	744	
85	7	Collins, Thomas	P.	Windham	Stark's	Woodbury's	14	54	28
81	8	Caldwell, Paul	P.	Londonderry	Stark's	Scott's	15	740	
99	9	Carleton, David [2]	P.	Lyndeborough	Reed's	Spaulding's	14	58	28
95	10	Carleton, George	P.	Rindge	Reed's	Thomas's	14	99	29
100	11	Cole, John	P.	Amherst	Reed's	Crosby's	14	102	28
80	12	Colbourne, Thomas	P.	Nashua	Prescott's	Moore'	15	745	
87	13	Dalton, Caleb	P.		Stark's	Richard's	14	57	28
102	14	Davis, John [3]	P.	Chesterfield	Reed's	Hinds's	14	85	28
82	15	French, William	P.	Nelson	Stark's	Scott's	15	740	
103	16	Farwell, Joseph	P.	Charlestown	Reed's	Marcy's	14	105	28
83	17	Howe, Jonas	P.	Marlborough	Stark's	Scott's	15	740	
107	18	Hills, Parker	P.	Candia	Reed's	H. Hutchins's	14	82	28
101	19	Hutchinson, James [4]	P.	Amherst	Reed's	Crosby's	14	103	28

APPENDIX B.

		Name	Rank	Town					
76	20	Hobart, Isaac [1]	P.			Prescott's	Dow's	15	74	
90	21	Lovejoy, Jonathan	P.	Ridge	Reed's	Thomas's	14	99	23
88	22	McClary, Andrew	Major	Epsom	Stark's		14	49	30
89	23	Mitchell, William	P.	Concord	Stark's	Abbot's	14	61	28
6	24	Manuel, John	P.	Bow	Stark's	Kinsman's	14	67	28
90	25	McIntosh, Archibald [5]	P.	Brookline	Prescott's	Gilbert's	15	745	28
73	26	Ninn, Asahel	Sergt.	Keene	Stark's	Stiles's	15	741	
86	27	Nevins, Phineas [6]	P.	Hollis	Prescott's	Dow's	15	744	20
75	28	Poor, Moses	P.		Stark's	Woodbury's	14	53	28
91	29	Poor, Peter	P.	Hollis	Prescott's	Dow's	15	744	
108	30	Shannon, George	P.	Canterbury	Stark's	G. Hutchins's	14	65	28
81	31	Scot, David	P.	Peterborough	Reed's	E. Towne's	14	91	28
74	32	Taylor, Joseph	P.	Peterborough	Stark's	Scott's	15	759	
79	33	Wheat, Thomas, Jr.	P.	Hollis	Prescott's	Dow's	15	744	
109	34	Youngman, Ebenezer	P.	Hollis	Prescott's	Moors'	15	745	
7	35	Clogstone, Paul [7]	P.	Nashua	Reed's	Walker's	14	95	
110	36	Couch, James [8]	P.	Brookline	Prescott's	Gilbert's	15	745	
111	37	Cram, Asa [?]	P.	Wilton	Reed's	Walker's	14	90	
92	38	Gray, Jonathan [10]	P.	Wilton	Reed's	Walker's	14	07	
112	39	McCrillis, William [11]	P.	Nottingham	Stark's	Pearborn's	14	09	
112	40	Russell, Jason [9]	P.	Nashua	Reed's	Walker's	14	05	
113	41	Wood, Oliver [9]	P.	Nashua	Reed's	Walker's	14	07	

[1] History Hollis, pp. 151, 265-205.
[2] Wounded, d. June 19; Swett's Notes, killed.
[3] In roll printed Paws; Swett's Notes, Isaac.
[4] Wounded, d. June 24; Swett's Notes, killed.
[5] Wounded, prisoner; d. August 10.
[6] Wounded, prisoner; in Swett's Notes printed Nevers, killed.
[7] Died July 15.
[8] Died July 21.
[9] State Papers, Vol. 14, p. 294, d. before Sept. 10.
[10] State Papers, Vol. 13, p. 691, d. before March 4, 1776.
[11] Died July 2.

93 — No. 42. Broderick, Joseph, private, of Captain Daniel Moore's company, Stark's regiment, enlisted May 1, and disappeared from the roll June 17, being allowed on roll pay for one month and eighteen days, but it appears no one ever took his money. — State Papers, Vol. 14, p. 70. Generally supposed to have been killed.

104 — No. 43. Patten, James, private, of Captain John Marcy's company, Reed's regiment, enlisted May 10; allowed on roll pay for one month and eleven days. On roll, D^d June 17.

105 — No. 44. Melvin, John, private, of Captain John Marcy's company, Reed's regiment, enlisted May 25; allowed on roll pay for twenty-four days. On roll, D^d June 17.

106 — No. 45. Chamberlain, Benjamin, private, of Captain John Marcy's company, Reed's regiment, enlisted May 26; allowed on roll pay for one month and three days; D^d June 25. — State Papers, Vol. 14, pp. 104, 105, for Nos. 43, 44, 45.

The last three men are supposed to have been wounded, and to have died, as on the same roll Joseph Farwell is marked D^d June 17.

GEORGE C. GILMORE.
Manchester, N.H., Jan. 30, 1889.

LIST OF PRISONERS TAKEN AT BUNKER HILL.

(From a revised copy printed in the New England Historical and Genealogical Register for April, 1858.)

*Lieut.-Colonel Parker, Chelmsford, dead.
*Capt. Benjamin Walker, Chelmsford, (died Aug. 15) dead.
*Lieut. Amaziah Fassett, Groton, dead.
81 Serg. Robert Phelps, Lancaster, dead.
84 Phineas Nevers [Neveus],*** Windsor, dead.
13 Oliver Stevens, Townsend, dead.
9 Daniel McGrath, dead.
134 Amasa Fisk, Pepperell, dead.
6 Archibald McIntosh, Townsend [Raby], dead.
36 David Kemp, Groton, dead.
135 William Robinson, unknown, dead.
128 Benjamin Ross, Ashford, Conn., dead.
136 John Dillon, Jersey, Eng., dead.
Unknown, unknown, dead.
93 William Kench, Peckerfield, dead. [Error for Wm. French.]
29 James Dodge, Edinburg, Scot., dead.
133 William Rollinson, Connecticut, dead.****
137 John Lord, unknown, dead.
51 James Milliken, Boston, dead.
30 Stephen Foster, Groton, dead.

Lieut. William Scott, Peterboro', alive. [Served through the war.]
John Perkins, New Rutland, alive. [See Mass. Rolls, vol. 70, p. 123.]
**Jacob Frost, Tewksbury, alive. [do. do. vol. 56, p. 178.]
**Daniel (Darius) Session, Andover, alive. [See Mass. Rolls, vol. 56, p. 4.]
Jonathan Norton, Newburyport, alive. [See Mass. Rolls, vol. 15, p. 85.
Philip Johnson Peck, Boston-Mansfield, alive.
**Benjamin Bigelow, Peckerfield (Packersfield, N.H.), alive.
Benjamin Wilson, Billerica, alive. [Died 10 June, 1776. Hist. of Billerica.]
John Deland, Charlestown, alive.
Lawrence Sullivan, Wethersfield, alive.
Twenty dead, ten living, September 14, 1775, as printed in the "Essex Gazette."

---

* These officers are all accounted for.
** These three are also on the Mass. Coat Rolls.
*** Judge Devens informs me that the name is Nevers.
**** Sec'y Hoadly informs me that this was doubtless Wilson Rowlandson of 2d Reg., 9th Co. The Connecticut roll says: "died, prisoner in Boston, July 1."

Having thus given the details of the evidence for the names placed on the tablets, it may be well to repeat, from City Document No. 73, of 1889, the action of the committee in charge.

The committee was appointed and confirmed Feb. 8, 1889. It met and organized February 27, and at once proceeded to work. March 8, Mr. Whitmore, Record Commissioner, was directed to prepare a list and submit it in print, and April 24 he reported. The committee deemed it unwise to take any decided action involving expense until the annual appropriations were passed. At this last date it was voted to have the City Architect (Mr. Bateman) prepare a design for the tablets; April 27, his design was received and approved; May 8, the bids for furnishing the bronze tablets and the iron frames were opened and contracts awarded.

The committee first proposed to place the tablets, reserving, of course, the property of the city therein, at the entrance to Monument square, opposite to Monument avenue. This idea was made known, informally, to members of the management of the Bunker Hill Monument Association, and at a meeting of the committee, on April 24, its chairman was directed to make a formal application. A letter was sent by Alderman Stacey to Hon. F. W. Lincoln, April 26, and a conference was held on Tuesday, May 14. The delays were in no way attributable to your committee.

The result of this application and conference is shown by the following communication sent to this committee : —

Whereas, at a meeting of the Directors of the Association of June 18, 1849, it was determined by a resolution reported by the Hon. Edward Everett, as the sense of the Board — "That the great object for which the obelisk was erected on Bunker Hill is monumental and not historical, and that it is not expedient that any record of names, dates, or events connected with the battle should be inscribed upon it, — "

Resolved, In view of this, and the fact that the list of names upon the intended tablets, of those who fell in the battle, is less perfect than, in the opinion of the Directors, it may be made, and that the inscriptions thereon are not wholly satisfactory, and of the further fact that one of the tablets is to be used for the vote of the city, and the names of the gentlemen comprising its committee, the Directors, who were only informed on April 26 of the wish of the City Council, are not now prepared to consent to the erection of the proposed tablets on the grounds of the Association.

Resolved, That if the preparation and erection of the tablets can be postponed until after June 17, the Directors will most willingly bring the whole subject to the consideration of the Association at its annual meeting on that day.

A true copy of the Resolves adopted at a meeting of the Directors of the Bunker Hill Monument Association, May 18, 1889.

    Attest:

               ANDREW C. FEARING, Jr.,
                                        Secretary.

Various attempts were made by the committee to come to some agreement with the Association, it being then supposed that this society had the virtual ownership of the monument and grounds. Nothing was obtained, not even leave to place the tablets against the outside fence surrounding the grounds.

The committee was therefore forced to seek another site, and its choice fell upon the well-known locality of Winthrop square, that being, in fact, a portion of Bunker Hill, and already adorned with the monument erected to the memory of the soldiers from Charlestown in the late war. In making this choice the committee followed the old rule of placing a city memorial upon land owned by the city, and the wisdom of this rule has been abundantly shown by the experience already related.

The committee, having been duly empowered, accordingly arranged to place these tablets at a new entrance made into Winthrop square, at its north-west corner. A smaller entrance has also been made at the south-east corner, and the paths have been re-located, so as to afford the most direct line of travel from City square to Hammond square.

The accompanying illustrations give a satisfactory idea of these tablets and their surroundings. The inscriptions upon them are repeated in the text, but the illustration facing page 133 is from a recent photograph and represents the present state of the tablet. In the first edition the reader was cautioned that the views were taken in August, and consequently the tablet which bore the names of "Soldiers unassigned" was represented as it *then* appeared, but the five names since recovered were properly entered in the printed page.

For this second edition new photographs and heliotypes have been made of the two general views, facing the title and page 11 respectively; and these, of course, give the winter aspect of these monuments.

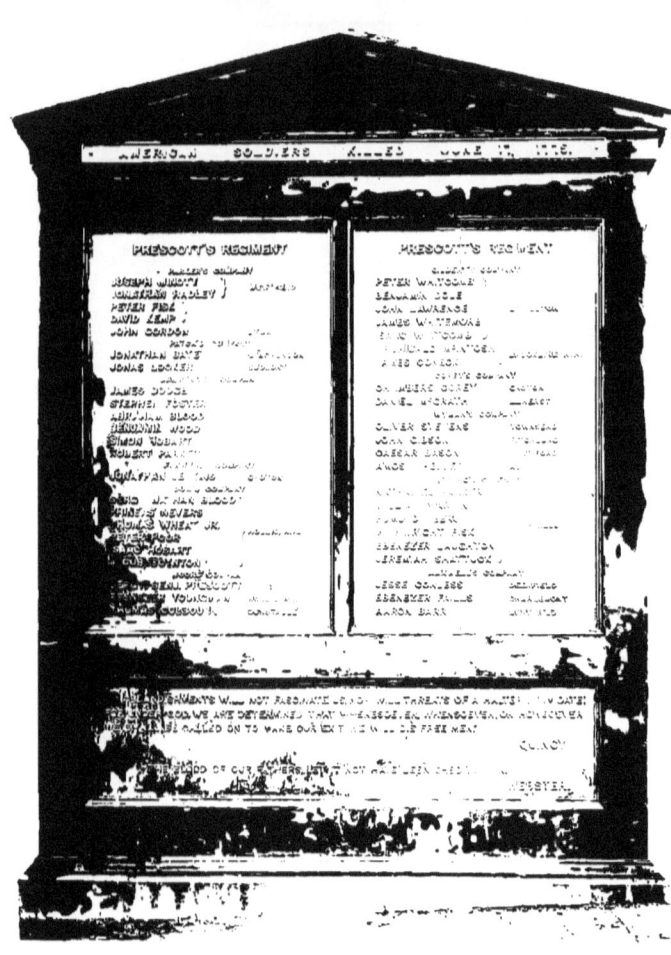

BRONZE TABLETS FACING WINTHROP SQUARE.

PRESCOTT'S REGIMENT.

Parker's company.

JOSEPH MINOTT, } Westford.
JONATHAN HADLEY, }
PETER FISK, } Groton.
DAVID KEMP, }
JOHN GORDON, Stow.

Patch's company.

JONATHAN BATE, Winchendon.
JONAS LOOKER, Sudbury.

Lawrence's company.

JAMES DODGE,
STEPHEN FOSTER,
ABRAHAM BLOOD,
BENJAMIN WOOD, } Groton.
SIMON HOBART,
ROBERT PARKER,

Farwell's company.

JONATHAN JENKINS, Groton.

Dow's company.

SERGT. NATHAN BLOOD,
PHINEAS NEVERS,
THOMAS WHEAT, JR.,
PETER POOR, } Hollis, N.H.
ISAAC HOBART,
JACOB BOYNTON,

Moors' company.

SERGT. BENJ. PRESCOTT, Groton.
EBENEZER YOUNGMAN, Hollis, N.H.
THOMAS COLBOURN, Dunstable.

PRESCOTT'S REGIMENT, Continued.

Gilbert's company.

PETER WHITCOMB,
BENJAMIN DOLE,
JOHN LAWRENCE, } Littleton.
JAMES WHITEMORE,
ISAAC WHITCOMB,
ARCHIBALD McINTOSH, } Brook-
JAMES CONECK, } line, N.H.

Corey's company.

CHAMBERS COREY, Groton.
DANIEL McGRATH, Amherst.

Wyman's company.

OLIVER STEVENS, Townsend.
JOHN GIBSON, Fitchburg.
CAESAR BASON, Westford.
AMOS WHEELER, Ashby.

Nutting's company.

NATHANIEL PARKER,
WILLIAM WARRIN,
EDMUND PEERS,
WAINWRIGHT FISK, } Pepperell.
EBENEZER LAUGHTON,
JEREMIAH SHATTUCK,

Maxwell's company.

JESSE CORLESS, Deerfield.
EBENEZER FAILLS, Charlemont.
AARON BARR, Meryfield.

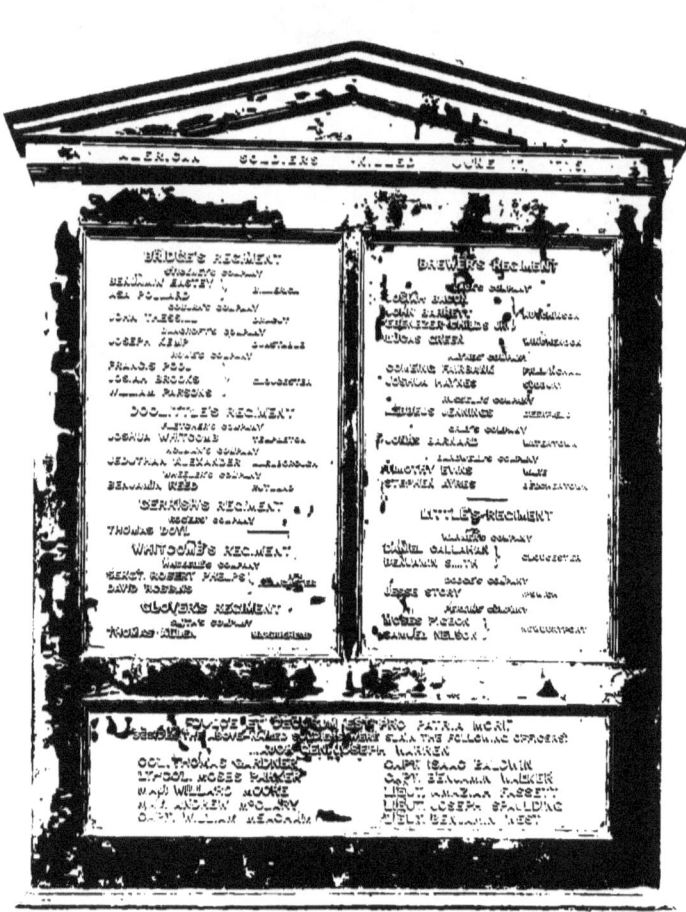

BRONZE TABLETS FACING WINTHROP SQUARE.

BRIDGE'S REGIMENT.
Stickney's company.
BENJAMIN EASTEY, } Billerica.
ASA POLLARD,

Coburn's company.
JOHN THESSILL,   Dracut.

Bancroft's company.
JOSEPH KEMP,   Dunstable.

Rowe's company.
FRANCIS POOL,
JOSIAH BROOKS,   } Gloucester.
WILLIAM PARSONS,

DOOLITTLE'S REGIMENT.
Fletcher's company.
JOSHUA WHITCOMB, Templeton.

Holman's company.
JEDUTHAN ALEXANDER, Marlborough.

Wheeler's company.
BENJAMIN REED,   Rutland.

GERRISH'S REGIMENT.
Rogers' company.
THOMAS DOYL,   ——

WHITCOMB'S REGIMENT.
Haskell's company.
SERGT. ROBERT PHELPS, } Lancaster.
DAVID ROBBINS,

GLOVER'S REGIMENT.
Smith's company.
THOMAS ALLEN,   Marblehead.

BREWER'S REGIMENT.

Black's company.

JOSIAH BACON,
JOHN BARRETT,   } Hutchinson.
EBENEZER CHILDS, JR.,
LUCAS GREEN,   Winchendon.

Haynes' company.

COMEING FAIRBANK,   Framingham.
JOSHUA HAYNES,   Sudbury.

Russell's company.

LEBBEUS JENNINGS,   Deerfield.

Gray's company.

JONAS BARNARD,   Watertown.

Bardwell's company.

TIMOTHY EVINS,   Ware.
STEPHEN AYRES,   Belchertown.

LITTLE'S REGIMENT.

Warner's company.

DANIEL CALLAHAN, } Gloucester.
BENJAMIN SMITH,

Dodge's company.

JESSE STORY,   Ipswich.

Perkins' company.

MOSES PIGEON, } Newburyport.
SAMUEL NELSON,

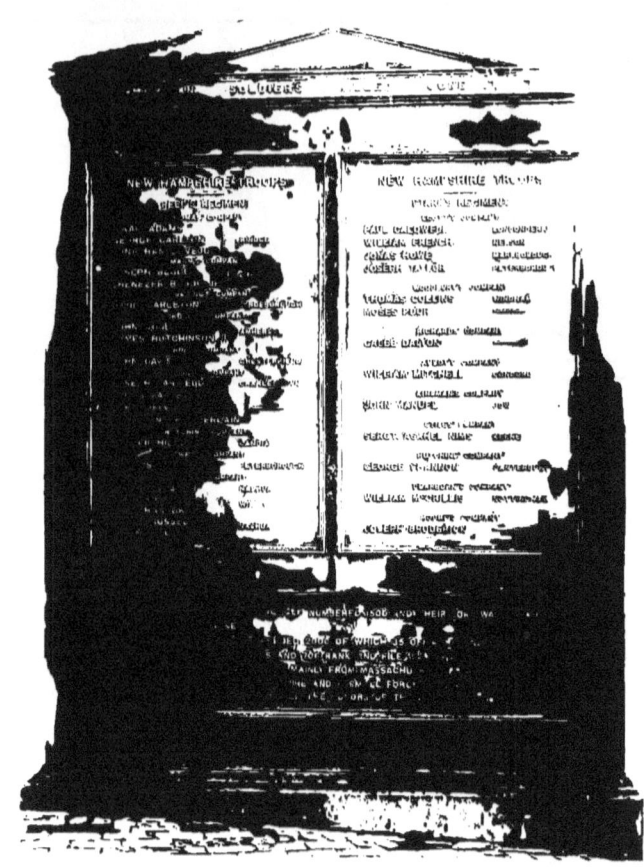

BRONZE TABLETS FACING ADAMS STREET.

THE HELIOTYPE PRINTING CO., BOSTON

NEW HAMPSHIRE TROOPS.

REED'S REGIMENT.

Thomas' company.

ISAAC ADAMS,
GEORGE CARLTON, } Rindge.
JONATHAN LOVEJOY,

Mann's company.

JOSEPH BLOOD,
EBENEZER BLOOD, JR., } Mason.

Spaulding's company.

DAVID CARLETON, Lyndeborough.

Crosby's company.

JOHN COLE,
JAMES HUTCHINSON, } Amherst.

Hinds' company.

JOHN DAVIS, Chesterfield.

Marcy's company.

JOSEPH FARWELL, Charlestown.
JAMES PATTEN,
JOHN MELVIN,
BENJAMIN CHAMBERLAIN, } ——

Hutchin's company.

PARKER HILLS, Candia.

Towne's company.

DAVID SCOTT, Peterborough.

Walker's company.

PAUL CLOGSTON, Nashua.
ASA CRAM,
JONATHAN GRAY, } Wilton.
JASON RUSSELL,
OLIVER WOOD, } Nashua.

NEW HAMPSHIRE TROOPS.

STARK'S REGIMENT.

Scott's company.
PAUL CALDWELL,   Londonderry.
WILLIAM FRENCH,   Nelson.
JONAS HOWE,   Marlborough.
JOSEPH TAYLOR,   Peterborough.

Woodbury's company.
THOMAS COLLINS,   Windham.
MOSES POOR,   ——

Richards' company.
CALEB DALTON,   ——

Abbot's company.
WILLIAM MITCHELL,   Concord.

Kinsman's company.
JOHN MANUEL,   Bow.

Stiles' company.
SERGT. ASAHEL NIMS,   Keene.

Hutchins' company.
GEORGE SHANNON,   Canterbury.

Dearborn's company.
WILLIAM McCRILLIS,   Nottingham.

Moore's company.
JOSEPH BRODERICK,   ——

BRONZE TABLETS FACING ADAMS STREET.

CONNECTICUT TROOPS.

ROGER FOX,   WILLIAM CHEENEY,
ASAHEL LYON,   BENJAMIN ROSS,
SAMUEL ASHBO,   GERSHOM SMITH,
MATTHEW CUMMINGS,   DANIEL MEMORY.
WILSON ROWLANDSON,

SOLDIERS UNASSIGNED.

AMASA FISK,	Pepperell.
WILLIAM ROBINSON,	—
JOHN DILLON,	Jersey, Eng.
JOHN LORD,	—
CORP. PHILIP FOWLER,	Tewksbury.
CORP. SAMUEL HILL,	Billerica.
SAMUEL BAILEY, JR.,	Andover.
DARIUS STEVENS,	Connecticut.
JOHN MEADS,	Ashby.

FRYE'S REGIMENT.

Currier's company.

DAVID HUNTINGTON,   Amesbury.

Sawyer's company.

JOHN EATON,
SIMEON PIKE,   Haverhill.
JOSEPH HIBBARD,   Dracut.

Richardson's company.

SAMUEL RUSSELL,
DANIEL EVENS,
JAMES MILLIKEN,
JOHN BLYTH,

Ballard's company.

ICHABOD MARCH,   Amesbury.

Perley's company.

JOSEPH SIMMONS,
JAMES BOYNTON,   Boxford.

Ames' company.

PHILIP ABBOT,
WILLIAM HAGGITT,
JOSEPH CHANDLER,   Andover.
JESSE HOLT,

Davis' company.

EBENEZER HERRICK,   Methuen.

WARD'S REGIMENT.

Drury's company.

SAMUEL HEARDS,   Grafton.

"Blandishments will not fascinate us, nor will threats of a halter intimidate; for under God, we are determined that wheresoever, whensoever, or howsoever we shall be called on to make our exit, we will die free men."

QUINCY.

"The blood of our fathers, let it not have been shed in vain."

WEBSTER.

"DULCE ET DECORUM EST PRO PATRIA MORI."

Besides the above-named soldiers, were slain the following officers:—

Major-Gen. JOSEPH WARREN.

Col. THOMAS GARDNER,	Capt. ISAAC BALDWIN,
Lt.-Col. MOSES PARKER,	Capt. BENJ. WALKER,
Major WILLARD MOORE,	Lieut. AMAZIAH FASSETT,
Maj. ANDREW MCCLARY,	Lieut. JOSEPH SPAULDING,
Capt. WILLIAM MEACHAM,	Lieut. BENJAMIN WEST.

The American troops engaged numbered 1,500, and their loss was 140 killed, 271 wounded, 30 prisoners.

The British forces exceeded 2,000, of which 35 officers and 191 rank and file were killed; 122 officers and 706 rank and file were wounded.

The American troops were mainly from Massachusetts, bravely assisted by two regiments from New Hampshire, and a small force from Connecticut.

Prescott and Putnam shared the honors of the day.

These tablets, in grateful recognition of the patriotic soldiers of the New England Army who fell June 17, 1775, were erected by order of the City Council of Boston, June 17, 1889.

THOMAS N. HART, *Mayor.*

COMMITTEE OF THE CITY GOVERNMENT.

BENJAMIN F. STACEY, ALBERT A. FOLSOM, HOMER ROGERS,
of the Aldermen.

THOMAS F. KEENAN, WILLIAM H. OAKES, FRANK E. BAGLEY, ISRAEL F. PEIRCE, WILLIAM J. DOHERTY,
of the Common Council.

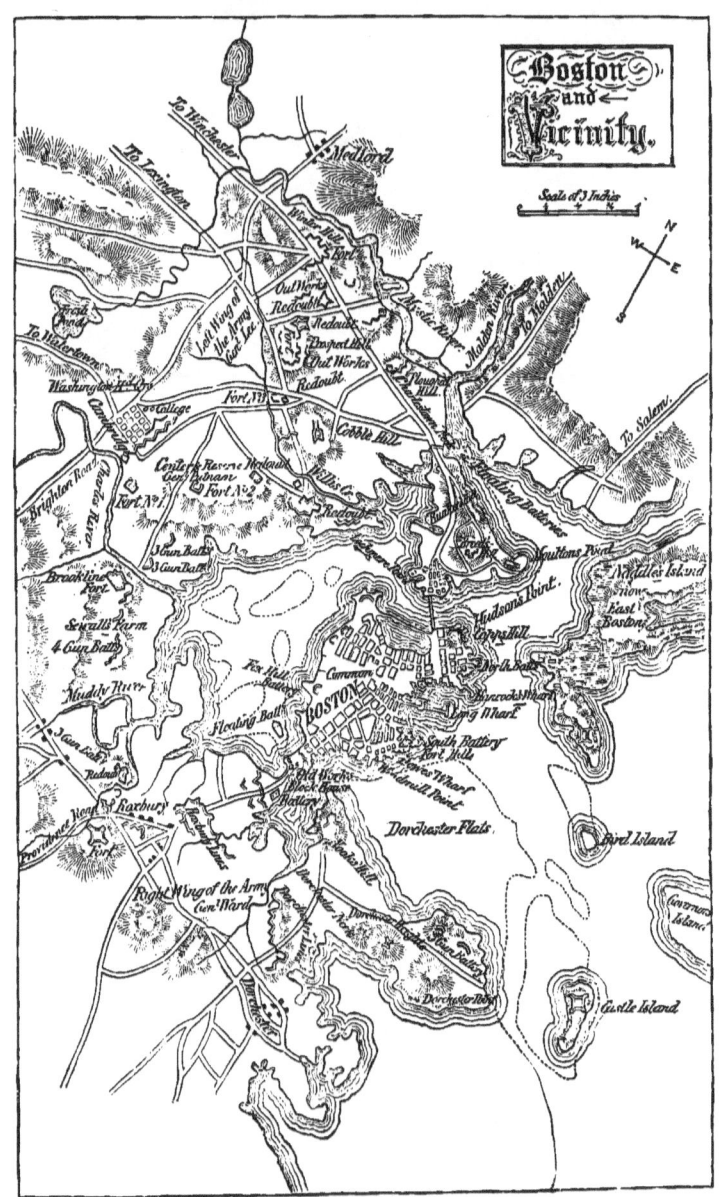

MAP SHOWING THE AMERICAN LINES, 1775.

APPENDIX C.

For some mysterious reason, the popular view in England just prior to the Revolution was, that the Colonists could not face regular troops. That such an idea was absurd was evident, indeed, to those who remembered the part taken only a few years before by the Colonial contingent in the French Wars. In fact, for a century New England had been harassed with incessant wars, and the inhabitants were especially familiar with the use of arms. Although at the beginning the Massachusetts colony was not forced to obtain land by conquest, a very considerable number of Indians inhabited this colony and Connecticut, while to the northward and eastward the savages were a constant menace.

In 1636, the Pequots in Connecticut broke out in open hostilities, and Captain Mason destroyed their stronghold near Stonington. The burden of the campaign fell upon Connecticut; but Massachusetts levied 160 men, and Plymouth 40 men, who took part in the pursuit and ultimate dispersion of the tribe.

The militia was soon placed on a thorough system in all the colonies. All males between the ages of sixteen and sixty were liable to military duty, and were equipped as infantry, with match-locks, pikes, and swords. In every town where there were sixty-four soldiers they were to constitute a company, and the officers were chosen by vote of the freemen, householders, and soldiers who had taken the oath of fidelity, subject to the approval of the County Court. The pikemen were to be armed " with a good pike well-headed, corslet, head-piece, sword, and snapsack; the musqueteers with a good fixed musquet, not under bastard-musquet bore, nor under three foot nine inches in length, nor above four foot three inches long, with a priming wire, worm, scourer, and mould, fitted to the bore of his musquet; also with a good sword, rest, bandaleres, one pound of powder, twenty bullets, and two fathoms of match." (Colonial Laws, 1660.)

The exceptions were few; only clergymen, teachers, physicians, deacons, captains of vessels, fishermen and herdsmen constantly employed, a few high officers, and the students and faculty at Harvard.

In 1636 we had three regiments of militia, Suffolk, Middlesex, and Essex; in 1671 three more were formed, Norfolk or Piscataqua, Yorkshire or Maine, and Hampshire. (Douglas, iii. 530.) In 1660 the militia consisted of about 4,000 foot and 400 horse. (Hutchinson, i. 244.)

Although for forty years from the Pequot war to King Philip's war, there was no open and recognized warfare, still the relations of England to Holland and France on several occasions threatened to embroil their respective colonies. It was necessary for the English colonies to be constantly prepared, and in several instances troops were voted, and perhaps collected, for expeditions against the New Netherlands or Canada.

After the Restoration of Charles II., the home authorities steadily endeavored to curtail the rights or privileges of the colonists, and to centralize the government. Accordingly, in 1668, a law was passed respecting the militia, that "for the time to come where new [officers] are to be chosen, it is only in the power of the General Court, or in case of emergency for the Council of the Commonwealth, to nominate, choose, appoint, and empower all commission military officers, except the Major-General and Admiral by Sea, the choice of whom are otherwise provided for by law; and for all inferior officers in companies, they are to be chosen and appointed by the commission officers of that company, and where no commission officer is, by the Major of the regiment." (Col. Laws, 1672.)

The horse-troopers, seventy of whom made a troop, were changed into a more select body in 1663, as it was enacted "that henceforth none shall be admitted to be a listed trooper, but such whom themselves or parents under whose government they are, do pay in a single country rate for one hundred pounds estate, and in other respects qualified as the law provides." (Col. Laws, 1672.)

In 1675 and 1676 the great Indian War took place, which resulted in the total extinction of the power of the aborigines in the southerly colonies of New England. During that time Massachusetts was a military camp, with every available man under arms. The result is thus summed up by Palfrey, iii. 215.

APPENDIX C.

"In Plymouth and Massachusetts there were eighty or ninety towns. Of these, ten or twelve were wholly destroyed, and forty others were more or less damaged by fire, making two-thirds of the whole number. Five or six hundred of the men of military age, one in every ten or twelve of the whole, were stealthily murdered, or fell in battle, or, becoming prisoners, were lost sight of forever, an unknown number of them being put to death with horrible tortures. . . . At the termination of hostilities the debt which had been incurred by that Colony is believed to have exceeded the value of the whole personal property of its people." In 1676, a rate of taxes was about £2,000. Sixteen rates were levied in this year amounting to nearly seven per cent. of the valuation. (*Ibid.*, iii. 230.)

Under Gov. Andros the military spirit was kept alive by a campaign against the Indians in Maine. When the colonists in 1689 rose in rebellion against King James, on the merest hope that William of Orange had succeeded, we are told that the force which captured Andros and his red-coats consisted of twenty companies collected in Boston, besides several hundred soldiers in Charlestown.

In 1690, war being waged between England and France, Massachusetts troops under Sir William Phips captured Port Royal (Annapolis) in Nova Scotia, and attempted the capture of Quebec. Thirty-two vessels, the largest mounting forty-four guns, conveyed 2,000 men; but the enterprise failed.

In 1703 hostilities with the Indians, who were incited thereto by the French, again began and kept the colony in constant alarm for some ten years. In 1711, Admiral Walker arrived at Boston with fifteen men-of-war and forty transports conveying more than 5,000 troops destined for another attack on Quebec. A levy of 900 men was ordered here. Owing to the lack of pilots the expedition failed disgracefully, many of the vessels being wrecked in the lower St. Lawrence, with great loss of life.

The Treaty of Utrecht in 1712 put an end to this war, in which "it was estimated that the eastern tribes had lost one-third of the whole number of their warriors during the past ten years and an equal number of women and children, and that the proportion of lives sacrificed had been little, if at all, less among the English population of Maine." (Palfrey, iv. 287.)

After some twenty-five years of peace, war against Spain was proclaimed by England in 1739. A requisition was made on Massachusetts for 1,000 men to serve in the expedition under Admiral Vernon against Carthagena. Of the five hundred troops who actually went, only fifty returned.

In March, 1744, the long-expected declaration of war was made by France, and Gov. Shirley, whose tastes were entirely military, promptly took measures to attack the French colonies. In 1745 Louisburg was taken by an expedition under the command of William Pepperrell, composed of 3,250 Massachusetts men, exclusive of officers, 304 New Hampshire troops, and 516 Connecticut troops. Commodore Warren assisted with a small fleet, but the main work and credit belonged to the colonists.

In April, 1748, the peace of Aix-la-Chapelle was signed, by which Cape Breton was restored to the French.

Douglas's Summary, i. 533, gives the rates of pay in 1748 as follows — in *old tenor*, then so depreciated as to be worth only one-tenth to one-eleventh of sterling money. Captains £18 per month; lieutenants £12; sergeant £6–8; chaplain £24; centinels £5; gunners £8. Bounties to privates £4, one month's advance wages, a blanket, and 30 shillings per week subsistence. The provisions were one pound of bread, a half pint of pease, and two-thirds of a pound of pork daily, one gallon of molasses for 42 days. Marching allowances, one pound of bread, one pound of pork, and one gill of rum.

He adds " the Alacrity of the New England Militia may be observed, by the Alarm from *d'Anville's* Brest French Squadron, end of September, 1746; in a very short time 6400 men from the Country, well armed, appeared in Boston Common, some of them (*v.g.* from Brookfield) travelled 70 Miles in two Days, each with a Pack (in which was Provision for 14 Days) of about a Bushel Corn weight."

In 1755 the colonists fitted out four expeditions against the French settlements, although war had not been formally declared. In three of these Massachusetts took part. Col. Monkton raised 2,000 men to go to Nova Scotia; for the Crown Point expedition, Massachusetts voted 1,200 men, New Hampshire 600, Rhode Island 400, Connecticut 1,000, and New York 800. This army under Gen. Johnson won

APPENDIX C.   143

a victory over the French under Dieskau at Lake George. Braddock's expedition was a terrible failure, and the colonial troops saved the retreat.

After two or three years of desultory fighting in which the French had the advantage, in 1758 Massachusetts voted 7,000 men to be joined to the regulars under Gen. Abercrombie to go to Lake George. 4,500 men were volunteers and 2,500 were drafted from the militia; the other colonies raised between 2,000 and 3,000 soldiers. This army met with a disgraceful repulse at Ticonderoga and fell back to Albany. Louisburg was however again captured this year by the fleet under Admiral Boscawen and the troops under Gen. Amherst.

In 1759 Massachusetts voted 5,000 men, and nearly 1,500 were added by voluntary enlistment. Gen. Amherst captured Ticonderoga and Crown Point; Johnson took Niagara, while Wolfe made himself immortal by the capture of Quebec.

Hutchinson writes (iii. 78), "The Massachusetts forces this year were of great service. Twenty-five hundred served in garrison at Louisburg and Nova Scotia, in the room of the regular troops taken from thence to serve under General Wolfe. Several hundred served on board the King's ships as seamen, and the remainder of the six thousand five hundred men, voted in the spring, served under General Amherst. Besides this force, upon application from General Wolfe, three hundred more were raised and sent to Quebec by the lieutenant-governor, in the absence of the governor at Penobscot. These served as pioneers and in other capacities, in which the regulars must otherwise have been employed."

In 1760, the colony voted 5,000 men who served this year in conjunction with other provincials and about 1,600 regulars, under Col. Haviland. They entered Canada from Crown Point by Lake Champlain, and joining the column under Gen. Amherst from Albany, and that under Gen. Murray from Quebec, they facilitated the reduction of Montreal and the whole province of Canada.

In 1762 "Massachusetts was again called upon for a like number of men as had been in service the last year, to serve upon the continent, while the regulars were to be employed in an important service elsewhere. The assembly determined to raise 3,200 men, which number was satisfactory. They also voted a bounty of seven pounds per man, to encourage the enlistment of 893 men into the regular troops. This is a singular instance.

"Men were raised with greater ease than ever. By habit, they became fond of the life of a soldier. The number now required not being half what had been required in several former years, there was not room for many who were inclined to serve, and who thus were obliged to remain at home." (Hutchinson, iii. 96.)

The Peace of Paris was signed Feb. 10, 1763, leaving Canada in the possession of the English and thus finally freeing the colonists from the danger which had been always menacing them for the past century.

This summary of matters which should in part have been entirely familiar to the English public at this time, may serve as a corrective to the slanders which follow, but which are worthy of our attention. The inconceivable blindness of the Englishmen on this point had an immense influence upon the action of the King and the Ministry.[1] The knowledge that such views were held in England was the main reason for fighting the battle which we are commemorating.

In the printed Parliamentary History (vol. 18, p. 226), I find in a debate, Feb. 2, 1775, on an Address to the King upon the Disturbances in North America, that Colonel Grant spoke as follows. "He had served in America, and knew the Americans well; was certain they would not fight. They would never dare to face an English army, and did not possess any of the quali-

---

[1] Among the more noted members of the House of Commons in the Parliament which met Nov. 29, 1774, were the Grenvilles; Sir John Borlace Warren; James Mansfield, Solicitor-General; Soame Jenyns; Edward Gibbon; Mollocux Shuldham, admiral; John and Thomas Pownal; Alexander Wedderburn, Attorney-General; Richard Rigby; Richard Fitzpatrick; Richard, viscount Howe, admiral; George Selwyn; Thomas Harley; Sir Horace Mann; Geo. John Burgoyne; John Wilkes, Richard Oliver, Frederick Bull, John Sawbridge, George Hayley, all of London; Charles Townshend; Gen. William Howe; Sir Henry Clinton; William Eden; Frederick, lord North; Henry Strachey; Henry Cruger; Edmund Burke; Edward Thurlow, Gen. Henry Seymour Conway; Sir Fletcher Norton, the Speaker; Lord George Germaine; Capt. George Johnstone, R.N.; John Dunning; Isaac Barré; Charles James Fox; Lord George Gordon; David Hartley; Charles Jenkinson; Lord Adam Gordon; Col. James Grant, Staats Long Morris, afterwards general; Col. John Maitland; and Sir George Macartney. W. H. W.

fications to make a good soldier; he repeated many of their common place expressions, ridiculed their enthusiasm in matters of religion, and drew a disagreeable picture of their manners and ways of living."

Col. James Grant was a member of the Parliament which met Nov. 24, 1774, and represented the burghs of Kirkwall, etc. He was Lt. Col. of the 40th Foot, 26 July, 1760; Colonel of the 55th Foot, Dec. 11, 1775; Maj. Gen., Aug. 29, 1777; Colonel of the 11th Foot, Nov. 9, 1791; Lieut. Gen., Nov. 26, 1792; full General, May 3, 1796. The Gentleman's Magazine (1806, i. 479) mentions April 13, the death at his seat at Ballendalloch, near Elgin, in Scotland, of Gen. Grant, "very old."

Hutchinson's Diary calls him *Gov.* Grant.

It is satisfactory to know that his slanders promptly returned to trouble him, as soon as the reports of actual fighting reached England. Hutchinson in his Diary (i. 461) notes as follows under date of May 31st, 1775.

"I called upon General Harvey, where I found Grant and Dalrymple. Harvey swore and reproached them — chiefly Dalrymple, because he wanted more forces — with this expression. ' How often have I heard you American Colonels boast that with four battalions you would march through America; and now you think Gage with 3,000 men and 40 pieces of cannon, mayn't venture out of Boston.' He was much heated in talking of the last advices from Boston."

In the debate in the House of Lords, March 16th, 1775, on the Bill restraining the Trade and Commerce of the New England Colonies, the Earl of Sandwich made a very ridiculous and insulting speech, of which quite a full abstract has been preserved. (Parl. History, vol. 18, p. 446.)

"The noble lord mentions the impracticability of conquering America; I cannot think the noble lord can be serious on this matter. Suppose the colonies do abound in men, what does that signify? They are raw, undisciplined, cowardly, men. I wish instead of 40,000 or 50.000 of these brave fellows, they would produce in the field at least 200,000, the more the better, the easier would be the conquest; if they did not run away, they would starve themselves into compliance with our measures. I will tell your lordships an anecdote that happened at the siege of Louisburgh: sir Peter Warren told me, that, in order to try the courage of the Americans, he ordered a great number of them to be placed in the front of the army; the Americans pretended at first to be very much elated at this mark of distinction, and boasted what mighty feats they would do upon the scene of action; however, when the moment came to put in execution this boasted courage, behold, every one of them ran from the front to the rear of the army, with as much expedition as their feet could carry them, and threatened to go off entirely, if the commander offered to make them a shield to protect the British soldiers at the expense of their blood; they did not understand such usage. Sir Peter finding what egregious cowards they were, and knowing of what importance such numbers must be to intimidate the French by their appearance, told these American heroes that his orders had been misunderstood, that he always intended to keep them in rear of the army to make the great push; that it was the custom of generals to preserve the best troops to the last; that this was always the Roman custom, and as the Americans resembled the Romans in every particular, especially in courage and love of their country, he should make no scruple of following the Roman custom, and made no doubt but the modern Romans would shew acts of bravery, equal to any in ancient Rome. 'By such discourses as these,' said sir Peter Warren, 'I made a shift to keep them with us, though I took care they should be pushed forward in no dangerous conflict.'

"Now, I can tell the noble lord, that this is exactly the situation of all the heroes in North America; they are all Romans: and are these the men to fright us from the post of honour? Believe me, my lords, the very sound of a cannon would carry them off, in sir Peter's words, 'as fast as their feet would carry them.' This is too trifling a part of the argument, to detain your lordships any longer. The noble earl then went on to abuse the Americans for not paying their debts; he made no doubt that the real motive of their associations was to defraud their creditors. That the congress, on which the noble lord had passed high encomiums, was a seditious and treasonable meeting of persons assembled to resist the legal and just authority of the supreme legislative power; and however dignified by his lordship, or any other noble lord, he should always continue to describe it by the latter appellation, as its only true and proper name. His lordship entered into a long examination of the purport of the evidence given at the bar by Messrs. Lister, Davis, Shuldham, and Paliser; and laboured to prove, that the present Bill, whatever other objects it might take in, was not, nor ought to be, a Bill of intimidation or experiment, but a perpetual law of commercial regulation, operating to extend our trade, to increase our seamen, and strengthen our naval power."

On the other side, the members of the Opposition praised very highly the conduct of the American troops. March 27th, 1775 (Parl. Hist., vol. 18, p. 556), David Hartley, a member from Kingston-upon-Hull, spoke as follows.

"To begin with the late war. The Americans turned the success of the war, at both ends of the line. Gen. Moukton took Beausejour in Nova Scotia with 1,500 provincial troops and about 200 regulars. Sir William Johnson in the other part of America, changed the face of the war to success with a provincial army, which took baron Dieskau prisoner. But, Sir, the glories of the war, under the united British and American arms, are recent in every one's memory. Suffice it to decide this question, that the Americans bore, even in our judgment, more than their full proportion. They kept, one year with another, 25,000 men on foot, and lost in the war the flower of their youth.

"Nor did they stint their services to North America; they followed their British arms out of their continent, to the Havannah and Martinique, after the complete conquest of America. And so had they done in the preceding war. They were not grudging of their exertions; they were at the siege of Carthagena: yet what was Carthagena to them, but as members of the common cause, of the glory of this country? In that war too, Sir, they took Louisbourg from the French, single-handed, without any European assistance; as mettled an enterprise as any in our history! an everlasting memorial of the zeal, courage and perseverance of the troops of New England."

October 26, 1775, on the Debate at the Opening of the Session (Parl. Hist., vol. 18, p. 751), Governor Johnstone (? Capt. George Johnstone, R.N., member for Appleby?) said

"I maintain that the sense of the best and wisest men in this country is on the side of the Americans; that three to one in Ireland are on their side; that the soldiers and sailors feel an unwillingness to the service; that you will never find the same exertions of spirit in this as in other wars. . . . I am well informed, that the four field officers in the four regiments now going from Ireland, have desired leave to retire or sell out. I do not mean that the soldiers or sailors in America have shown any signs of cowardice, this is below their spirit; I only assert they in general proclaim it a disagreeable service; most of the army feel it as such; that numbers have not deserted is owing to their situation. There is a wide difference between the English officer or soldier who barely does his duty, and the general exertions of the New England army, where every man is thinking what further service he can perform; where every soldier is a Scævola."

Col. Barré, the well-known member from Calne, in the same debate (Parl. History, vol. 18, p. 767) said

"The Americans had been called cowards; that the noble lord at the head of the Admiralty [Sandwich] had wantonly raked up the ashes of a deceased admiral to confirm his hasty assertions; but now he had sent for a living admiral home, to give the departed one the lie. As to cowards, they were certainly the greatest to his knowledge; for the 47th regiment of foot, which behaved so gallantly at Bunker's Hill (an engagement which smacked more of defeat than victory) — the very corps that broke the whole French column and threw them into such disorder at the siege of Quebec — were three parts composed of these cowards."

In the Debate on the American Prohibitory Bill, Dec. 1, 1775 (Parl. History, vol. 18, p. 1033), Hon. Richard Fitzpatrick (member from Tavistock, and brother to the Earl of Upper Ossory),

"Complained of the conduct of administration in keeping everything secret; it was very probable, if administration could have kept it a secret that the King's troops were defeated at Lexington in April, or that they suffered worse than a defeat at Bunker's Hill,

— we should have never heard of these mortifying occurrences; nor that an army of 10,000 men, with a most formidable train of artillery, and commanded by four generals of reputation, have been blocked up during the whole summer by a body of people who have been described in this House, ever since their names have been first mentioned, as a mere cowardly rabble."

Dec. 7th, 1775, on the Debate on Mr. Hartley's Proposition for Conciliation (Parl. Hist., vol. 18, p. 1055), Ald. John Sawbridge (member from London) said

"It has been very fashionable both within and without doors, to stigmatize the Americans as cowards and poltroons, but he believed the truth would be on the other side; for he was well informed that the King's troops at the action of Bunker Hill consisted of 2,500 men, and the provincials not quite 1,500; and even those 1,500 men would have completely defeated the King's troops, if their ammunition had not been totally spent."

Lord North in reply estimated the American force at 8,000 men; to which Gov. Johnstone replied, "At all events there was something fatal to the noble lord's argument either way; for either the works were weak and therefore the provincials defended them bravely; or being strong, it showed what a dangerous enemy they must be who could raise and so judiciously construct such works, from 11 o'clock at night on a summer's evening till day-break the next morning."

Col. Morris placed the American force engaged at fully 5,000, which was two to one.

In a debate Feb. 20, 1776 (Parl. Hist., vol. 18, p. 1155), Col. Barré said "that the troops, from an aversion to the service, misbehaved at Bunker's-hill on the 17th of June."

General Burgoyne, who was a member from Preston, "rose with warmth, and contradicted the last honorable member in the flattest manner. He allowed that the troops gave way a little at one time, because they were flanked by the fire out of the houses, etc., at Charles-Town; but they soon rallied and advanced; and no men on earth ever behaved with more spirit, firmness and perseverance, till they forced the enemy out of their entrenchments."

That Burgoyne must have spoken, as above reported, with some mental reservations, will appear from the following copies of his confidential letters, written at the time from Boston. They will be found in the volume of his "Life and Correspondence," edited by Fonblanque, and printed in London in 1876, at pp. 142-154 and 191-199. These letters, I believe, have not been copied in full before, although extracts were printed in Dr. Ellis's Oration in 1876, on the Centennial Anniversary of the Evacuation of Boston.

"TO LORD ROCHFORT.

"My Lord, — I take the first opportunity of a safe conveyance to enter upon the confidential correspondence which your Lordship permitted me to hold with you. And while I lament the untoward state of things, which, in consistency with such an intercourse, I may often be bound to impart, it is truly satisfactory to me to reflect that my communications and opinions will be safe and sacred under the guard of your honour and friendship: the one will secure me from being discovered by those who might consider my intelligence with jealousy or prejudice: to the other I trust for a candid and generous interpretation of the freedoms my pen may take.

"The end I aim at is to convey truth to the King. My heart disavows a single sentiment of asperity or ill-will towards any servant of the Crown in America; and in regard to that servant in particular to whom, in stating facts, I must necessarily and principally allude, I desire to be considered as one who bears high respect to his private virtues: and who, in commenting upon the circumstances of his public conduct, finds reason to justify him in some, to excuse him in others, and to pity him in all.

"I arrived at Boston, together with Generals Howe and Clinton, on the 25th May. It would be unnecessary were it possible, to describe our surprise or other feelings, upon the appearances which at once and on every side, were offered to our observation. The town, on the land side, invested by a rabble in arms, who flushed with success and insolence, had advanced their sentries to pistol-shot of our out-guards; the ships in the harbour exposed to, and expecting a cannonade or bombardment; — in all companies, whether of officers or inhabitants, men still lost in a sort of stupefaction which the events of the 19th of April had occasioned, and venting expressions of censure, anger, or despondency.

"The principle of seizing arms, and thereby bringing the designs of the malcontents to a test and a decision was certainly just. We can only wonder that it was not sooner adopted. Had General Gage held himself authorised by his instruction, sufficient in force, and unimpeded by other difficulties, to have acted upon this principle early in the preparations of hostility, and at the same time to have seized the persons of Adams, Hancock, and other leaders who were then within his reach, it would probably have tended to the best effects; but even then means should have been found, such as at a later time he made use of, to obtain secret intelligence of the enemy's counsels; military precautions should have been used to prepare the troops for the sort of combat they were to expect, and so prevent a possibility of insult to the troops, or at least of advantage over them. Posts should have been occupied for keeping open the adjacent country for the supply of the town; and above all, plentiful stores should have been provided of every article that, in failure of common supplies, every exigency might require. Perhaps the town and harbour of Boston are more advantageously situated for the establishment of magazines, supposing the command of the sea, than any spot that could be found upon the map of the world.

"It is not therefore from the principle of the measure of the 19th of April, but from the plan of the execution, and the want of preparation for the consequences, that I think may be derived great part of the perplexity and disgrace which have followed.

"The news of this miscarriage, aggravated with misrepresentation and inflammatory suggestions, were dispersed, it is incredible how swiftly, from one end of the continent to the other. A total suppression of those who were acting in favour of Government followed everywhere; and from the neighbouring provinces reinforcements flocked to the victorious insurgents by thousands a day. The cattle upon the neighbouring islands in the harbour (a poor stock it must be confessed) were taken off with triumph; the houses of those who had dared to supply provisions to the garrison, were burnt; an armed vessel of the fleet was burnt, and her guns taken away in the view of an admiral and lieutenant-general; and in the unfortunate situation to which things were then reduced, I do not know that they could have prevented these insults. At last, the enemy advanced works upon the height which commands the town and harbour; and there seemed to want only the opening of batteries to produce a more singular and shameful event than can be found in the history of the world — a paltry skirmish (for the affair of the 1£th of April was no more) inducing circumstances as rapid and as decisive as the battle of Pharsalia; and the colours of a fleet and army of Great Britain, not wrested from us, but without a conflict kicked out of America.

" The sentiments of Howe, Clinton, and myself have been unanimous from the beginning. We have alike endeavoured to palliate past omissions; to conceal present irremediable wants; to press vigorous undertakings. At the same time, we have been obliged in justice to acknowledge that the reasons for waiting to the last moment for the expected reinforcements which it was known were near, were justly founded.

" At the time when the exigencies above stated had nearly reached their consummation, the troops of the first embarkation happily arrived. The effect on the spirits of the army was visible. Nevertheless, the proceedings of the enemy did not manifest any intimidation on their part. They pushed on their work on the heights on both sides of the town with double diligence. We lost no time in preparation, and on the 17th instant, General Howe was detached with a considerable corps, to attack on the heights of Charlestown.

" It would be waste of your Lordship's time to enter into the detail of an action that will of course be conveyed at large to the King's servants by General Gage's letters; and my friend Howe's conduct will not want my testimony to do it justice. Clinton had the good fortune in the course of the action to be actively employed, and acquitted himself, as I am persuaded he will ever do, much to his honour. For my part, the inferiority of my station as youngest Major-General upon the staff, left me almost a useless spectator, for my whole business lay in presiding during part of the action over a cannonade to assist the left.

"This situation, you well know, my Lord, I foresaw, and felt, before I left England. In the general regular course of business in this army, Major-Generals are absolute cyphers. The small number of brigades and large number of Brigadiers perhaps makes them necessarily so. We have not even the little employment of inspection; and for commands of detachments of consequence like the last, should they go in rotation, I am afraid the sphere of our campaign must be too bounded to furnish one to each of the triumvirate. My lot in justice and propriety must come last, and in the meantime my rank only serves to place me in a motionless, drowsy, irksome medium, or rather vacuum, too low for the honour of command, too high for that of execution. This correspondence is the single gratification my mind receives in its activity and zeal; but while I declare it single, I acknowledge it sufficient, provided it can furnish any useful lights in so great a cause; and in that hope I will stifle the regret of being otherwise unemployed.

"I have supposed the King's servants to be apprised by General Gage's letters of the general circumstances of the success of the 17th; and I now congratulate you, my dear Lord, upon an event that effaces the stain of the 19th of April, and will, I hope stand a testimony and a record in America of the superiority of regular troops over those of any other description. It is certain our detachment had to struggle with more than treble numbers, assisted with all that nature and art could do to strengthen a post; intoxicated with zeal; and instigated, during the action by the presence of one of their most favourite and able demagogues (Warren), who at last sealed his fanaticism with his blood before their eyes.

"In this point of view the action is honourable in itself; and whatever measures his Majesty's councils may now pursue, it must be of important assistance by the impression it will make, not only in America, but universally upon public opinion. It may be wise policy to support this impression to the utmost, both in writing and discourse; but when I withdraw the curtain, your Lordship will find much cause for present reflection, much for the exercise of your judgment, upon the future conduct of the scene.

"Turn your eyes first, my Lord, to the behaviour of the enemy. The defence was well conceived and obstinately maintained; the retreat was no flight; it was even covered with bravery and military skill, and proceeded no farther than to the next hill, where a new post was taken, new intrenchments instantly begun, and their numbers affording constant reliefs of workmen, they have been continued day and night ever since.

"View now, my Lord, the side of victory; and first the list of killed and wounded. If fairly given, it amounts to no less than ninety-two officers, many of them an irreparable loss — a melancholy disproportion to the number of the private soldiers — and there is a melancholy reason for it. Though my letter passes in security, I tremble while I write it; and let it not pass even in a whisper from your Lordship to more than one person: the zeal and intrepidity of the officers, which was without exception exemplary, was ill-seconded by the private men. Discipline, not to say courage, was wanting. In the critical moment of carrying the redoubt, the officers of some corps were almost alone; and what was the worst part of the confusion of these corps — all the wounds of the officers were not received from the enemy. I do not mean to convey any suspicion of backwardness in the cause of Government among the soldiery, which ignorant people in England are apt to imagine; and as little would I be understood to imply any dislike or ill-will to their officers. I believe the men attached to their regiments, and exasperated against the enemy — that there has not been a single desertion since the 19th of April is a proof of it — I only mean to represent that the men in the *defective* corps being ill-grounded in the great points of discipline, and the men in *all* the corps having twice felt their enemy to be more formidable than they expected, it will require some training under such generals as Howe and Clinton before they can prudently be intrusted in many exploits against such odds as the conduct and spirit of the leaders enabled them in this instance to overcome.

"But suppose that point of confidence in the troops attained. Look my Lord, upon the country near Boston — it is all fortification. Driven from one hill, you will see the enemy continually retrenched upon the next; and every step we move must be the slow step of a siege. Could we at last penetrate ten miles, perhaps we should not obtain a single sheep or an ounce of flour by our laborious progress, for they remove every article of provisions as they go. Does any man extend his expectations to a further scope of country, and against such an enemy, who in composition and system are all light troops, they are not more than requisite to secure our convoys and communnications between the army and the great deposit of magazines; or if that difficulty were got over by great and active genius, look into our state once more, and you will find us totally unprovided with bread waggons, hospital carriages, bat-horses, sufficient artillery horses, and many other articles of *attirail* indispensably necessary for an army to proceed by land to a great distance.

" I am apprehensive lest this representation, taken upon the gross, should seem to carry more of imputation than I professed at setting out. But I do not mean it, and would explain myself upon that subject once for all.

" I think General Gage possessed of every quality to maintain quiet government with honour to himself and happiness to those he governs; his temper and his talents, of which he has many, are calculated to dispense the offices of justice and humanity. In the military I believe him capable of figuring upon ordinary and given lines of conduct, but his mind has not resources for great, and sudden, and hardy exertions, which spring self-suggested in extraordinary characters, and generally overbear all opposition. In short, I think him a contrast to that cast of men, somewhere described, —

> " ' Fit to disturb the peace of all the world
> And rule it when 'tis wildest.'

" Unfortunately for us that cast of character, at least the latter part of it, is precisely what we want here; and I hope I shall not be thought to disparage my general and my friend in pronouncing him unequal to his situation, when I add that I think it one in which Cæsar might have failed.

" The lamentable point with which I shall close the state of our affairs (one, indeed, in which Cæsar would not have erred) is the parsimonious extreme to which our system of caution has extended in point of money. Your Lordship is better placed than I am to discover whether any part of that blame lies at home; some may possibly be due to those at the head of subordinate departments here. The general may have excuses for the rest, but the miserable result of the whole is that the interest of the treasury has been managed, or mismanaged, till we are destitute, not only of cattle and magazines of forage, but of the most important of all circumstances in war or negotiation, — *intelligence*. We are ignorant, not only of what passes in congresses, but want spies for the hill half a mile off. And what renders the reflection truly provoking is that there was hardly a leading man among the rebels, in councils or in the field, but, at a proper time and by proper management, might have been bought.

"It is now time to consider, my Lord — and the question will naturally be asked in the King's councils at home, — can nothing then be done this campaign? I think something may, and my colleagues and General Gage I believe, will agree in my opinion. When the four battalions of the second embarkation arrive (and they are expected daily, one vessel being come in), and such of the wounded men as we may expect speedily to recover have joined their regiments, our army will consist of about five thousand two hundred effective men, exclusive of officers. If you, in England, reckon upon more, you are mistaken. With this force, and perhaps before it all arrives, we cannot fail possessing the whole peninsula on the south of Boston, called Dorchester Neck. It is proposed afterwards to fortify it with redoubts. To occupy this ground when so fortified, on one side, the heights of Charlestown on the other, and the lines and other works of Boston in the centre, will take, in the opinion of our best officers, upwards of three thousand men. I will suppose, therefore, about two thousand left to be employed upon expeditions. I would embark this force, and unite to it all the ships of war that can be safely spared from the protection of Boston.

"I should think one probable and immediate effect would be the separation of a great part of the Massachusetts army, which is composed of the forces of Connecticut, Rhode Island, and Hampshire. The Bostonians alone would remain before Boston. This possibly might give an opening to those affected by their inclinations (for such I still believe there are), and to a much larger number affected by their interest, to move in our favour. And if they did not open a direct communication with the town, in the starving condition it is in at present, even smuggling a quantity of fresh provisions would be of great consequence to the health and spirits both of army and inhabitants; the former live entirely upon salt meat, and I hardly guess how some of the latter live at all.

"The expedition at sea, the whole coast of America, equally ignorant of its destination, would be equally in alarm. The real points for acting with effect must depend upon circumstances. My idea would be to try the temper and strength of places, by degrees, to the southward. Rhode Island ought to feel chastisement; Connecticut river, if practicable, would afford ample contribution; Long Island will, I hope, be found deserving of encouragement, and can hardly fail, under protection of force, to become an excellent market for supplies. As for New York, do not let me be thought positive or chimerical if I still retain the sentiments I so much pressed in London. That province is lost for want of management, and a proper force to second it. I continue to lament that I was not thought worthy of undertaking that business. I might have failed, but with the temper which prevailed in the Assembly, and the different uses which might have been made of the military power, to encourage and to terrify, I would have been content to forfeit all pretensions to discretionary trust hereafter if I had. Even now, notwithstanding the use that has been made of the 19th of April, I do not despair of great effects from an expedition there, if wise measures are taken to work upon men's minds.

"As one previous step to that purpose, my advice to General Gage had been to treat the prisoners taken in the late action, most of whom are wounded, with all possible kindness, and to dismiss them without terms. 'You have been deluded; return to your homes in peace; it is your duty to God and your country to undeceive your neighbors.'

"I have had opportunities to sound the minds of these people. Most of them are men of good understandings, but of much prejudice, and still more credulity; they are yet ignorant of their fate, and some of them expect, when they recover, to be hanged. Such an act of mercy as I have proposed may make an impression, and it may spread.

Should it fail, it will at least serve to justify acts of a different nature hereafter; and you are no further dupes of it in the meantime than by adding about thirty men now in your power to a stock of as many thousands who are out of it.

"Another and more material prelude to an expedition will be a manifesto; and I heartily wish a proper one, framed in England by the King's ablest counsellors, could arrive in time.

"Large contributions of cattle, forage, and other requisite stores for winter magazines, must, I think, be obtained. Should some towns be burned, and others be deserted, it will be warning and alarm to the yet more southern provinces; and should the enthusiasm of the time and the control of the seditious leaders be indeed general, Government will at least have clear lights to proceed by.

"If the continent is to be subdued by arms, his Majesty's councils will find, I am persuaded, the proper expedients; but I speak confidently as a soldier, because I speak the sentiments of those who know America best, that you can have no probable prospect of bringing the war to a speedy conclusion with any force that Great Britain and Ireland can supply. A large army of such foreign troops as might be hired, to begin operations up the Hudson river; another army composed partly of old disciplined troops and partly of Canadians, to act from Canada; a large levy of Indians, and a supply of arms for the blacks, to awe the southern provinces, conjointly with detachments of regulars; and a numerous fleet to sweep the whole coast, might possibly do the business in one campaign.

"Should it be thought more expedient to the nation, and reconcilable to its honour, to relinquish the claims in question, I doubt not the wisdom of those councils of which your Lordship is so distinguished a part, will propose such relinquishment as will be at once effectual. But I am fully persuaded that any intermediate measure between these disagreeable extremes (except that of withdrawing your army, and leaving the restraints of trade enforced by a fleet to operate, which would be a work of long protraction), I repeat my full persuasion — that any intermediate measure, supposing the confederation to be general, will be productive of much fruitless expense, great loss of blood, and a series of disappointments.

"I have delivered this sentiment firmly, but I rely upon your Lordship's candour to receive it as intelligence collected by personal observation of men and things which those at home have not opportunity to make; and not as a presumption of my private judgment acting in competition with those to whom the King has entrusted the great direction of the state."

"TO LORD GEORGE GERMAIN.

"Boston, 20th August, 1775.

"My Lord, — I have never lost the remembrance of the honour you did me in permitting me to write to you, and I rely upon your Lordship's candour not to consider my silence hitherto as inconsistent with that profession. The occasions of writing confidentially have been few, and those generally so sudden as barely to leave time to despatch letters of business and family concern.

"The notoriety of the event of the 19th of April; the general revolt which ensued; the blockade of Boston; the action of the 17th of June upon Charlestown heights, and many other occurrences previous to the return of the "Cerberus," necessarily stated in all public letters, and commented upon in all private ones, will much abridge my undertaking at present.

"Your Lordship's insight into men and things will make my reflections equally superfluous upon the parts of our present dilemma imputable at home. Whatever party in America may father this rebellion, all parties in England have contributed to nurse it into strength. Inconsistencies and contradictions, by a strange fatality of the times, have lost their usual nature. Ministry and Opposition, faction and meekness of spirit, principles the most incongruous, have in effect operated to the same end; — till after a fatal procrastination, not only of vigorous measures, but of preparation for such, we took a step as decisive as the passage of the Rubicon, and found ourselves plunged at once in a most serious war, without a single requisite, gunpowder excepted, for carrying it on.

"Such was the beginning of the campaign; and the almost only circumstance upon which the mind can rest with a moment's satisfaction since, is the victory obtained at Charlestown by the spirit and conduct of Mr. Howe, and the exemplary, I might almost say unexampled, bravery of the officers under him.

"It would depreciate this victory to estimate only its immediate effects. Great as they are, they do not more than compensate the heavy loss by which it was bought. But in one consideration it may be esteemed most important; it re-establishes the ascendency of the King's troops in public opinion, and enables us to rest upon our arms, or even to close the war, should the enemy so incline, with an impression, not only beneficial to the present circumstances of England, but to the general repose of mankind. I believe in most states of the world, as well as our own, the respect and control and subordination of Government at this day, in great measure depends upon the idea that trained troops are invincible against any number or any position of undisciplined rabble, and this idea was a little in suspense since the 19th of April.

"I have one remaining subject of congratulation for your Lordship and other friends of Government, and with that I am afraid I must close all the agreeable part of my intelligence. It is however, highly satisfactory. The army is firmly attached in principle to the cause of Britain; the private men, a very few rascally drafts and recruits from Irish jails excepted, have not deserted. On the contrary they appear in general exasperated against their enemy; and as to the officers, no men ever fought or endured hardship with more alacrity and distinguished fortitude.

"Occasion will doubtless be taken in England, as well as in America, to extol the defence of the rebels at Charlestown, and the report of our loss will assist prejudices. But nothing happened there, or in any of the little affairs since, that raised them in my opinion one jot above the level of all men expert in the use of firearms; Corsicans, Miquelets, Croats, Tartars, mountaineers, and borderers, in almost all countries, have in their turns done more hardy things than defend one of the strongest posts that nature and art combined could make, and then run away. In short, it is as preposterous to recur to Sparta and Athens for comparisons to their courage, as it is to suppose their spring of action in this revolt analogous to the genuine spirit of liberty that guided those states. But the multitude are zealous, and the leaders, though often the most profligate hypocrites, have among them very able men. I believe Adams to be as great a conspirator as ever subverted a state. I cannot help quoting a passage of a letter from him to his wife, intercepted the other day, and which I conclude is transmitted with some others, to Lord Dartmouth: —

"'The business' (says he) 'I have had upon my mind has been as great and important as can be entrusted to man, and the difficulty and intricacy of it is prodigious — a constitution to form for a great empire — a country of fifteen hundred miles in extent to fortify — millions to train and arm — a naval power to begin — an extensive commerce to regulate — a standing army of twenty-seven thousand men to raise, pay, and victual, and officer, &c.'

"In another confidential letter to a friend, intercepted at the same time, after expressing great dissatisfaction against one of his tools (I conclude he means Handcock, president of the Continental Congress, whom he calls a piddling genius), he goes on thus; — ' We ought to have had in our hands a month ago the whole legislative, executive and judicial of the whole continent, and have completely modelled a constitution; to have raised a naval power, and opened all our ports wide; to have arrested every friend of Government on the Continent, and held them as hostages for the poor victims in Boston. Shall I hail you Speaker of the House' (meaning a Provincial Congress), or councillor, or what? What sort of magistrates do you intend to make? Will your new legislative and executive feel bold or irresolute? Will your judicial hang, and whip and fine, and imprison without scruple? &c. &c.

" The bare effort of investigating such objects argues an aspiring and vigorous mind : but when it is considered that with a profligate character, a very unpopular origin in party, neither supported by pecuniary nor political interest, nor ascending to factious eminence by the footsteps of any leader or patron ; that merely by the exercise of his parts, availing himself of the temper and prejudices of the times, he has cajoled the opulent, drawn in the wary, deluded the vulgar till all parties in America, and some in Great Britain, are puppets in his string; when the contrivance, and extent, and execution of his present plans as far as they appear or are conceived, are examined, I am persuaded your Lordship will, with me, lose sight of Catiline or Cromwell in passing judgment upon his character.

"Be assured, my Lord, this man soars too high to be allured by any offer Great Britain can make to himself or to his country. America, if his counsels continue in force, must be subdued or relinquished. She will not be reconciled.

"I will not presume to suggest measures for proceeding in either of the extremes with honour to Britain. Your Lordship's acute discernment will best point them out. Nor would I willingly lead your attention from objects of that magnitude to the very inferior ones of this campaign. I shall therefore say very little upon it.

"The blockade of Boston cannot be effectually relieved. Not that I think it impossible, even with our disparity of numbers, to dislodge the enemy from their present posts; but that neither having bread-waggons, bat-horses, sufficient artillery horses, nor other articles of *attirail* necessary for an army to move at a distance; nor numbers to keep up posts of communication and convoys (had we even magazines to be convoyed), it would be impossible after success to open the country so as to force supplies.

"Conceiving therefore that an attack upon the adjacent entrenchments might be attended with considerable loss and no possible advantage, my colleagues and I have been unanimous (as indeed we have been upon every other matter) to advise operations at a distance.

"My own favourite plan is a descent at Rhode Island, where I would entrench; and I think it might be effected with two thousand men and some frigates. I have set forth in a memorandum to General Gage the advantages that I think possessing that post would afford, not only as a diversion that might probably disperse the army before Boston, but likewise as it is of importance to cover and facilitate greater designs.

"I confess a despair of seeing this or any other enterprise take place — our efforts at best have but the disappointed vigour of a dream:

"' Nequicquam extendere cursus
Velle videmur, et in mediis conatibus ægri
Succidimus.'

APPENDIX C.

"The representation I have touched may seem to carry imputation to General Gage. I check my pen whenever that thought comes across me, for I have a most sincere value for his character, which is replete with virtues and with talents. That it is not of a cast proper for his present situation, I allow; and hence many, though far from all, of our misfortunes. To have prevented, or to have redeemed the circumstances of this war, required a man of the greatest resources of mind — of a spirit not to be overborne by difficulties; but above all of a resolution to act upon the occasion; in events which the King's servants at home could not have foreseen, to substitute reason and principle for orders — to state his motives — and whatever were the fortune of his undertaking, to submit his honour and his head to the judgment of his country.

"If this character in the present age be not quite ideal, it is at least so rare as to admit us to mention where it fails without disparagement or offence to a respectable officer and friend.

"It may be asked in England, 'What is the Admiral doing?'

"I wish I were able to answer that question satisfactorily; but I can only say what he is *not* doing.

"That he is *not* supplying us with sheep and oxen, the dinners of the best of us bear meagre testimony; the state of our hospitals bears a more melancholy one.

"He is *not* defending his own flocks and herds, for the enemy have repeatedly plundered his own islands.

"He is *not* defending the other islands in the harbour, for the enemy in force landed from a great number of boats, and burned the lighthouse at noonday (having first killed and taken the party of marines which was posted there) almost under the guns of two or three men-of-war.

"He is *not* employing his ships to keep up communication and intelligence with the King's servants and friends at the different parts of the continent, for I do not believe General Gage has received a letter from any correspondent out of Boston these six weeks.

"He is intent upon greater objects, you will think, — supporting in the great points the dignity of the British flag, — and where a number of boats have been built for the enemy; privateers fitted out; prizes carried in; the King's armed vessels sunk; the crews made prisoners, the officers killed, — he is doubtless enforcing instant restitution and reparation by the voice of his cannon and laying the towns in ashes that refuse his terms? Alas! he is not. British thunder is diverted or controlled by pitiful attentions and mere Quaker-like scruples; and under such influences, insult and impunity, like righteousness and peace, have kissed each other.

"I should have hesitated in giving an account that may appear invidious, had not the facts been too notorious to expose me to that censure, and my feelings in this great cause too sensible to observe them without some impatience. Upon the whole, when the supineness of this department is added to the diffidence of the other; and the defects of Quartermaster-Generals, Adjutant-Generals, Secretaries, and Commissaries, are superadded to both, they will make altogether a mass of inefficiencies that I am afraid would counteract and disappoint the ablest counsels in the world.

"You will now, my Lord, indulge me with a moment's patience if I say one word of myself. I have experienced, in fact, all I foresaw of an irksome situation before I left England, and much more. It is hard to conceive so absolute a cypher in a military light as the youngest Major-General in this army. I have been brought from the most interesting concerns, pleasures, duties of life, to partake of every inconvenience that can be supposed to exist in a town invested on one side, asleep on the other; and from both those and some other causes destitute of fresh provision, money, and all those common comforts which habit makes almost necessaries, and with scarcely any other employment than to contemplate errors that I cannot redress.

"I do not complain of this rough lot of service. I only lament the little use that is made of me. Every sentiment I feel in this great cause tells me (and I trust I am free from vanity in those sensations) I deserve a more active station. My private motives, therefore, are not more prevalent than public ones when I solicit leave to return to England. A proposal for making myself serviceable was transmitted to Lord North some time ago, and I conclude it has been communicated to your Lordship. I mean to be a faithful intelligencer to Government, and, if I can, a useful one to Parliament; and shall be ready to cross the Atlantic back again in the spring, should the war continue, and be extended enough to make my presence useful.

"I have delivered my opinion of our circumstances with freedom, my Lord, but I hope without acrimony. I bear sincere friendship to some, and enmity to none of the persons to whom I have alluded. I have not withheld important truths, because I am persuaded that the knowledge of them under your Lordship's management may be beneficial to this great national crisis; and confiding in your Lordship's discretion, and I venture to add friendship, not to commit the author, I have only to finish this long intrusion upon your time with sincere profession of the very profound respect with which

"I have the honour to be

"Your Lordship's, &c., &c.

"P. S. — Since writing the above, a provision of cattle is come in, and I hope it will have speedy effect upon the health of the camp: but we owe it to the transports armed and sent out by General Gage, and not to any assistance from the fleet."

These confidential letters show very clearly that Burgoyne had a very profound respect for the bravery and skill of his undisciplined opponents, but that he deemed it essential to keep the English public deceived on this point; and to even claim Bunker Hill as a British success, whilst his private conviction was strongly the opposite.

W. H. W.

APPENDIX D.

BUNKER-HILL MONUMENT.

The history of the Monument, which now marks the site of the redoubt where the battle raged most furiously, deserves to be made available to all our citizens. Much of it is set forth in the "History of the Bunker-Hill Monument Association," by the late George W. Warren (Boston, 1877); but a short sketch will give the main points.

The first effort to raise a fitting memorial was made by King Solomon's Lodge of Free and Accepted Masons, in Charlestown, who, in December, 1794, erected in Mr. Russell's pasture, a Tuscan pillar, built of wood, 18 feet high, placed upon a platform 8 feet high and 8 feet square, and surmounted by a gilt urn marked J. W. Æ. 34. The land required was given by James Russell, Esq., and the monument cost about one thousand dollars. A model of it is preserved in the entrance floor of the present Monument.

The following resolve was passed by our Legislature, Feb. 3, 1796 (Special Laws, ii. 52) : —

AN ACT FOR THE PRESERVATION OF A MONUMENT ERECTED ON THE HEIGHTS OF CHARLESTOWN.

WHEREAS, the Society of Freemasons, in Charlestown, in the county of Middlesex, designated by the name of King Solomon's Lodge, have erected a Monument in memory of Major-General Joseph Warren and his associates, who were slain on the heights of said Charlestown, on the seventeenth of June, one thousand seven hundred and seventy-five; and have been presented by the Hon. James Russell with a piece of land for that purpose :

VIEW OF THE MONUMENT AS PROPOSED, FROM THE CERTIFICATE OF MEMBERSHIP, 1854.

SECTION 1. Be it enacted by the Senate and House of Representatives, in General Court assembled, and by the authority of the same, That any legal deed or conveyance of the said land, duly recorded, shall enable the said King Solomon's Lodge of Freemasons to hold the same in fee-simple, for the purpose aforesaid, forever.

SECT. 2. And be it further enacted by the authority aforesaid, That the Master or Treasurer of the said Lodge for the time being shall have power and authority to sue for and recover damages, in any court of law suitable to try the same, from any person or persons who shall be convicted of defacing, injuring, or destroying the said Monument; and the person or persons thus convicted shall, in addition to such damages as may be legally awarded, pay to the Master or Treasurer of the said Lodge a fine not exceeding twenty dollars, nor less than two dollars, at the discretion of the court before whom the action for damages shall be finally tried; which fines shall be appropriated for the necessary repairs of the said Monument.

The annexed view, from the "Massachusetts Magazine" for June, 1791, shows the appearance of the hill.

Here the matter rested for a quarter of a century, but in 1818 a controversy sprang up in regard to the conduct of the battle, which led to a renewed interest in the subject. Daniel Webster, in the "North American Review," took a part in the discussion, and William Tudor, the editor, was also warmly interested therein. In 1822, a portion of the land on the hill was offered for sale. Mr. Tudor conferred with several friends, one of whom, Dr. John C. Warren, purchased the lot and held it until the Association was formed. The prime movers in the enterprise, besides these two, were Col. Thomas H. Perkins, Daniel Webster, William Sullivan, and George Blake. In May, 1823, these gentlemen and twenty others joined together to obtain an Act of Incorporation for the purpose of "erecting such a monument as shall endure to future ages and be a permanent memorial, consecrated by the gratitude of the present generation, to the memory of those statesmen and soldiers who led the way in the American Revolution."

The petition was promptly presented to the Legislature and the following Act was passed June 7, 1823 (Special Laws, vi. 95) : —

AN ACT TO INCORPORATE THE BUNKER HILL MONUMENT ASSOCIATION.

SECTION 1. Be it enacted, by the Senate and House of Representatives, in General Court assembled, and by the authority of the same, That Joseph Story, Jesse Putnam, Daniel Webster, Edward Everett, Samuel D. Harris, Samuel Swett, Theodore Lyman, Jr., Stephen Gorham, Jr., Thomas H. Perkins, William Tudor, Henry A. S. Dearborn, Benjamin Gorham, Franklin Dexter, William Sullivan, George Ticknor, Charles R. Codman, Warren Dutton, Isaac P. Davis, Thomas Harris, Seth Knowles, Benjamin Welles, John C. Warren, George Blake, and Francis C. Gray, their associates and successors, be and they are hereby made a body politic and corporate, by the name of the " Bunker Hill Monument Association," with all the powers and subject to all the duties of aggregate corporations, and for the purposes hereinafter named.

SECT. 2. Be it further enacted, That said corporation shall have power to take and hold, by gift, grant, or devise, such real and personal estate and property as may be necessary or convenient to promote the object of the incorporation, the construction of a Monument in Charlestown, to perpetuate the memory of the early events of the American Revolution.

SECT. 3. Be it further enacted, That the said Henry A. S. Dearborn, William Tudor, and Theodore Lyman, Jr., or any two of them, may call the first meeting of said corporation, by giving three days' previous notice thereof in two public newspapers printed in Boston ; at which, or at any subsequent meeting, the said corporation may choose such officers, agents, and trustees as they may think proper, and establish such by-laws and regulations for their own government and the management of their concerns, not repugnant to the laws and constitution of this Commonwealth, as they may deem necessary, and the same may modify and annul at pleasure.

SECT. 4. Be it further enacted, That said corporation may, at any time after said monument shall be completed, assign and transfer the same, with the land on which it stands, and the appurtenances, to the Commonwealth; and that the Commonwealth will accept the same, provided that the Commonwealth shall not thereby become liable for debts contracted by said corporation.

On June 13, 1823, the incorporators met, at the Exchange Coffee-House in Boston, and on June 17 they adopted by-laws and chose officers. The number of Directors was fixed at twenty-five, and that body appointed a Standing Committee of five, to manage the affairs of the corporation. It was also decided that any one who subscribed five dollars should become a member of the Association.

The original Act of Incorporation did not seem entirely sufficient. Governor Eustis, who had served as surgeon at the battle of Bunker Hill, felt very strongly the propriety of the State's ownership of the completed Monument. In his address to the Legislature, Jan. 24, 1825, he spoke as follows: —

"The erection of a Monument on Bunker's Hill is another work of a public nature, in which our fellow-citizens have taken a great interest. For this purpose an Act of Incorporation was granted, and it is believed that adequate funds will be raised by voluntary subscription. I recommend a revision of the Act, that two conditions may be added: first, that a plan or model be submitted to the Legislature for their approbation previous to the construction of the Monument; and, secondly, that when it is completed, it shall revert to the Commonwealth. Should the funds prove insufficient for the completion of such a work as is worthy of the occasion and becoming the character of the State, I do not permit myself to doubt that aid will be afforded by an enlightened Legislature.

"To commemorate one of the principal events of the Revolution; to consecrate the field in Massachusetts, on which, in the first stages of the war, our heroes and statesmen sealed with their blood the principles they had sworn to maintain; where a disciplined enemy received from a hardy, untutored yeomanry a lesson which produced the most beneficial consequences through the whole of the Revolutionary War, — is worthy the care of the patriot and statesman. The splendid column on Bunker Hill will unite principles with history, patriotism with glory. It will be read by all; its moral will strike deep in the heart, and leave an indelible impression on the mind. The trust is too sacred, the work too important, to rest exclusively in the charge of individuals; it should be a common property, in which every citizen should have a right; as it will be the pride, it should also be the property, of the Commonwealth."

Governor Eustis died Feb. 6, 1825, but his wishes were met in substance by the passage of the following law. The Association appeared as petitioners to the State, first, for aid in the form of money or its equivalent; secondly, for some cannon; thirdly, for the right to take land by right of eminent domain,[1] as some parcels on the Hill could not easily be obtained by purchase. These conditions in favor of the Association were granted; but coupled with them was the provision, curtailing the former grant, that the Monument when completed, with all the land purchased and then held by the Corporation, should be conveyed to the Commonwealth.

AN ACT TO AID THE BUNKER HILL MONUMENT ASSOCIATION.

Passed Feb. 26, 1825 (Special Laws, vi. 280).

SECTION 1. Be it enacted by the Senate and House of Representatives in General Court assembled, and by the authority of the same, That the Bunker Hill Monument Association shall be entitled to have the stone, of which their intended monument may be constructed, hammered and prepared to be used at the state prison in Charlestown; and the proper officers of the prison are hereby authorized and required to cause the same stone to be hammered and prepared accordingly, and in such form and manner as the directors of said association may request. Provided, that the hammering of stone, under the provisions of

---

[1] Warren says that this right was used only in one case, that of a party under guardianship, who was owner of an undivided sixth part of a lot.

this section, shall never exceed in value the sum of ten thousand dollars; and, provided further, that nothing herein contained, shall be so construed as to prevent or retard the fulfilment of any contract for stone work with any other person or persons whatever.

SECT. 2. Be it further enacted, that whenever the directors of said association shall apply therefor, the governor and council be, and they hereby are authorized and empowered, to cause to be delivered to said association, the two cannon called the Hancock and Adams, to adorn the intended monument, and to be preserved as the earliest of the reliques of the revolutionary struggle, and to deliver, also, for the same purpose, any two other cannon, used in the Revolutionary War, and now belonging to the state, as to the governor and council may seem proper.

SECT. 3. Be it further enacted, that the Bunker Hill Monument Association be, and the directors thereof, acting for said association, hereby are, authorized and empowered to take and to appropriate to the legal uses of said association, any land on Breed's Hill, in Charlestown, which said directors may find to be necessary in the design of erecting a monument, and laying out the surrounding ground in the appropriate manner, not exceeding five acres: Provided always that the said corporation shall, before the title to said land which shall be so taken shall vest in said corporation, apply by petition to the court of common pleas, in the county of Middlesex, to have a committee of five disinterested freeholders within the same county, appointed to appraise the land which may be so taken for the uses aforesaid, and the said committee shall be commissioned by said court to perform that duty, and shall be duly sworn to the performance thereof, and having notified all persons known to be interested in said land, to appear, at a time and place, to be by said committee appointed, shall proceed to appraise the same, and shall make return into said court under their hand and seals of their doings, and shall describe the lands taken by said corporation, by metes and bounds, and the just value thereof in money to each and every individual proprietor thereof, and the return of said committee being accepted by the court, and ordered to be recorded, the said corporation shall be holden to pay unto said court the full appraised value of the land taken, with all the costs of appraisement, and on making such payment into court, the title to said land shall vest in said corporation. Provided always, that any person or persons, who may be aggrieved by the appraisement of said committee, may move the court that a jury may be empanelled to appraise the value, by their verdict, of the land which may have been taken from such person or persons, and the said court shall proceed to enquire of the said value by the said jury, and it shall be lawful for any two or more of the proprietors from whom land shall have been taken, to join in submitting their joint or respective claims to such jury. And if the said jury shall not, by their verdict, find the value of the land to be greater than said committee shall have appraised the same at, the said former owner or owners shall not recover costs for the trial by jury. But if the said jury shall find the value of the land to be greater than the said committee shall have appraised the same at, the said corporation shall be adjudged to pay the costs of the trial; that the verdict of the jury being accepted and recorded by the court, the said corporation shall be entitled to have and to hold the land taken, on paying the value found by the jury, into court, with or without costs, as aforesaid.

SECT. 4. Be it further enacted, that the money paid into court shall be paid out to such person or persons as the court shall find to have been the lawful owners of the land taken by said corporation, or to the legal representatives of such owners, according to the respective rights which such owners or their legal representatives, shall make to appear to said court, and that said corporation shall pay the legal costs of such application to the court.

SECT. 5. Be it further enacted, that when the said monument shall have been completed by the said corporation, the same shall be, together with all the lands purchased and then held by said corporation, conveyed to the Commonwealth of Massachusetts, to be had and held by said Commonwealth, on the condition that the Commonwealth shall keep the said monument, and any buildings for public use connected therewith, in good repair forever.

The purchases of land by the Association at this time, as given by Warren (p. 101), were as follows: —

	Price.
Of Nathaniel Austin	$5,000 00
Timothy Walker	4,500 00
Andrew Kettell	2,600 00
Ephraim Frost	2,200 00
Parnell Brooks	3,450 00
Benjamin Adams	1,000 00
Samuel Spring	600 00
William Austin	400 00
Heirs of Mary Beaman	2,232 42
Dr. John C. Warren (Russell lot).	1,250 00
Total	$23,232 42

for which sum the Association obtained fifteen acres. The money was furnished, in advance of subscription, by a note on which twenty gentlemen, including Mr. Webster, Mr. George Blake, and Judge Prescott were sureties.

Although neither the form nor the size of the Monument had been decided upon, it was thought best, in 1825, to lay the corner-stone under such circumstances as should demonstrate that work had begun and should stimulate contributions towards its completion. Accordingly this was done on June 17, under the most auspicious surroundings, Gen. Lafayette being present as an honored guest, and Daniel Webster being the orator.

The managers of the Association were long in doubt as to the best form for the proposed Monument. Many preferred a pillar; but the subject was referred to a sub-committee composed of Daniel Webster, Gilbert Stuart, Washington Allston, Loammi Baldwin, and George Ticknor. Four of this committee, on April 25, 1825, submitted a report, recommending the plan for an obelisk as proposed by Horatio Greenough. On the 7th of June the matter was disposed of finally, by the following order: —

"Voted, That the form of an obelisk shall be adopted for the proposed Monument, or, in other words, a pyramidal structure such as may be hereafter agreed on."

The estimate made July 1, 1825, was for an Obelisk, 220 feet high, on a square base of 30 feet, built of Chelmsford granite, to cost $100,000.

The amount of money collected to September 1 was $54,433.07; expenditures for land, laying corner-stone, engraving certificates, etc., amounted to $29,416.03, and the Directors voted to proceed with the erection of the building. Solomon Willard was appointed superintendent, and to his unceasing and unselfish exertions, as much as to any other single cause, the eventual success of the enterprise was due. At the very outset he sought out and obtained the right to use the quarry at Quincy from which the stone was taken. His great knowledge and fertility of invention were brought into use at every step, and he consented to receive in payment only his bare expenses.

After the auspicious beginning, however, the great enterprise seemed to lag. As too often happens in such affairs, not enough money was raised at the start to complete the undertaking, public interest waned, and subscriptions ceased. The Directors mortgaged the land, and the Building Committee, with this collateral, gave their individual notes for over $25,000. But in February, 1829, the order was given to suspend work when only fourteen courses of stone had been completed, raising the monument but 37 feet 4 inches. The expenditures by Mr. Willard amounted to $56,525.19.

The following view taken from Snow's "Geography of Boston," published in 1830, gives an idea of its appearance at that time: —

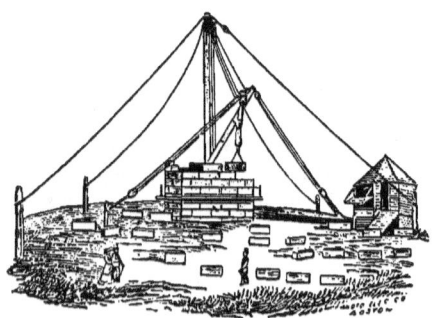

After several years' idleness, an arrangement was made with the Massachusetts Charitable Mechanic Association of Boston, to take charge of the enterprise. Although the exact terms of this agreement do not seem to be recorded in G. W. Warren's History, the Legislative Report of 1836 gives the essential point. It says that the Bunker Hill Association, by a formal vote, "authorized the Massachusetts Charitable Mechanic Association to take the building of the Monument into their own hands, and to expend whatever money they had already collected, or thereafter might collect in the building, and by their own committees, subject merely to a general supervision of the Executive Committee of the Bunker Hill Monument Association."

This coöperation is fully shown in the second form of Certificate issued to subscribers of Five Dollars. It is headed "By the Bunker Hill Monument Association, founded in 1823, and aided in 1833 in completing the original design, by the Massachusetts Charitable Mechanic Association."

Work was resumed under the charge of the Charitable Association on June 17, 1834, and continued until November, 1835. During this time eighteen more courses were laid, making the total height 85 feet, at a cost of over $20,421.17, of which about $16,000 was raised by this society.

This episode is worthy of notice, as it breaks the continuous chain of services rendered by the Bunker Hill Monument Association, and also most strongly points out the almost insurmountable difficulties which that public-spirited society had to encounter, and its freedom from any selfish or vain-glorious feelings.

That the Mechanics' Association could not succeed, notwithstanding that it held a public meeting in Faneuil Hall, at which Daniel Webster appealed to the generosity of the city, is only an evidence of the magnitude of the enterprise. In 1834 they reported that "the general depression, arising from the state of the country, has been unfavorable to these exertions." Unfortunately, business affairs progressed from bad to worse, and the panic of 1837 would certainly have proved fatal in any stage of the incomplete undertaking.

The following cut, copied from the "American Magazine of Useful and Entertaining Knowledge," Vol. III., p. 402 (Boston, 1837), shows its appearance when progress was stopped for the second time: —

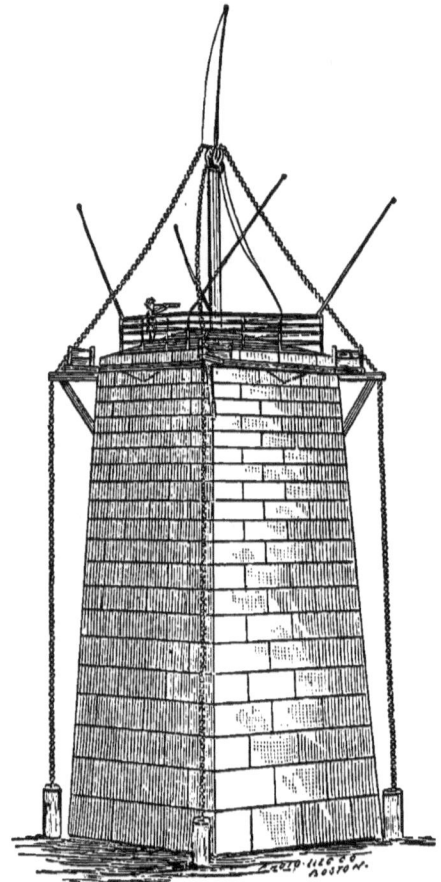

VIEW OF THE MONUMENT IN 1837.

In 1836 an attempt was made to interest the State in the completion of the Monument. As supplementing the official account, the following Report to the Legislature will be found very interesting: —

[*Columbian Centinel, Saturday, April 23, 1836.*]

[OFFICIAL.]

BUNKER-HILL MONUMENT.

COMMONWEALTH OF MASSACHUSETTS.

Senate, March 8, 1836.

Ordered, That Messrs. Gray, Parmenter and Fairbanks, with such as the House may join, be a Committee to consider the expediency of purchasing on behalf of the Commonwealth, the Battle Ground on Bunker Hill.   Sent down for concurrence.

CHAS. CALHOUN, Clerk.

House of Representatives, April 9, 1836.

Concurred; and Messrs. Park of Boston, Hitchcock of Southbridge, Ruggles of Fall River, Lucas of Plymouth and Peabody of Salem are joined.

L. S. CUSHING, Clerk.

Senate, April 16, 1836.

The Special Joint Committee appointed to consider the expediency of purchasing on behalf of the Commonwealth, the Battle Ground on Bunker-Hill, having attended to their duty, ask leave to report as follows:

The Bunker-Hill Monument Association was incorporated by the statute of 1823, c. 1. An Additional Act was passed in the year

1826 (Stat. of 1825, c. 122,) extending in some respects the powers of the Association, and making to them on the part of the Commonwealth a donation of two pieces of cannon, which had been employed in the war of the Revolution, and of labor in hammering stone to the value of $10,000, which last donation was subsequently commuted into a grant of seven thousand dollars in money for the purpose of erecting a Monument. Under the provisions of these acts, the Association procured a tract of land, of the extent of about fifteen acres, comprising the greater portion of Breed's Hill, property so called, and containing the celebrated Redoubt. The Monument was commenced on the scite of this redoubt, in the year 1825, and has been since carried on with a long interruption at one period, till it has reached the height of eighty feet, being a little more than one third of the height originally contemplated, though considering the extent and depth of the foundation, it is thought by the best judges that more than half of the work is accomplished. In the prosecution of this work, and other incidental expenses previous to the year 1829, the funds of the Association, including the donation of seven thousand dollars by the Commonwealth were exhausted, and a debt incurred to the amount of about thirty thousand dollars. It was proposed in the year 1834 to pay off the greater part of this debt by the sale of a large portion of the land of the Association, with the reservation, however, of the right of redemption. Accordingly the land immediately round the Monument, to the extent of about four acres, was reserved by the Association to be forever kept open. The remainder of the field of fifteen acres, being nearly three-fourths of the whole, was sold to a company of individuals, to be laid out in streets and house lots, according to a specified plan. The sum received for this land was twenty-five thousand dollars, which sum was faithfully appropriated to the reduction of the debt of the Association.

The indenture by which this sale was effected is dated October 30, 1834.

It contains several conditions, one of which authorizes the redemption of the land at any time previous to the seventeenth day of June, A.D. 1837, on prepayment of the purchase money of $25,000, with interest. Of such a redemption, however, the Association entertain no hope.

The public have been twice appealed to with the greatest earnestness; first, by the corporation itself, and more recently by the Massachusetts Charitable Mechanic Association. The members of this last named Association, more especially, have for the last two years exerted themselves to the utmost, both in the way of request and of example, to procure a sum sufficient for the completion of the Monument in the first instance, and in the next, for the redemption of the Land conveyed as above. All that can be effected by individual liberality, and it should be added, all that could be reasonably expected from that source has been done, but without effecting the desired object. The Monument has been carried, as above stated, to the height of eighty feet, and all expectation of completing it as originally contemplated, or even of carrying it to any height at which it could be properly terminated, is for the present at an end.

In a little more than a year from the present time the right of redeeming the land sold for house lots will expire, and the land will be forthwith applied to private uses.

Your committee have annexed to this Report a document containing a succinct and interesting history of the present condition of the Land and Monument in question, being an extract from a report of the Executive Committee of the Massachusetts Charitable Mechanic Association made early in January last.

Under these circumstances your committee have good reason to believe that the Bunker-Hill Monument Association would readily convey, or cause to be conveyed to the Commonwealth, the Monument together with the whole real estate heretofore purchased by the Association, on receiving a sum sufficient to redeem the portion of the land sold as above (being twenty-five thousand dollars) with interest from October 30, 1834, and also pay of the remaining debt of the Corporation, being five thousand dollars with interest from the same period. For, although this last mentioned debt is not, strictly speaking a charge on the land, it would obviously be unjust in the Corporation to divest themselves of their property, without providing for its payment.

The question, therefore, before the Legislature is simply this: Will the Commonwealth purchase the whole land in question, being fifteen acres, with the granite Monument of eighty feet in height, standing thereon, and the whole personal property of the Corporation, provided the same can be procured for the sum of thirty thousand dollars, with interest from October 1834, making an amount of a little less than thirty-three thousand dollars? Your committee can conceive of but one proper answer to this question.

It is, in their judgment, matter of serious regret, that the whole ground on which the battle of Bunker-Hill was fought, was not long since rendered the property of the Commonwealth, and that the right of purchasing and ornamenting any portion of that ever memorable spot, should ever have been relinquished by our public authorities to any other hands. Your committee do not deem it necessary to dilate on the many circumstances which rendered the battle of Bunker-Hill second in importance to none in our revolution. This has been often done with an ability and an eloquence which would render such an attempt on their part not only unnecessary, but presumptuous. As little necessity can there be for showing that the spot where so much was achieved for the glory of New-England and the independence of our country, must be an object of intense and increasing interest, not only to all Americans, but to all lovers of rational liberty through all future time.

The deep feeling which the view of this spot must excite in the bosom of every reflecting observer is founded on the great principle of the Association of ideas, — a principle as prevalent and as powerful in the intellectual world as is that of gravitation in the physical.

It is true that it is no longer practicable to procure and set apart from private uses the whole battle ground of Bunker-Hill.

But it is in the power of the Commonwealth to acquire the control of a large portion of it, and that too, the portion most interesting to the citizens of our own State. The tract in question is of more than one third the extent of the common in Boston, and forming as it does, the very crest of the Hill, furnishes to the spectator an unobstructed view of a great portion of the scenery of the environs. It is the portion of the original battle-ground where the Massachusetts troops were chiefly posted, and contains the remains of the redoubt where Prescott commanded and Warren fell. To preserve every portion of this tract from becoming a mere site for private dwelling-houses; — to prevent the magnificent landscape visible from its summit from being obstructed by masses of brick or stone, are surely objects which the Commonwealth will not hesitate to secure at a moderate and reasonable expense. For it might easily be shown that the land which it is proposed to the Commonwealth to redeem is worth far more than the sum requisite for that purpose, if we could suppose that this spot could ever be regarded by the Legislature as mere property. But this is a supposition which your committee will not allow themselves to entertain.

What further arrangement shall be made either with respect to the ground or the Monument is a question which may be safely left to the wisdom and magnanimity of future Legislatures, and on which your committee do not presume to offer any suggestions. But they feel assured that should the tract in question become the property of the Commonwealth, it will be sacredly retained by those who succeed us as the inheritance of their fathers, and that the great events and noble deeds of which it has pleased Heaven to render it the scene, will effectually preserve every part of it from all common and ordinary uses. Your committee therefore hope that this interesting, it ought rather to be said, this hallowed spot, will be placed at once in the keeping of those to whom of all others it should belong — the people of this Commonwealth.

They conceive that no considerations of economy, — considerations which in their proper place and to a proper extent, are respected by none more than by your committee, ought to induce the Commonwealth to forego an opportunity which cannot be recalled and the loss of which may prove a source of deep and unavailing regret to every citizen of New-England in all succeeding times.

In conformity to the above suggestions, your committee respectfully submit the subjoined Resolve: —

JOHN C. GRAY,
WM. PARMENTER,
STEPHEN FAIRBANKS,
JOHN C. PARK,
SAM'L. A. HITCHCOCK,
JOSEPH LUCAS,
GEO. PEABODY.

Commonwealth of Massachusetts. In the year of our Lord one Thousand eight Hundred and thirty-six.

A Resolve for purchasing a certain Tract of Land on Breed's Hill.

Resolved, That the Governor be authorized to purchase, on behalf of the Commonwealth, all the land on Breed's Hill, heretofore purchased and held by the Bunker-Hill Monument Association; together with the Monument standing thereon, and all the personal property of said corporation, provided that the same can be procured, free of all incumbrance, for a sum not exceeding thirty-three thousand dollars; provided also that a good and sufficient deed of conveyance of the whole of said real and personal property, without condition or restriction, be executed by the Bunker-Hill Monument Association, and by all other persons and corporations, if any, who may be interested in any portion of said property at the time of such conveyance; such deed to be delivered to the Governor on or before the seventeenth day of June next.

Resolved, That the Governor be authorized to draw his warrant on the Treasury for any sum necessary to carry into effect the preceding Resolve.

EXTRACT referred to in the preceding Report:

In presenting a report of the present condition of the Monument, and the state of the funds collected for the purpose of its completion, it may not be impertinent to the occasion, to take a brief review of the proceedings of the Association in relation to that subject.

APPENDIX D.

In the month of May, 1833, it was agreed, after mature deliberation, and at a full meeting of this Association, to make an attempt to gather, by subscription, a sum of money sufficient to complete the Monument, and to relieve the battle ground on Bunker-Hill, from all incumbrances of a pecuniary nature. It was then understood, from the best information that could be obtained from the Bunker-Hill Monument Association, that the debt of that corporation was about $22,000; as security for this debt, the battle ground, with the exception of an oblong square, had been mortgaged to five gentlemen, who had become security for the payment of the sum before mentioned, to a Bank in this city. It was supposed at that time, that $50,000 would be amply sufficient to discharge this debt, and to carry the Monument to the height of 220 feet, agreeably to the original plan.

The Association appointed various committees to collect subscriptions, all of which entered upon the labor assigned them, with cheerfulness and industry; the subscriptions were made on the condition, that the full sum of fifty thousand dollars should be raised, within a given time; at the expiration of that limited time, it was found that only about $21,000 had been subscribed; a considerable portion of this amount had been subscribed in small sums, and paid to the committees, at the time of subscription. This money, from time to time, was placed as a special deposite in one of the banks in this city, the Directors of which allowed for it an interest of five per cent. during its continuance in the bank.

In the meantime, it had been found by more strict investigation into the affairs of the Bunker-Hill Monument Association, and the expense of procuring and laying the materials of the Monument, that even the whole sum of $50,000, had it been collected, would have been insufficient for the purposes proposed; the debt of the corporation, with the interest, already accumulated, amounted to about $30,000; and the calculations of the committee appointed to estimate the expense of completing the Monument, manifested beyond all doubt, that very erroneous impressions had existed in regard to the cost of labor, and transportation of material.

Difficulties seemed thus to accumulate at every step, and the Executive Committee began to feel somewhat disheartened; but the desire of completing the Monument, and thus erecting an imperishable memorial of the patriotism and virtue of their fathers, encouraged them to pursue their object with renewed zeal, and to devise means that should ensure success.

A negotiation was then opened with the Bunker-Hill Monument Association, the details of which it would be tedious and useless to present in this report; it is sufficient for the present purpose to state the result. The Bunker-Hill Monument Association, by a formal vote of the corporation, authorized the Massachusetts Charitable Mechanic Association, to take the building of the Monument into their own hands, and to expend whatever moneys they had already collected, or thereafter might collect, in the building, and by their own committees, subject merely to a general supervision of the Executive Committee of the Bunker-Hill Monument Association.

It was also voted by that corporation, that the land then under mortgage, should be sold to discharge the debt due the bank, from which the loan was obtained, and thus relieve the Monument from all incumbrance. To effect this at the least possible sacrifice, it was proposed to open a subscription for fifty shares, at 500 dollars each, the subscribers to be entitled to a lot for each share subscribed. This subscription, the committee understand, is now filled up — many of the gentlemen who subscribed the largest sums on the terms of the subscription offered in May, 1833, took these shares, with the understanding, that our Association would not demand of them the payment of the original subscription; and as the original terms of subscription were such, that the payment could not be enforced, (the sum of $50,000 not having been subscribed during the limited period,) it seemed that no other course was left to be adopted; consequently, one subscription of $5000, another of 2000, several of 1000, and several others of 500 dollars, have never been paid to this Association, and are altogether unavailable for the purpose of completing the Monument.

Thus it will be seen by the Association, that after two years labor, and an expenditure of more than $20,000, the Monument

VIEW OF THE MONUMENT, AS PROPOSED IN 1836.

is not much more than half finished, and it cannot in the opinion of your committee be raised to the height of 160 feet, short of about $25,000.

In Senate, April 16, 1836. Referred to the next General Court, and to be printed in the papers in which the laws of the Commonwealth are published.

Sent down for concurrence.

CHAS. CALHOUN, Clerk.

House of Representatives, April 16, 1836. Concurred.

L. S. CUSHING, Clerk.

A true copy — Attest,

CHAS. CALHOUN, Clerk of the Senate.

☞ The Editors of the several newspapers which publish the laws of this Commonwealth will please give the above Report one insertion.

The accompanying view, copied from the title page of the "Bunker-Hill Quickstep," copyrighted in 1836 by H. Prentiss, is of interest as showing, like all the other views of earlier date, the design of the Monument, for which subscriptions were solicited. There is no indication of "a lodge," either of wood or granite, and the obelisk itself is evidently the only monument then contemplated.

From 1836 to 1840, the prospects of the Association were indeed gloomy. The financial condition of the country was very bad, the panic causing failures which brought distress to all classes, in New England especially. The country was poor, to a degree which now seems incredible. Under these circumstances, after one or two renewals of time, the Association was obliged to abandon all hopes of redeeming the ten acres of land which it had pledged, and was forced to content itself with preserving the five acres immediately surrounding the Monument.

In 1840, however, began the final effort to collect funds, which happily resulted in success. The ladies of Boston and vicinity decided to hold a fair in aid of the object in Faneuil Hall. The committee in charge consisted of Mrs. Sarah J. Hale, Mrs. Jonathan Chapman, Mrs. William H. Prescott, Mrs. John C. Warren, Mrs. George Darracott, and Mrs. Thomas B. Wales. The Fair was opened Sept. 8, 1840, and lasted seven days; the nett proceeds were $30,035.53.

On the 10th of September, a Whig mass meeting was held at Bunker Hill. Daniel Webster, as President, marched on foot at the head of the great procession. The annexed view is from the frontispiece to the "Freemen's Quickstep" composed for the occasion by George Hews. It is said to be "sketched on the spot by W. Sharp" and printed by Sharp, Michelin & Co. It is also inscribed — "as this print will remain long after all who beheld the brilliant spectacle shall have passed away, it may not be amiss to stamp upon it the interesting fact, that this same 10th of September a Fair was held by Ladies in the City of Boston, for the purpose of obtaining funds for the completion of the Monument (which is here presented in its unfinished state). The object was entirely successful. This drawing was taken from Mr. Phipps' house, South East of the Monument, and represents the moment of time when the Cavalcade, having counter-marched, are about returning to the City, while a portion only of the Delegates on foot here have yet reached the hill."

As already stated, the impetus given by the Fair was sufficient to carry the project to success. Besides the $30,000 thus raised, Amos Lawrence gave $10,000, Judah Touro gave $10,000, Messrs. Wales, Stone, and Bowditch, trustees, gave $1,500, A. L. Forestier gave $987, from Philadelphia came $794, Fanny Elssler contributed $569, and small amounts brought the total to $55,153.27, and a nett sum remained of $47,189.54.

A contract was accordingly made Nov. 4, 1840, with James S. Savage, "for the completion of the Monument to its full original height of 220 feet, for the sum of $43,800, the top to be finished according to a plan drawn by Mr. Willard, and the whole work to be done under his direction as architect." (Warren's History, p. 304.)

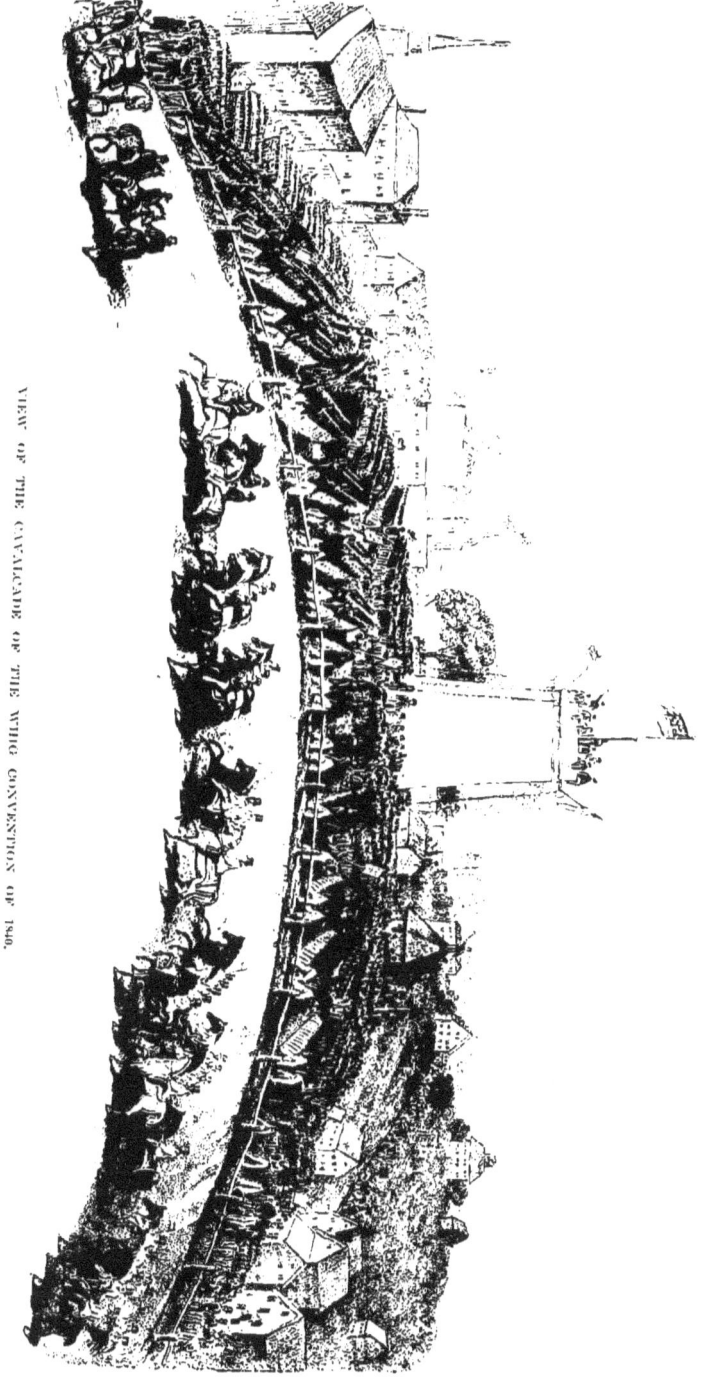

VIEW OF THE CAVALCADE OF THE WHIG CONVENTION OF 1840.

"On Saturday, July 23, 1842, at 6 o'clock in the morning, pursuant to public notice, the Directors and several hundred citizens assembled on Bunker Hill to witness the laying on of the top-stone upon the Monument. As the clock struck six a signal gun was fired by the members of the Charlestown Artillery, and the cap-stone, which had been previously adjusted to the hoisting apparatus connected with the steam-engine, immediately began to ascend. It was surmounted by the American flag. In sixteen minutes, the cap-stone reached the place of its destination on the top of the Monument. At half-past six, it was embedded in cement, and a national salute fired by the Charlestown Artillery *announced the complete erection of the Monument.*" This extract from the Records of the Bunker Hill Monument Association, printed in Warren's History, p. 304, effectually disposes of any claim that the Monument is still unfinished.

The formal ceremonies were held on Saturday, June 17, 1843, President Tyler and his cabinet being among the invited guests, and Daniel Webster the orator at the completion, as he had been at the beginning of the work. The matchless orations on these two occasions are reprinted in Appendix E.

After the completion of the Monument, a contract was made with Mr. Savage "under which he held possession of the Monument, with the right to take the usual fees from visitors; and for this privilege he laid a granite walk ten feet wide on each side of the Monument, erected an iron fence on the outer line of the same, and also laid a brick side-walk on the streets upon the four sides of the square." (Warren's History, p. 340.) "The Secretary, as one of the Committee on the Fair, raised a subscription of $5,300 towards erecting the iron fence to enclose Monument Square, and the granite steps leading to it." About $4,000 was spent in planting trees and ornamenting the grounds.

In 1850, the seventy-fifth anniversary was celebrated, Edward Everett being the orator. In 1861, Governor Andrew presided at the ceremony of hoisting the national flag on the Monument. In 1875, a centennial celebration was held under the auspices of the City Government of Boston, Charlestown having been joined to that city in 1874. The orator on this occasion was Gen. Charles Devens, whose eloquent address was published by the city.

The Annual Meeting in 1881 was noteworthy on account of the dedication of the statue of Col. William Prescott, which, was placed in the grounds in front of the Monument. This statue, which is the work of W. W. Story, was presented by a number of citizens, acting through Rev. George E. Ellis. The address, delivered in presence of Gov. Long and a distinguished body of guests, was by Hon. Robert C. Winthrop.

The subsequent history of the Association is set forth in its Annual Reports.

No one can desire for a moment to undervalue the great services of the original members of the Bunker Hill Monument Association, especially of the small number who were the directors and active officers from 1824 to 1843. But as these men have passed away, and as even their labors ceased with the completion of the Monument, the acts of their successors are to be viewed irrespective of the past of the Association.

The original Association collected money from every source, and every contributor of five dollars became thereby a life member.

We therefore pass from the time and the men who built the Monument, to the gentlemen who have since so kindly taken upon them the duties of administering this great public trust.

The constitution of the present Bunker Hill Monument Association is not very plainly set forth in any of its publications. Prior to 1843 the nominal membership was several hundreds, perhaps thousands, comprising every contributor of five dollars. According to the reports, "before 1861 no new members had been admitted since 1834." It is understood, however, that out of the great number of nominal members, those resident in Boston and Charlestown kept up the form of electing officers annually. In 1861 there was a revival of interest, and members were again made on the payment of five dollars. From 1861 to 1873, 110 members joined; and up to the present year 566 members seem to have been elected. It is believed that the Association holds only one meeting in the year, the work being carried on by the directors or committees.

The printed reports give little information as to the finances prior to 1861, but the receipts seem to have been about $2,700 a year. For the twenty-eight years from 1862 to 1889, the sum of $140,633.49 has been received from the tolls of 20 cents for adults, and 10 cents for children, levied upon all who ascended the Monument. To this must be added the payments of 566 members, at $5 = $2,830, and some amounts for interest.

The expenses have been for the care of the grounds and of the Monument, and the expenditures of the Association itself. It should be noted that the one item of printing the annual reports of the Association far exceeds the total of $2,830 paid in by the members, and consequently the public has had to contribute not only to the care of the Monument, but to the preservation of the society.

After all the expenditures there has remained a surplus, which has been allowed to accumulate, with the intent of building a stone lodge for the use of the society, and the preservation of such relics as it may possess. This sum is about $15,000.

The natural result of the position taken by the officials of the Association adverse to the wishes of the City Council, was to lead to a scrutiny into the rights of all parties, especially of the citizens in general. The following order was passed: —

"IN BOARD OF ALDERMEN, May 31, 1889.

Ordered, That the Committee on Bunker Hill Tablets be requested to report the cost, method, and advisability of laying out Monument square, Charlestown, as a public park.

Referred to Committee on Bunker Hill Tablets.

E. U. CURTIS,
City Clerk."

The result was a report (City Doc. 1889, No. 111), from which the following extracts are taken: —

REPORT.

In the discharge of the duties imposed upon your committee by the foregoing order, they sent through their chairman the following inquiries to the Corporation Counsel: —

CITY HALL, BOSTON, June 7, 1889.

JAMES B. RICHARDSON, ESQ., *Corporation Counsel:* —

DEAR SIR, — The committee of which I am chairman has been instructed to report upon the method, cost, and advisability of taking, for the purposes of a public park, the land in Charlestown known as Monument square. I desire, therefore, to have your opinion on the following points: —

1. Is the fee of the land in the Bunker Hill Monument Association, a corporation established by Chap. 1 of Acts of 1823, and Chap. 122 of Acts of 1824?

2. Has said corporation been released from the provisions of Sect. 5 of the said Chap. 122 of Acts 1824? If not, is the fee in the Commonwealth, although no conveyance of the land has been made to it?

3. In either case, does the land come within the provisions of the acts establishing Public Parks in Boston, and can the Commissioners proceed to take such land, by "purchase or otherwise," if they deem it desirable?

4. In case the fee is in the said Association, what would be the *measure* of damages (not the amount), in your opinion, due regard being had to the language of the acts under which said Association has obtained the land?

5. In case the city took the land for a public park, would it be competent for it also to assume the care and maintenance of the Monument, statues, etc., now standing thereon, and would it be lawful for the city to pay to the said Association, for an amicable settlement of any presumed rights, a sum of money to be used by said Association in continuing its organization and taking charge of the relics intrusted to it by the State or by individuals?

I shall be obliged if you will reply at your earliest convenience, in order that the committee may make its report in season to allow of any desired action thereon, and remain

Yours very truly,
B. F. STACEY,
Chairman Com. B. H. Tablets.

At that time the Committee supposed, in common with all other citizens, that the Bunker Hill Monument Association was in lawful possession of Monument square, and that the city would have to deal with that society in order to obtain the land for a public park.

The reply of Mr. Richardson was as follows: —

OFFICE OF THE CORPORATION COUNSEL,
June 22, 1889.

HON. B. F. STACEY, *Chairman Committee on Bunker Hill Tablets:* —

DEAR SIR, — In reply to your request for information concerning the title to the lands known as "Monument square," in the Charlestown district of the City of Boston; and as to whether the city has a right to purchase or take said land for the purposes of a public park; and, if taken, the measure of damages therefor; and whether it would be competent for the city to enter into an obligation for the care of the Monument and relics intrusted to the Association by the State and others, — I have the honor to say, that I find, upon an examination made by Mr. Day of this office, in the records of titles to lands in the registries of deeds for the Counties of Suffolk and Middlesex, that the fee of said land in Monument square appears to be in the Bunker Hill Monument Association; but, by Sect. 5 of Chap. 122 of the Special Acts of the General Court for the year 1824, in an act entitled "An Act to aid the Bunker Hill Monument Association," it was provided that "when the said Monument shall have been completed by the said corporation, the same shall be, together with all the land purchased and then held by said corporation, conveyed to the Commonwealth of Massachusetts, to be had and held by said Commonwealth on the condition that the Commonwealth shall keep the said Monument and any buildings for public use connected therewith, in good repair forever."

The Monument, according to general historical evidence, was completed in 1843, and the event was celebrated on the 17th of June of that year.

I ought, perhaps, to state that it appears that, "in lieu of the provision in favor of the Bunker Hill Monument Association, made and provided" in said Chap. 122 of the Acts of 1824, "the sum of seven thousand dollars in money" was authorized, by Chap. 78 of the Resolves of the General Court of the year 1827, to be paid by the treasurer of the Commonwealth to said Bunker Hill Monument Association.

We do not find on said records any conveyance by said Association to the Commonwealth of said Monument or land, as provided by said act of 1824;

nor do we find that any release of said obligation to so convey it has been made or given by the Commonwealth to said Association. I am informed that said Association claims that "they have not finished its original design, the erection on the grounds, as one of the appurtenances connected with the Monument, the granite lodge for statues, and for a museum of revolutionary relics connected with the battle."

I think that the fee in the land comprising said square is in the said Association, but subject to said obligation of said Association, to convey it, with the Monument, to the Commonwealth, if said Monument now is, or whenever it is, completed. Further replying to your inquiries, I think that the city has the power to acquire said land by purchase for the purposes of a public park; but I do not think that the city has the power, at the present time, without further authority from the Legislature, to take said land for park purposes, under the right of eminent domain. It is therefore not necessary, at the present time, to undertake to state what the measure of damages of such a taking might be.

In case the city acquires title to the land by purchase, or in any other way, when authorized, I do not see any objection to the city entering into an obligation for the care of the Monument, relics, and other property connected therewith, such obligation being considered as part compensation for the land.

Very respectfully yours,
JAMES B. RICHARDSON,
Corporation Counsel.

Your committee understand, from the necessarily guarded opinion of the Corporation Counsel, that the charter of the Association, in 1825, expressly stipulated that the Monument and lands adjacent were to be turned over to the Commonwealth on the completion of the Monument. This intent was fully set forth in the message of Governor Eustis in that year, as well as in the act itself. It is also beyond question that, in the common sense of the words, the Monument was finished in 1843. Webster's glorious oration bears on its title, "Delivered at Bunker Hill June 17, 1843, on the Completion of the Monument." One of the well-known sentences of that address is as follows: —

"The Bunker Hill Monument is finished. Here it stands. Fortunate in the high natural eminence on which it is placed, —

higher, infinitely higher in its objects and purpose, it rises over the land and over the sea, and visible at their homes to three hundred thousand of the people of Massachusetts, it stands a memorial of the last, and a monitor to the present and to all succeeding generations."

Your committee has been unable to discover the reasons which prevented the formal transfer of the Monument at that date, in accordance with the law. It may easily be seen, however, that in 1843 the want of a public park in Charlestown had not been felt. The care of the Monument and the grounds was a burden, which, though really light, may have seemed heavy to our legislators. Very probably, also, the provisions of the charter, already eighteen years old, had passed out of mind. That the result of this neglect to make a conveyance to the State has been for awhile beneficial, no one will deny. If the State had taken title in 1843 it is not improbable that some part of the land might have passed into private hands.

Believing that the time has come when the public interest demands that the Commonwealth should assert its rights and assume its duties, your committee feel that no hardship is done to the members of the Association. For forty-five years the Association has mistakenly assumed and rigorously exercised the rights of ownership over five acres of land in the heart of a city, and over the most noted monument in the country. Its administration of the land has not been to the satisfaction of the citizens of Charlestown, who desired a freedom and an accommodation entirely incompatible with the interests of the Association. As the land was the cause only of expense, and the Monument was the only source of revenue, it was natural and proper that visitors should be encouraged mainly to the latter object.

But the time has come when the public needs are great and pressing. Public parks have become a necessity, and Charlestown is peculiarly unfortunate as lacking vacant land within its boundaries which could be applied to this purpose. The only spot heretofore suggested lies at the very extremity of its limits. It was this urgent need which led to the offering of the order under which your committee has acted. For the past ten years or more the desire of the residents of Charlestown has been to have these five acres, so admirably situated for a local park, thrown open to the public on the same conditions as the Public Garden and the other smaller public grounds are.

And now that it has become manifest that for forty-five years the public has been kept out of its own, either by a misunderstanding or a legal technicality, it is certain that the public hopes must be fulfilled and the public rights asserted and secured. The care of the Monument itself is at a merely nominal cost; the expense of taking care of the grounds and of providing the necessary police attendance will be felt neither by the State nor by the city.

Another gain, by no means insignificant, will result from the assertion by the Commonwealth of its rights in this land. For forty-five years visitors have been obliged to pay a toll, by no means merely nominal, for ascending the Monument. This has been held up as a reproach to us, especially as a large proportion of the visitors were not our citizens. The Association was not to blame, as it had no other source of revenue. It was the result of the unfortunate blunder which left the Monument in private hands, that a tax or toll was inevitable. But the reputation of the Commonwealth has suffered thereby.

Your committee feel that the result of the present fulfilment of the law will be, a free Monument for the country, and a free park for the citizens of Boston and all visitors. They are advised that the proper step to be taken is, for the Governor to demand, in behalf of the Commonwealth, a conveyance from the Bunker Hill Monument Association of the Monument itself, and of all the land owned by the Association, on June 17, 1843, at which date the Monument was completed, on the evidence of Daniel Webster.

APPENDIX D. 195

As the City of Boston is so greatly interested in this measure, it seems proper that the City Council should officially call the attention of the Governor to these facts, and, moreover, to render any assistance which it can give.

Your committee therefore recommend the passage of the annexed orders.

Respectfully submitted,

BENJAMIN F. STACEY,
ALBERT A. FOLSOM,
HOMER ROGERS,
THOMAS F. KEENAN,
WILLIAM H. OAKES,
FRANK E. BAGLEY,
ISRAEL F. PIERCE,
WILLIAM J. DOHERTY.

Committee.

"*Ordered,* That His Honor the Mayor be, and he hereby is, requested, in behalf of the City of Boston, to respectfully represent to his Excellency the Governor, that by law the Bunker Hill Monument Association was bound to convey to the Commonwealth of Massachusetts the Monument when completed, together with all the land purchased and then held by said corporation; that the Monument was completed on June 17, 1843, and that the public welfare requires that the Commonwealth should now make a demand for an immediate transfer of the property.

Ordered, That His Honor the Mayor be, and he hereby is, authorized to tender to the Governor, in case the Commonwealth shall obtain possession of the Monument and land, the assistance of any and all of the departments and officers of the city, free of expense, in the care and maintenance of such land and building until the first day of March, A.D. 1890, or until the Legislature shall have sooner provided for such charge."

This report was accepted and the order passed, in Common Council, June, 27, 1889, in Board of Aldermen, July 1, and approved

196   HISTORY OF THE MONUMENT.

by Mayor Hart, July 2. The copy of the orders was promptly forwarded to Gov. Ames, and by him referred to the Attorney-General, whose report had not been made at the date of the completion of this review.

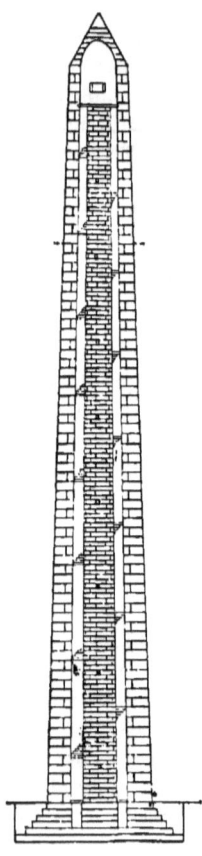

DIAGRAM OF MONUMENT.   FROM WILLARD'S MEMORIAL.

APPENDIX E.

AN ADDRESS[1]

DELIVERED AT

THE LAYING OF THE CORNER-STONE

OF THE

BUNKER HILL MONUMENT,

JUNE 17TH, 1825.

BY DANIEL WEBSTER.

This uncounted multitude before me, and around me, proves the feeling which the occasion has excited. These thousands of human faces, glowing with sympathy and joy, and, from the impulses of a common gratitude, turned reverently to heaven, in this spacious temple of the firmament, proclaim that the day, the place, and the purpose of our assembling have made a deep impression on our hearts.

If, indeed, there be anything in local association fit to affect the mind of man, we need not strive to repress the emotions which agitate us here. We are among the sepulchres of our fathers.

---

[1] It seemed most appropriate and desirable to reprint in this volume the two well-known and admirable orations delivered by Daniel Webster, respectively at the Laying of the Corner-Stone of the Monument, and at its Completion. These orations have become classics, and many of his sentences are still the delight and instruction of our youth. But in their complete form they are not easily attainable, certainly not by the majority of our citizens.

Permission to print these orations in this memorial volume only was kindly given by the courtesy of the owners of the copyright, and is gratefully acknowledged by the Committee.

In the Appendix which treats of the history of the Monument, a full account will be found of the proceedings attending the delivery of these Addresses. W. H. W.

We are on ground distinguished by their valor, their constancy, and the shedding of their blood. We are here, not to fix an uncertain date in our annals, nor to draw into notice an obscure and unknown spot. If our humble purpose had never been conceived, if we ourselves had never been born, the 17th of June, 1775, would have been a day on which all subsequent history would have poured its light, and the eminence where we stand a point of attraction to the eyes of successive generations. But we are Americans. We live in what may be called the early age of this great continent; and we know that our posterity, through all time, are here to suffer and enjoy the allotments of humanity. We see before us a probable train of great events; we know that our own fortunes have been happily cast; and it is natural, therefore, that we should be moved by the contemplation of occurrences which have guided our destiny before many of us were born, and settled the condition in which we should pass that portion of our existence which God allows to men on earth.

We do not read even of the discovery of this continent without feeling something of a personal interest in the event; without being reminded how much it has affected our own fortunes and our own existence. It is more impossible for us, therefore, than for others, to contemplate with unaffected minds that interesting, I may say, that most touching and pathetic scene, when the great discoverer of America stood on the deck of his shattered bark, the shades of night falling on the sea, yet no man sleeping; tossed on the billows of an unknown ocean, yet the stronger billows of alternate hope and despair tossing his own troubled thoughts; extending forward his harassed frame, straining westward his anxious and eager eyes, till Heaven at last granted him a moment of rapture and ecstasy, in blessing his vision with the sight of the unknown world.

Nearer to our times, more closely connected with our fates, and therefore still more interesting to our feelings and affections, is the settlement of our own country by colonists from England. We cherish every memorial of these worthy ancestors; we celebrate their patience and fortitude; we admire their daring enterprise;

we teach our children to venerate their piety; and we are justly proud of being descended from men who have set the world an example of founding civil institutions on the great and united principles of human freedom and human knowledge. To us, their children, the story of their labors and sufferings can never be without its interest. We shall not stand unmoved on the shore of Plymouth while the sea continues to wash it; nor will our brethren in another early and ancient colony forget the place of its first establishment till their river shall cease to flow by it. No vigor of youth, no maturity of manhood, will lead the nation to forget the spots where its infancy was cradled and defended.

But the great event, in the history of the continent, which we are now met here to commemorate; that prodigy of modern times, at once the wonder and the blessing of the world, is the American Revolution. In a day of extraordinary prosperity and happiness, of high national honor, distinction, and power, we are brought together, in this place, by our love of country, by our admiration of exalted character, by our gratitude for signal service and patriotic devotion.

The Society, whose organ I am, was formed for the purpose of rearing some honorable and durable monument to the memory of the early friends of American Independence. They have thought that for this object no time could be more propitious, than the present prosperous and peaceful period; that no place could claim preference over this memorable spot; and that no day could be more auspicious to the undertaking, than the anniversary of the battle which was here fought. The foundation of that Monument we have now laid. With solemnities suited to the occasion, with prayers to Almighty God for his blessing, and in the midst of this cloud of witnesses, we have begun the work. We trust it will be prosecuted; and that springing from a broad foundation, rising high in massive solidity and unadorned grandeur, it may remain, as long as Heaven permits the works of man to last, a fit emblem, both of the events in memory of which it is raised, and of the gratitude of those who have reared it.

We know, indeed, that the record of illustrious actions is most safely deposited in the universal remembrance of mankind. We know that if we could cause this structure to ascend, not only till it reached the skies, but till it pierced them, its broad surfaces could still contain but part of that which, in an age of knowledge, hath already been spread over the earth, and which history charges itself with making known to all future times. We know that no inscription on entablatures less broad than the earth itself, can carry information of the events we commemorate where it has not already gone; and that no structure which shall not outlive the duration of letters and knowledge among men, can prolong the memorial. But our object is, by this edifice, to show our own deep sense of the value and importance of the achievements of our ancestors; and, by presenting this work of gratitude to the eye, to keep alive similar sentiments, and to foster a constant regard for the principles of the Revolution. Human beings are composed not of reason only, but of imagination also, and sentiment; and that is neither wasted nor misapplied, which is appropriated to the purpose of giving right direction to sentiments, and opening proper springs of feeling in the heart. Let it not be supposed that our object is to perpetuate national hostility, or even to cherish a mere military spirit. It is higher, purer, nobler. We consecrate our work to the spirit of national independence, and we wish that the light of peace may rest upon it forever. We rear a memorial of our conviction of that unmeasured benefit which has been conferred on our own land, and of the happy influences which have been produced, by the same events, on the general interests of mankind. We come as Americans to mark a spot which must forever be dear to us and our posterity. We wish that whosoever, in all coming time, shall turn his eye hither, may behold that the place is not undistinguished, where the first great battle of the Revolution was fought. We wish that this structure may proclaim the magnitude and importance of that event, to every class and every age. We wish that infancy may learn the purpose of its erection from maternal lips, and that weary and withered age may behold it, and be solaced by the recollections which it suggests. We wish that labor may look up here, and be proud in the midst of its toil. We wish that, in those days of disaster, which, as they come on all nations, must be expected to come on us also, desponding patriotism may turn its eyes hitherward, and be assured that the foundations of our national power still stand strong. We wish that this column, rising towards heaven among the pointed spires of so many temples dedicated to God, may contribute also to produce, in all minds, a pious feeling of dependence and gratitude. We wish, finally, that the last object on the sight of him who leaves his native shore, and the first to gladden his who revisits it, may be something which shall remind him of the liberty and the glory of his country. Let it rise till it meets the sun in his coming; let the earliest light of the morning gild it, and parting day linger and play on its summit.

We live in a most extraordinary age. Events so various and so important that they might crowd and distinguish centuries are, in our times, compressed within the compass of a single life. When has it happened that history has had so much to record, in the same term of years, as since the 17th of June, 1775? Our own Revolution, which, under other circumstances, might itself have been expected to occasion a war of half a century, has been achieved; twenty-four sovereign and independent States erected; and a general government established over them, so safe, so wise, so free, so practical, that we might well wonder its establishment should have been accomplished so soon, were it not far the greater wonder that it should have been established at all. Two or three millions of people have been augmented to twelve; and the great forests of the West prostrated beneath the arm of successful industry; and the dwellers on the banks of the Ohio and the Mississippi, become the fellow-citizens and neighbors of those who cultivate the hills of New England. We have a commerce that leaves no sea unexplored; navies which take no law from superior force; revenues, adequate to all the exigencies of government, almost without taxation; and peace with all nations, founded on equal rights and mutual respect.

Europe, within the same period, has been agitated by a mighty revolution, which, while it has been felt in the individual condition and happiness of almost every man, has shaken to the centre her political fabric, and dashed against one another thrones which had stood tranquil for ages. On this, our continent, our own example has been followed; and colonies have sprung up to be nations. Unaccustomed sounds of liberty and free government have reached us from beyond the track of the sun; and, at this moment, the dominion of European power, in this continent, from the place where we stand to the south pole, is annihilated forever.

In the meantime, both in Europe and America, such has been the general progress of knowledge; such the improvements in legislation, in commerce, in the arts, in letters, and, above all, in liberal ideas, and the general spirit of the age, that the whole world seems changed.

Yet, notwithstanding that this is but a faint abstract of the things which have happened since the day of the battle of Bunker Hill, we are but fifty years removed from it; and we now stand here to enjoy all the blessings of our own condition, and to look abroad on the brightened prospects of the world, while we hold still among us some of those who were active agents in the scenes of 1775, and who are now here, from every quarter of New England, to visit, once more, and under circumstances so affecting,— I had almost said so overwhelming,—this renowned theatre of their courage and patriotism.

VENERABLE MEN! you have come down to us from a former generation. Heaven has bounteously lengthened out your lives that you might behold this joyous day. You are now where you stood, fifty years ago this very hour, with your brothers and your neighbors, shoulder to shoulder, in the strife for your country. Behold, how altered! The same heavens are indeed over your heads; the same ocean rolls at your feet; but all else how changed! You hear now no roar of hostile cannon, you see no mixed volumes of smoke and flame rising from burning Charlestown. The ground strewed with the dead and the dying; the impetuous charge; the steady and successful repulse; the loud call to repeated assault; the summoning of all that is manly to repeated resistance; a thousand bosoms freely and fearlessly bared in an instant to whatever of terror there may be in war and death; — all these you have witnessed, but you witness them no more. All is peace. The heights of yonder metropolis, its towers and roofs, which you then saw filled with wives and children and countrymen in distress and terror, and looking with unutterable emotions for the issue of the combat, have presented you to-day with the sight of its whole happy population, come out to welcome and greet you with an universal jubilee. Yonder proud ships, by a felicity of position appropriately lying at the foot of this monut, and seeming fondly to cling around it, are not means of annoyance to you, but your country's own means of distinction and defence. All is peace; and God has granted you this sight of your country's happiness, ere you slumber in the grave forever. He has allowed you to behold and to partake the reward of your patriotic toils; and he has allowed us, your sons and countrymen, to meet you here, and in the name of the present generation, in the name of your conntry, in the name of liberty, to thank you!

But, alas! you are not all here! Time and the sword have thinned your ranks. Prescott, Putnam, Stark, Brooks, Read, Pomeroy, Bridge! our eyes seek for you in vain amidst this broken band. You are gathered to your fathers, and live only to your country in her grateful remembrance and your own bright example. But let us not too much grieve that you have met the common fate of men. You lived at least long enough to know that your work had been nobly and successfully accomplished. You lived to see your country's independence established, and to sheathe your swords from war. On the light of Liberty you saw arise the Light of Peace, like

"another morn,
Risen on mid-noon;"—

and the sky on which you closed your eyes was cloudless.

But — ah! — Him! the first great Martyr in this great cause! Him! the premature victim of his own self-devoting heart! Him! the head of our civil councils and the destined leader of our military bands; whom nothing brought hither but the unquenchable fire of his own spirit. Him! cut off by Providence, in the hour of overwhelming anxiety and thick gloom; falling ere he saw the star of his country rise; pouring out his generous blood like water, before he knew whether it would fertilize a land of freedom or of bondage! How shall I struggle with the emotions that stifle the utterance of thy name! — Our poor work may perish; but thine shall endure! This monument may moulder away; the solid ground it rests upon may sink down to a level with the sea; but thy memory shall not fail! Wheresoever among men a heart shall be found that beats to the transports of patriotism and liberty, its aspirations shall be to claim kindred with thy spirit![1]

But the scene amidst which we stand does not permit us to confine our thoughts or our sympathies to those fearless spirits who hazarded or lost their lives on this consecrated spot. We have the happiness to rejoice here in the presence of a most worthy representation of the survivors of the whole Revolutionary Army.

VETERANS! you are the remnant of many a well-fought field. You bring with you marks of honor from Trenton and Monmouth, from Yorktown, Camden, Benningtou, and Saratoga. VETERANS OF HALF A CENTURY! when in your youthful days you put everything at hazard in your country's cause, good as that cause was, and sanguine as youth is, still your fondest hopes did not stretch onward to an hour like this! At a period to which you could not reasonably have expected to arrive; at a moment of national prosperity such as you could never have foreseen, you are now met here to enjoy the fellowship of old soldiers, and to receive the overflowings of an universal gratitude.

But your agitated countenances and your heaving breasts inform me that even this is not an unmixed joy. I perceive that a tumult of contending feelings rushes upon you. The images of the dead, as well as the persons of the living, throng to your embraces. The scene overwhelms you, and I turn from it. May

---

[1] Gen. Joseph Warren, born at Roxbury, Mass., June 11, 1741. Killed June 17, 1775.— W. H. W.

the Father of all mercies smile upon your declining years and bless them! And when you shall here have exchanged your embraces; when you shall once more have pressed the hands which have been so often extended to give succor in adversity, or grasped in the exultation of victory, then look abroad into this lovely land, which your young valor defended, and mark the happiness with which it is filled; yea, look abroad into the whole earth, and see what a name you have contributed to give to your country, and what a praise you have added to freedom, and then rejoice in the sympathy and gratitude which beam upon your last days from the improved condition of mankind.

The occasion does not require of me any particular account of the battle of the 17th of June, nor any detailed narrative of the events which immediately preceded it. These are familiarly known to all. In the progress of the great and interesting controversy, Massachusetts and the town of Boston had become early and marked objects of the displeasure of the British Parliament. This had been manifested in the Act for altering the Government of the Province, and in that for shutting up the Port of Boston. Nothing sheds more honor on our early history, and nothing better shows how little the feelings and sentiments of the colonies were known or regarded in England, than the impression which these measures everywhere produced in America. It had been anticipated that while the other colonies would be terrified by the severity of the punishment inflicted on Massachusetts, the other seaports would be governed by a mere spirit of gain; and that as Boston was now cut off from all commerce, the unexpected advantage which this blow on her was calculated to confer on other towns, would be greedily enjoyed. How miserably such reasoners deceived themselves! How little they knew of the depth, and the strength, and the intenseness of that feeling of resistance to illegal acts of power which possessed the whole American people! Everywhere the unworthy boon was rejected with scorn. The fortunate occasion was seized, everywhere, to show to the whole world that the colonies were swayed by no local interest, no partial interest, no selfish interest. The temptation to profit by the punishment of Boston was strongest to our neighbors of Salem. Yet Salem was precisely the place where this miserable proffer was spurned in a tone of the most lofty self-respect and the most indignant patriotism. "We are deeply affected," said its inhabitants. "with the sense of our public calamities; but the miseries that are now rapidly hastening on our brethren in the capital of the Province greatly excite our commiseration. By shutting up the port of Boston, some imagine that the course of trade might be turned hither, and to our benefit; but we must be dead to every idea of justice, lost to all feelings of humanity, could we indulge a thought to seize on wealth, and raise our fortunes on the ruin of our suffering neighbors." These noble sentiments were not confined to our immediate vicinity. In that day of general affection and brotherhood, the blow given to Boston smote on every patriotic heart, from one end of the country to the other. Virginia and the Carolinas, as well as Connecticut and New Hampshire, felt and proclaimed the cause to be their own. The Continental Congress, then holding its first session in Philadelphia, expressed its sympathy for the suffering inhabitants of Boston, and addresses were received from all quarters assuring them that the cause was a common one, and should be met by common efforts and common sacrifices. The Congress of Massachusetts responded to these assurances; and in an address to the Congress at Philadelphia, bearing the official signature, perhaps among the last, of the immortal Warren, notwithstanding the severity of its suffering and the magnitude of the dangers which threatened it, it was declared, that this colony "is ready at all times to spend and to be spent in the cause of America."

But the hour drew nigh which was to put professions to the proof, and to determine whether the authors of these mutual pledges were ready to seal them in blood. The tidings of Lexington and Concord had no sooner spread, than it was universally felt that the time was at last come for action. A spirit pervaded all ranks, not transient, not boisterous, but deep, solemn, determined,

"totamque infusa per artus
Mens agitat molem, et magno se corpore miscet."

War, on their own soil and at their own doors, was, indeed, a strange work to the yeomanry of New England; but their consciences were convinced of its necessity, their country called them to it, and they did not withhold themselves from the perilous trial. The ordinary occupations of life were abandoned; the plough was stayed in the unfinished furrow; wives gave up their husbands, and mothers gave up their sons, to the battles of a civil war. Death might come, in honor, on the field; it might come, in disgrace, on the scaffold. For either and for both they were prepared. The sentiment of Quincy was full in their hearts. "Blandishments," said that distinguished son of genius and patriotism, "will not fascinate us, nor will threats of a halter intimidate; for, under God, we are determined, that wheresoever, whensoever, or howsoever we shall be called to make our exit, we will die free men."

The 17th of June saw the four New England colonies standing here, side by side, to triumph or to fall together; and there was with them from that moment to the end of the war, what I hope will remain with them forever, one cause, one country, one heart.

The battle of Bunker Hill was attended with the most important effects beyond its immediate results as a military engagement. It created at once a state of open public war. There could now be no longer a question of proceeding against individuals, as guilty of treason or rebellion. That fearful crisis was past. The appeal now lay to the sword; and the only question was, whether the spirit and the resources of the people would hold out till the object should be accomplished. Nor were its general consequences confined to our own country. The previous proceedings of the colonies, their appeals, resolutions, and addresses, had made their cause known to Europe. Without boasting, we may say, that in no age or country has the public cause been maintained with more force of argument, more power of illustration, or more of that persuasion which excited feeling and elevated principle can alone bestow, than the revolutionary State papers exhibit. These papers will forever deserve to be studied, not only for the spirit which they breathe, but for the ability with which they were written.

To this able vindication of their cause, the colonies had now added a practical and severe proof of their own true devotion to it, and evidence also of the power which they could bring to its support. All now saw that if America fell, she would not fall without a struggle. Men felt sympathy and regard, as well as surprise, when they beheld these infant States, remote, unknown, unaided, encounter the power of England, and in the first considerable battle, leave more of their enemies dead on the field, in proportion to the number of combatants, than they had recently known in the wars of Europe.

Information of these events, circulating through Europe, at length reached the ears of one who now hears me. He has not forgotten the emotion which the fame of Bunker Hill, and the name of Warren, excited in his youthful breast.

Sir,[1] we are assembled to commemorate the establishment of great public principles of liberty, and to do honor to the distinguished dead. The occasion is too severe for eulogy to the living. But, sir, your interesting relation to this country, the peculiar circumstances which surround you and surround us, call on me to express the happiness which we derive from your presence and aid in this solemn commemoration.

Fortunate, fortunate man! with what measure of devotion will you not thank God for the circumstances of your extraordinary life! You are connected with both hemispheres and with two generations. Heaven saw fit to ordain that the electric spark of Liberty should be conducted, through you, from the New World to the Old; and we, who are now here to perform this duty of patriotism, have all of us long ago received it in charge from our fathers to cherish your name and your virtues. You will account it an instance of your good fortune, sir, that you crossed the seas to visit us at a time which enables you to be present at this solemnity. You now behold the field, the renown of which reached you in the heart of France, and caused a thrill in your ardent bosom. You see the lines of the little redoubt thrown up by the

---

[1] Marie Jean Paul Roch Yves Gilbert Motier, Marquis de Lafayette, born 6 Sept., 1757, died at Paris, May 19, 1834. — W. H. W.

incredible diligence of Prescott; defended to the last extremity by his lion-hearted valor; and within which the corner-stone of our monument has now taken its position. You see where Warren fell, and where Parker, Gardner, McCleary, Moore, and other early patriots fell with him. Those who survived that day, and whose lives have been prolonged to the present hour, are now around you. Some of them you have known in the trying scenes of the war. Behold! they now stretch forth their feeble arms to embrace you. Behold! they raise their trembling voices to invoke the blessing of God on you and yours forever.

Sir, you have assisted us in laying the foundation of this edifice. You have heard us rehearse, with our feeble commendation, the names of departed patriots. Sir, monuments and eulogy belong to the dead. We give them, this day, to Warren and his associates. On other occasions they have been given to your more immediate companions in arms, to Washington, to Greene, to Gates, Sullivan, and Lincoln. Sir, we have become reluctant to grant these, our highest and last honors, further. We would gladly hold them yet back from the little remnant of that immortal band. *Serus in cœlum redeas.* Illustrious as are your merits, yet far, oh, very far distant be the day when any inscription shall bear your name, or any tongue pronounce its eulogy!

The leading reflection to which this occasion seems to invite us, respects the great changes which have happened in the fifty years since the battle of Bunker Hill was fought. And it peculiarly marks the character of the present age, that, in looking at these changes, and in estimating their effect on our condition, we are obliged to consider, not what has been done in our own country only, but in others also. In these interesting times, while nations are making separate and individual advances in improvement, they make, too, a common progress; like vessels on a common tide, propelled by the gales at different times, according to their several structure and management, but all moved forward by one mighty current beneath, strong enough to bear onward whatever does not sink beneath it.

A chief distinction of the present day is a community of opinions and knowledge amongst men, in different nations, existing in a degree heretofore unknown. Knowledge has, in our time, triumphed and is triumphing, over distance, over difference of languages, over diversity of habits, over prejudice, and over bigotry. The civilized and Christian world is fast learning the great lesson, that difference of nation does not imply necessary hostility, and that all contact need not be war. The whole world is becoming a common field for intellect to act in. Energy of mind, genius, power, wheresoever it exists, may speak out in any tongue, and the *world* will hear it. A great chord of sentiment and feeling runs through two continents, and vibrates over both. Every breeze wafts intelligence from country to country; every wave rolls it; all give it forth, and all in turn receive it. There is a vast commerce of ideas; there are marts and exchanges for intellectual discoveries, and a wonderful fellowship of those individual intelligences which make up the mind and opinion of the age. Mind is the great lever of all things; human thought is the process by which human ends are ultimately answered; and the diffusion of knowledge, so astonishing in the last half century, has rendered innumerable minds, variously gifted by nature, competent to be competitors, or fellow-workers, on the theatre of intellectual operation.

From these causes important improvements have taken place in the personal condition of individuals. Generally speaking, mankind are not only better fed, and better clothed, but they are able also to enjoy more leisure; they possess more refinement and more self-respect. A superior tone of education, manners, and habits prevails. This remark, most true in its application to our own country, is also partly true when applied elsewhere. It is proved by the vastly augmented consumption of those articles of manufacture and of commerce, which contribute to the comforts and the decencies of life; an augmentation which has far outrun the progress of population. And while the unexampled and almost incredible use of machinery would seem to supply the place of labor, labor still finds its occupation and its reward; so wisely has Providence adjusted men's wants and desires to their condition and their capacity.

APPENDIX E.

Any adequate survey, however, of the progress made in the last half century in the polite and the mechanic arts, in machinery and manufactures, in commerce and agriculture, in letters and in science, would require volumes. I must abstain wholly from these subjects, and turn, for a moment, to the contemplation of what has been done on the great question of politics and government. This is the master topic of the age; and during the whole fifty years it has intensely occupied the thoughts of men. The nature of civil government, its ends and uses, have been canvassed and investigated; ancient opinions attacked and defended; new ideas recommended and resisted, by whatever power the mind of man could bring to the controversy. From the closet and the public halls the debate has been transferred to the field; and the world has been shaken by wars of unexampled magnitude and the greatest variety of fortune. A day of peace has at length succeeded; and now that the strife has subsided, and the smoke cleared away, we may begin to see what has actually been done, permanently changing the state and condition of human society. And without dwelling on particular circumstances, it is most apparent that, from the beforementioned causes of augmented knowledge and improved individual condition, a real, substantial, and important change has taken place, and is taking place, greatly beneficial, on the whole, to human liberty and human happiness.

The great wheel of political revolution began to move in America. Here its rotation was guarded, regular, and safe. Transferred to the other continent, from unfortunate but natural causes, it received an irregular and violent impulse; it whirled along with a fearful celerity; till at length, like the chariot wheels in the races of antiquity, it took fire from the rapidity of its own motion, and blazed onward, spreading conflagration and terror around.

We learn from the result of this experiment how fortunate was our own condition, and how admirably the character of our people was calculated for making the great example of popular governments. The possession of power did not turn the heads of the American people, for they had long been in the habit of exercising a great portion of self-control. Although the paramount authority of the parent State existed over them, yet a large field of legislation had always been open to our colonial assemblies. They were accustomed to representative bodies and the forms of free government; they understood the doctrine of the division of power among different branches, and the necessity of checks on each. The character of our countrymen, moreover, was sober, moral, and religious; and there was little in the change to shock their feelings of justice and humanity, or even to disturb an honest prejudice. We had no domestic throne to overturn, no privileged orders to cast down, no violent changes of property to encounter. In the American Revolution no men sought or wished for more than to defend and enjoy his own. None hoped for plunder or for spoil. Rapacity was unknown to it; the axe was not among the instruments of its accomplishment; and we all know that it could not have lived a single day under any well-founded imputation of possessing a tendency adverse to the Christian religion.

It need not surprise us that, under circumstances less auspicious, political revolutions elsewhere, even when well intended, have terminated differently. It is, indeed, a great achievement, it is the master work of the world, to establish governments entirely popular on lasting foundations; nor is it easy, indeed, to introduce the popular principle at all into governments to which it has been altogether a stranger. It cannot be doubted, however, that Europe has come out of the contest in which she has been so long engaged, with greatly superior knowledge, and, in many respects, a highly improved condition. Whatever benefit has been acquired, is likely to be retained, for it consists mainly in the acquisition of more enlightened ideas. And although kingdoms and provinces may be wrested from the hands that hold them, in the same manner they were obtained; although ordinary and vulgar power may, in human affairs, be lost as it has been won; yet it is the glorious prerogative of the empire of knowledge, that what it gains it never loses. On the contrary, it increases by the multiple of its own power; all its ends become means; all its attainments helps to new conquests. Its whole abundant harvest is but so much seed wheat, and nothing has ascertained, and nothing can ascertain, the amount of ultimate product.

Under the influence of this rapidly increasing knowledge, the people have begun, in all forms of government, to think and to reason on affairs of State. Regarding government as an institution for the public good, they demand a knowledge of its operations, and a participation in its exercise. A call for the Representative system, wherever it is not enjoyed, and where there is already intelligence enough to estimate its value, is perseveringly made. Where men may speak out, they demand it; where the bayonet is at their throats, they pray for it.

When Louis XIV. said, "I am the State," he expressed the essence of the doctrine of unlimited power. By the rules of that system, the people are disconnected from the State; they are its subjects; it is their lord. These ideas, founded in the love of power, and long supported by the excess and the abuse of it, are yielding, in our age, to other opinions; and the civilized world seems at last to be proceeding to the conviction of that fundamental and manifest truth, that the powers of government are but a trust, and that they cannot be lawfully exercised but for the good of the community. As knowledge is more and more extended, this conviction becomes more and more general. Knowledge, in truth, is the great sun in the firmament. Life and power are scattered with all its beams. The prayer of the Grecian combatant, when enveloped in unnatural cloud and darkness, is the appropriate political supplication for the people of every country not yet blessed with free institutions;

"Dispel this cloud, the light of heaven restore,
Give me TO SEE — and Ajax asks no more."

We may hope that the growing influence of enlightened sentiments will promote the permanent peace of the world. Wars, to maintain family alliances, to uphold or to cast down dynasties, to regulate successions to thrones, which have occupied so much room in the history of modern times, if not less likely to happen at all, will be less likely to become general and involve many nations, as the great principle shall be more and more established, that the interest of the world is peace, and its first great statute, that every nation possesses the power of establishing a government for itself. But public opinion has attained also an influence over governments which do not admit the popular principle into their organization. A necessary respect for the judgment of the world operates, in some measure, as a control over the most unlimited forms of authority. It is owing, perhaps, to this truth that the interesting struggle of the Greeks has been suffered to go on so long without a direct interference, either to wrest that country from its present masters, and add it to other powers, or to execute the system of pacification by force, and, with united strength, lay the neck of Christian and civilized Greece at the foot of the barbarian Turk. Let us thank God that we live in an age when something has influence besides the bayonet, and when the sternest authority does not venture to encounter the scorching power of public reproach. Any attempt of the kind I have mentioned should be met by one universal burst of indignation; the air of the civilized world ought to be made too warm to be comfortably breathed by any who would hazard it.

It is, indeed, a touching reflection, that while, in the fulness of our country's happiness, we rear this monument to her honor, we look for instruction, in our undertaking, to a country which is now in fearful contest, not for works of art or memorials of glory, but for her own existence. Let her be assured that she is not forgotten in the world; that her efforts are applauded, and that constant prayers ascend for her success. And let us cherish a confident hope for her final triumph. If the true spark of religious and civil liberty be kindled, it will burn. Human agency cannot extinguish it. Like the earth's central fire, it may be smothered for a time; the ocean may overwhelm it; mountains may press it down; but its inherent and unconquerable force will heave both the ocean and the land, and at some time or another, in some place or another, the volcano will break out and flame up to heaven.

Among the great events of the half century, we must reckon, certainly, the revolution of South America; and we are not likely to overrate the importance of that revolution, either to the people of the country itself or to the rest of the world. The late Spanish colonies, now independent States, under circumstances less favorable, doubtless, than attended our own Revolution, have yet successfully commenced their national existence. They have accomplished the great object of establishing their independence; they are known and acknowledged in the world; and although, in regard to their systems of government, their sentiments on religious toleration, and their provisions for public instruction, they may have yet much to learn, it must be admitted that they have risen to the condition of settled and established States more rapidly than could have been reasonably anticipated. They already furnish an exhilarating example of the difference between free governments and despotic misrule. Their commerce, at this moment, creates a new activity in all the great marts of the world. They show themselves able, by an exchange of commodities, to bear an useful part in the intercourse of nations. A new spirit of enterprise and industry begins to prevail; all the great interests of society receive a salutary impulse; and the progress of information not only testifies to an improved condition, but constitutes itself the highest and most essential improvement.

When the battle of Bunker Hill was fought, the existence of South America was scarcely felt in the civilized world. The thirteen little colonies of North America habitually called themselves the "Continent." Borne down by colonial subjugation, monopoly, and bigotry, these vast regions of the south were hardly visible above the horizon. But in our day there hath been, as it were, a new creation. The southern hemisphere emerges from the sea. Its lofty mountains begin to lift themselves into the light of heaven; its broad and fertile plains stretch out, in beauty, to the eye of civilized man, and at the mighty bidding of the voice of political liberty, the waters of darkness retire.

And, now, let us indulge an honest exultation in the conviction of the benefit which the example of our country has produced, and is likely to produce, on human freedom and human happiness. And let us endeavor to comprehend, in all its magnitude, and to feel, in all its importance, the part assigned to us in the great drama of human affairs. We are placed at the head of the system of representative and popular governments. Thus far our example shows that such governments are compatible, not only with respectability and power, but with repose, with peace, with security of personal rights, with good laws, and a just administration.

We are not propagandists. Wherever other systems are preferred, either as being thought better in themselves, or as better suited to existing condition, we leave the preference to be enjoyed. Our history hitherto proves, however, that the popular form is practicable, and that with wisdom and knowledge men may govern themselves; and the duty incumbent on us is, to preserve the consistency of this cheering example, and take care that nothing may weaken its authority with the world. If, in our case, the Representative system ultimately fail, popular governments must be pronounced impossible. No combination of circumstances more favorable to the experiment can ever be expected to occur. The last hopes of mankind, therefore, rest with us; and if it should be proclaimed, that our example had become an argument against the experiment, the knell of popular liberty would be sounded throughout the earth.

These are excitements to duty; but they are not suggestions of doubt. Our history and our condition, all that is gone before us, and all that surrounds us, authorize the belief, that popular governments, though subject to occasional variations, perhaps not always for the better, in form, may yet, in their general character, be as durable and permanent as other systems. We know, indeed, that, in our country, any other is impossible. The *principle* of free governments adheres to the American soil. It is bedded in it; immovable as its mountains.

And let the sacred obligations which have devolved on this generation, and on us, sink deep into our hearts. Those are daily dropping from among us, who established our liberty and our government. The great trust now descends to new hands. Let us apply ourselves to that which is presented to us, as our appropriate object. We can win no laurels in a war for independence. Earlier and worthier hands have gathered them all. Nor are

APPENDIX E. 217

there places for us by the side of Solon, and Alfred, and other founders of States. Our fathers have filled them. But there remains to us a great duty of defence and preservation; and there is opened to us, also, a noble pursuit, to which the spirit of the times strongly invites us. Our proper business is improvement. Let our age be the age of improvement. In a day of peace, let us advance the arts of peace and the works of peace. Let us develop the resources of our land, call forth its powers, build up its institutions, promote all its great interests, and see whether we also, in our day and generation, may not perform something worthy to be remembered. Let us cultivate a true spirit of union and harmony. In pursuing the great objects which our condition points out to us, let us act under a settled conviction, and an habitual feeling, that these twenty-four States are one country. Let our conceptions be enlarged to the circle of our duties. Let us extend our ideas over the whole of the vast field in which we are called to act. Let our object be, OUR COUNTRY, OUR WHOLE COUNTRY, AND NOTHING BUT OUR COUNTRY. And, by the blessing of God, may that country itself become a vast and splendid monument, not of oppression and terror, but of Wisdom, of Peace, and of Liberty, upon which the world may gaze with admiration forever!

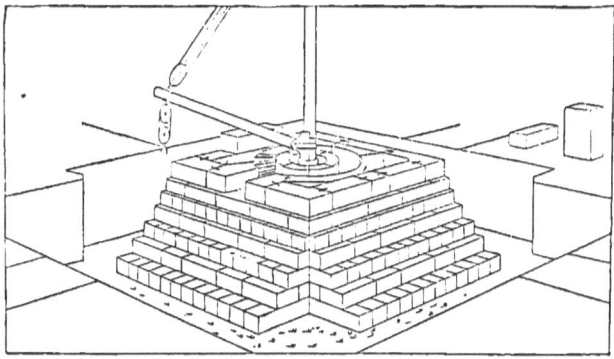

DETAIL OF FOUNDATION. FROM WILLARD'S MEMORIAL.

ADDRESS

DELIVERED AT

BUNKER HILL, JUNE 17, 1843,

ON THE

COMPLETION OF THE MONUMENT.

By DANIEL WEBSTER.

A DUTY has been performed. A work of gratitude and patriotism is completed. This structure, having its foundations in soil which drank deep of early revolutionary blood, has at length reached its destined height, and now lifts its summit to the skies.

We have assembled to celebrate the accomplishment of this undertaking, and to indulge, afresh, in the recollection of the great event which it is designed to commemorate. Eighteen years, more than half the ordinary duration of a generation of mankind, have elapsed since the corner-stone of this monument was laid. The hopes of its projectors rested on voluntary contributions, private munificence, and the general favor of the public. These hopes have not been disappointed. Donations have been made by individuals, in some cases of large amount, and smaller sums have been contributed by thousands. All who regard the object itself as important, and its accomplishment, therefore, as a good attained, will entertain sincere respect and gratitude for the unwearied efforts of the successive presidents, boards of directors, and committees of the association which has had the general control of the work. The architect, equally entitled to our thanks and commendation, will find other reward, also, for his labor and skill, in the beauty and elegance of the obelisk itself, and the distinction which, as a work of art, it confers on him.

At a period when the prospects of further progress in the undertaking were gloomy and discouraging, the Mechanic Association, by a most praiseworthy and vigorous effort, raised new funds for carrying it forward, and saw them applied with fidelity, economy, and skill. It is a grateful duty to make public acknowledgments of such timely and efficient aid.

The last effort, and the last contribution, were from a different source. Garlands of grace and elegance were destined to crown a work which had its commencement in manly patriotism. The winning power of the sex addressed itself to the public, and all that was needed to carry the monument to its proposed height, and give to it its finish, was promptly supplied. The mothers and the daughters of the land contributed thus, most successfully, to whatever of beauty is in the monument itself, or whatever of utility and public benefit and gratification in its completion.

Of those with whom the plan of erecting, on this spot, a monument worthy of the event to be commemorated, originated, many are now present; but others, alas! have themselves become subjects of monumental inscription. William Tudor,[1] an accomplished scholar, a distinguished writer, a most amiable man, allied, both by birth and sentiment, to the patriots of the Revolution, died while on public service abroad, and now lies buried in a foreign land. William Sullivan,[2] a name fragrant of Revolutionary merit, and of public service and public virtue, who himself partook, in a high degree, of the respect and confidence of the community, and yet was always most loved where best known, has also been gathered to his fathers. And last, George Blake,[3] a lawyer of

---

[1] William Tudor, son of Judge William T., was born in Boston, 28 Jan. 1779, died at Rio Janeiro, 9 Mch. 1830. He was distinguished in many ways, as a merchant, orator, author and diplomatist, and for his public spirit.— W. H. W.

[2] William Sullivan, son of Gen. James S., born at Saco, 30 Nov. 1774, died at Boston, 3 Sept. 1839. He was a lawyer, frequently in the legislature, a noted writer and orator.— W. H. W.

[3] George Blake, son of Joseph, born at Hardwick, Mass. 16 April, 1769, died at Boston, 6 to 4 1841. He was a prominent lawyer, and orator, and U. S. District Attorney.— W. H. W.

learning and eloquence, a man of wit and of talent, of social qualities the most agreeable and fascinating, and of gifts which enabled him to exercise large sway over public assemblies, has closed his human career. I know that in the crowds before me there are those from whose eyes copious tears will flow at the mention of these names. But such mention is due to their general character, their public and private virtues, and especially, on this occasion, to the spirit and zeal with which they entered into the undertaking which is now completed.

I have spoken only of those who are no longer numbered with the living. But a long life, now drawing towards its close, always distinguished by acts of public spirit, humanity, and charity, forming a character which has already become historical and sanctified by public regard and the affection of friends, may confer, even on the living, the proper immunity of the dead, and be the fit subject of honorable mention and warm commendation. Of the early projectors of the design of this monument, one of the most prominent, the most zealous, and the most efficient, is Thomas H. Perkins.[1] It was beneath his ever hospitable roof that those whom I have mentioned, and others yet living and now present, having assembled for the purpose, adopted the first step towards erecting a monument on Bunker Hill. Long may he remain, with unimpaired faculties, in the wide field of his usefulness. His charities have distilled, like the dews of heaven; he has fed the hungry and clothed the naked; he has given sight to the blind; and for such virtues there is a reward on high, of which all human memorials, all language of brass and stone, are but humble types and attempted imitations.

Time and nature have had their course in diminishing the number of those whom we met here on the 17th of June, 1825. Most of the Revolutionary characters then present have since deceased; and Lafayette sleeps in his native land. Yet the name

---

[1] Thomas Handasyde Perkins, born at Boston 15 Dec. 1764, died there 11 January, 1854. With his brother James, he established a great commercial house, trading especially with the East Indies. Both brothers were splendid examples of mercantile honor and enterprise, and equally distinguished by their public spirit and grand munificence. The Blind Asylum and the Boston Athenæum are evidences of their wisdom as well as their generosity. — W. H. W.

and blood of Warren are with us; the kindred of Putnam are also here; and near me, universally beloved for his character and his virtues, and now venerable for his years, sits the son of the noble-hearted and daring Prescott.[1] Gideon Foster, of Danvers; Enos Reynolds, of Boxford; Phineas Johnson, Robert Andrews, Elijah Dresser, Josiah Cleaveland, Jesse Smith, Philip Bagley, Needham Maynard, Roger Plaisted, Joseph Stephens, Nehemiah Porter, and James Harvey, who bore arms for their country, either at Concord and Lexington, on the 19th of April, or on Bunker Hill, all now far advanced in age, have come here to-day to look once more on the field of the exercise of their valor, and to receive a hearty outpouring of our respect.

They have long outlived the troubles and dangers of the Revolution; they have outlived the evils arising from the want of a united and efficient government; they have outlived the pendency of imminent dangers to the public liberty; they have outlived nearly all their contemporaries; but they have not outlived — they cannot outlive — the affectionate gratitude of their country. Heaven has not allotted to this generation an opportunity of rendering high services, and manifesting strong personal devotion, such as they rendered and manifested, and in such a cause as that, which roused the patriotic fires of their youthful breasts and nerved the strength of their arms. But we may praise what we cannot equal, and celebrate actions which we were not born to perform. *Pulchrum est benefacere reipublicæ, etiam bene dicere haud absurdum est*.

The Bunker Hill monument is finished. Here it stands. Fortunate in the high natural eminence on which it is placed — higher, infinitely higher in its objects and purpose, it rises over the land, and over the sea, and visible, at their homes, to three hundred thousand of the people of Massachusetts, — it stands a memorial of the last, and a monitor to the present, and to all succeeding generations. I have spoken of the loftiness of its purpose. If it had been without any other design than the creation of a work of art, the granite of which it is composed would have slept in its

---

[1] Judge William Prescott, son of Col. William P., was born at Pepperrell, Mass. 19 Aug. 1762, died at Boston, 8 Dec. 1844. He was distinguished as a lawyer and a legislator. — W. H. W.

native bed. It has a purpose; and that purpose gives it its character. That purpose enrobes it with dignity and moral grandeur. That well-known purpose it is which causes us to look up to it with a feeling of awe. It is itself the orator of this occasion. It is not from my lips, — it could not be from any human lips, — that that strain of eloquence is this day to flow, most competent to move and excite the vast multitudes around me. The powerful speaker stands motionless before us.

It is a plain shaft. It bears no inscriptions, fronting to the rising sun, from which the future antiquarian shall wipe the dust. Nor does the rising sun cause tones of music to issue from its summit. But at the rising of the sun, and at the setting of the sun, in the blaze of noonday, and beneath the milder effulgence of lunar light, it looks, it speaks, it acts, to the full comprehension of every American mind, and the awakening of glowing enthusiasm in every American heart. Its silent, but awful utterance; its deep pathos, as it brings to our contemplation the 17th of June, 1775, and the consequences which have resulted to us, to our country, and to the world, from the events of that day, and which we know must continue to rain influence on the destinies of mankind to the end of time; the elevation with which it raises us high above the ordinary feelings of life: surpass all that the study of the closet, or even the inspiration of genius can produce.

To-day it speaks to us. Its future auditories will be the successive generations of men, as they rise up before it, and gather around it. Its speech will be of patriotism and courage; of civil and religious liberty; of free government; of the moral improvement and elevation of mankind; and of the immortal memory of those who with heroic devotion have sacrificed their lives for their country.

In the older world, numerous fabrics still exist, reared by human hands, but whose object has been lost in the darkness of ages. They are now monuments of nothing but the labor and skill which constructed them.

The mighty pyramid itself, half buried in the sands of Africa, has nothing to bring down and report to us but the power of kings and the servitude of the people. If it had any purpose beyond that of a mausoleum, such purpose has perished from history and from tradition. If asked for its moral object, its admonition, its sentiment, its instruction to mankind, or any high end in its erection, it is silent — silent as the millions which lie in the dust at its base, and in the catacombs which surround it. Without a just moral object, therefore, made known to man, though raised against the skies, it excites only conviction of power, mixed with strange wonder. But if the civilization of the present race of men, founded as it is in solid science, the true knowledge of nature, and vast discoveries in art, and which is stimulated and purified by moral sentiment, and by the truths of Christianity, be not destined to destruction before the final termination of human existence on earth, the object and purpose of this edifice will be known till that hour shall come. And even if civilization should be subverted, and the truths of the Christian religion obscured by a new deluge of barbarism, the memory of Bunker Hill and the American Revolution will still be elements and parts of the knowledge which shall be possessed by the last man, to whom the light of civilization and Christianity shall be extended.

This celebration is honored by the presence of the Chief Executive Magistrate of the Union.[1] An occasion so national in its object and character, and so much connected with that Revolution from which the government sprang, at the head of which he is placed, may well receive from him this mark of attention and respect. Well acquainted with Yorktown, the scene of the last great military struggle of the Revolution, his eye now surveys the field of Bunker Hill, the theatre of the first of those important conflicts. He sees where Warren fell, where Putnam, and Prescott, and Stark, and Knowlton, and Brooks fought. He beholds the spot where a thousand trained soldiers of England were smitten to the earth, in the first effort of Revolutionary war, by the arm of a bold and determined yeomanry, contending for

---

[1] President John Tyler and his cabinet were present. — W. H. W.

liberty and their country. And while all assembled here entertain towards him sincere personal good wishes, and the high respect due to his elevated office and station, it is not to be doubted that he enters, with true American feeling, into the patriotic enthusiasm, kindled by the occasion, which animates the multitudes which surround him.

His Excellency the Governor of the Commonwealth,[1] the Governor of Rhode Island, and the other distinguished public men, whom we have the honor to receive as visitors and guests to-day, will cordially unite in a celebration connected with the great event of the Revolutionary war.

No name in the history of 1775 and 1776 is more distinguished than that borne by an ex-President of the United States, whom we expected to see here, but whose ill-health prevents his attendance. Whenever popular rights were to be asserted, an Adams was present; and when the time came for the formal Declaration of Independence, it was the voice of an Adams that shook the halls of Congress. We wish we could have welcomed to us this day the inheritor of Revolutionary blood, and the just and worthy representative of high Revolutionary names, merit, and services.

Banners and badges, processions and flags, announce to us that amidst this uncounted throng are thousands of natives of New England, now residents in other States. Welcome, ye kindred names, with kindred blood! From the broad savannas of the South, from the newer regions of the West, from amidst the hundreds of thousands of men of Eastern origin, who cultivate the rich valley of the Genesee, or live along the chain of the Lakes, from the mountains of Pennsylvania, and the thronged cities of the Coast, welcome, welcome! Wherever else you may be strangers, here you are all at home. You assemble at this shrine of liberty, near the family altars, at which your earliest devotions were paid to Heaven; near to the temples of worship, first entered by you, and near to the schools and colleges in which your education was received. You come hither with a glorious ancestry of liberty.

---

[1] Gov. Marcus Morton of Massachusetts and Gov. James Fenner of Rhode Island were on the platform. — W. H. W.

You bring names which are on the rolls of Lexington, Concord, and Bunker Hill. You come, some of you, once more to be embraced by an aged Revolutionary Father, or to receive another, perhaps, a last blessing, bestowed in love and tears, by a mother, yet surviving to witness, and to enjoy, your prosperity and happiness.

But if family associations and the recollections of the past bring you hither with greater alacrity, and mingle with your greeting much of local attachment and private affection, greeting, also, be given, — free and hearty greeting, — to every American citizen who treads this sacred soil with patriotic feeling, and respires with pleasure, in an atmosphere perfumed with the recollections of 1775. This occasion is respectable — nay, it is grand, it is sublime, by the nationality of its sentiment. In the seventeen millions of happy people who form the American community, there is not one who has not an interest in this monument, as there is not one that has not a deep and abiding interest in that which it commemorates.

Woe betide the man who brings to this day's worship feeling less than wholly American! Woe betide the man who can stand here with the fires of local resentments burning, or the purpose of fomenting local jealousies, and the strifes of local interests, festering and rankling, in his heart. Union, established in justice, in patriotism, and the most plain and obvious common interest; union, founded on the same love of liberty, cemented by blood shed in the same common cause; union has been the source of all our glory and greatness thus far, and is the ground of all our highest hopes. This column stands on Union. I know not that it might not keep its position if the American Union, in the mad conflict of human passions, and in the strife of parties and factions, should be broken up and destroyed. I know not that it would totter and fall to the earth, and mingle its fragments with the fragments of Liberty and the Constitution, when State should be separated from State, and faction and dismemberment obliterate forever all the hopes of the founders of our Republic and the great inheritance of their children. It might stand. But who, from beneath the weight of mortification and shame that would oppress him, could look up to behold it? Whose eyeballs would not be seared by such a spectacle? For my part, should I live to such a time, I shall avert my eyes from it forever.

It is not as a mere military encounter of hostile armies, that the battle of Bunker Hill presents its principal claim to attention. Yet, even as a mere battle, there were circumstances attending it, extraordinary in character, and entitling it to peculiar distinction. It was fought on this eminence; in the neighborhood of yonder city; in the presence of more spectators than there were combatants in the conflict. Men, women, and children, from every commanding position, were gazing at the battle, and looking for its result with all the eagerness natural to those who knew that the issue was fraught with the deepest consequences to themselves, personally, as well as to their country. Yet, on the 16th of June, 1775, there was nothing around this hill but verdure and culture. There was, indeed, the note of awful preparation in Boston. There was the provincial army at Cambridge, with its right flank resting on Dorchester and its left on Chelsea. But here all was peace. Tranquillity reigned around.

On the 17th, everything was changed. On this height had arisen, in the night, a redoubt, built by Prescott, and in which he held command. Perceived by the enemy at dawn, it was immediately cannonaded from the floating batteries in the river and from the opposite shore. And then ensued the hurry of preparation in Boston, and soon the troops of Britain embarked in the attempt to dislodge the colonists. In an hour everything indicated an immediate and bloody conflict. Love of liberty on one side, proud defiance of rebellion on the other; hopes and fears, and courage and daring, on both sides, animated the hearts of the combatants as they hung on the edge of battle.

I suppose it would be difficult, in a military point of view, to ascribe to the leaders on either side any just motive for the engagement which followed. On the one hand, it could not have been very important to the Americans to attempt to hem the British within the town, by advancing one single post a quarter of a mile; while on the other hand, if the British found it essential to dislodge the American troops, they had it in their power, at no expense of life. By moving up their ships and batteries, they could have completely cut of all communication with the main land over the neck, and the forces in the redoubt would have been reduced to a state of famine in forty-eight hours.

But that was not the day for any such considerations, on either side. Both parties were anxious to try the strength of their arms. The pride of England would not permit the rebels, as she termed them, to defy her to the teeth; and without for a moment calculating the cost, the British general determined to destroy the fort immediately. On the other side, Prescott and his gallant followers longed and thirsted for a decisive trial of strength and of courage. They wished a battle, and wished it at once. And this is the true secret of the movements on this hill.

I will not attempt to describe that battle. The cannonading — the landing of the British — their advance — the coolness with which the charge was met — the repulse — the second attack — the second repulse — the burning of Charlestown — and finally the closing assault, and the slow retreat of the Americans — the history of all these is familiar.

But the consequences of the battle of Bunker Hill are greater than those of any ordinary conflict, although between armies of far greater force, and terminating with more immediate advantage, on the one side or the other. It was the first great battle of the Revolution; and not only the first blow, but the blow which determined the contest. It did not, indeed, put an end to the war, but in the then existing hostile state of feeling, the difficulties could only be referred to the arbitration of the sword. And one thing is certain: that after the New England troops had shown themselves able to face and repulse the regulars, it was decided that peace never could be established but upon the basis of the independence of the colonies. When the sun of that day went down, the event of independence was no longer doubtful. In a few days Washington heard of the battle, and he inquired if the militia had stood the fire of the regulars. And when told that they had not only stood that fire, but reserved their own till the enemy was within eight rods, and then poured it in with tremendous effect, — "Then," exclaimed he, "the liberties of the country are safe!"

The consequences of this battle were just of the same importance as the Revolution itself.

If there was nothing of value in the principles of the American Revolution, then there is nothing valuable in the battle of Bunker Hill and its consequences. But if the Revolution was an era in the history of man, favorable to human happiness, — if it was an event which marked the progress of man, all over the world, from despotism to liberty — then this monument is not raised without cause. Then the battle of Bunker Hill is not an event undeserving celebrations, commemorations, and rejoicings now, and in all coming times.

What, then, is the true and peculiar principle of the American Revolution, and of the systems of government which it has confirmed and established? The truth is, that the American Revolution was not caused by the instantaneous discovery of principles of government before unheard of, or the practical adoption of political ideas such as had never before entered into the minds of men. It was but the full development of principles of government, forms of society, and political sentiments, the origin of all which lay back two centuries in English and American history.

The discovery of America, its colonization by the nations of Europe, the history and progress of the colonies, from their establishment to the time when the principal of them threw off their allegiance to the respective States which had planted them, and founded governments of their own, constitute one of the most interesting trains of events in human annals. These events occupied three hundred years; during which period civilization and knowledge made steady progress in the Old World; so that Europe, at the commencement of the nineteenth century, had become greatly changed from that Europe which began the colonization of America at the close of the fifteenth, or the commencement of the sixteenth. And what is most material to my present purpose is, that in the progress of the first of these centuries, that is to say, from the discovery of America to the settlements of Virginia and Massachusetts, political and religious events took place which most materially affected the state of society and the sentiments of mankind, especially in England and in parts of continental Europe.

After a few feeble and unsuccessful efforts by England, under Henry VII. to plant colonies in America, no designs of that kind were prosecuted for a long period, either by the English government or any of its subjects. Without inquiring into the causes of this delay, its consequences are sufficiently clear and striking. England in this lapse of a century, unknown to herself, but under the providence of God and the influence of events, was fitting herself for the work of colonizing North America, on such principles, and by such men, as should spread the English name and English blood, in time, over a great portion of the Western hemisphere.

The commercial spirit was greatly fostered by several laws passed in Henry the Seventh's reign; and in the same reign, encouragement was given to arts and manufactures in the Eastern counties, and some not unimportant modifications of the feudal system took place, by allowing the breaking of entails. These, and other measures, and other occurrences, were making way for a new class of society to emerge and show itself, in a military and feudal age; a middle class, — between the barons or great landholders and the retainers of the crown, on the one side, and the tenants of the crown and barons, and agricultural and other laborers, on the other side. With the rise and growth of this new class of society, not only did commerce and the arts increase, but better education, a greater degree of knowledge, juster notions of the true ends of government, and sentiments favorable to civil liberty, began to spread abroad, and become more and more common. But the plants springing from these seeds were of slow growth. The character of English society had indeed begun to undergo a change; but changes of national character are ordinarily the work of time. Operative causes were, however, evidently in existence, and sure to produce, ultimately, their proper effect.

From the accession of Henry VII. to the breaking out of the civil wars, England enjoyed much more exemption from war, foreign and domestic, than for a long period before, and during, the controversy between the houses of York and Lancaster. These years of peace were favorable to commerce and the arts. Commerce and the arts augmented general and individual knowledge; and knowledge is the only fountain, both of the love and the principles of human liberty. Other powerful causes soon came into active play. The Reformation of Luther broke out, kindling up the minds of men afresh, leading to new habits of thought, and awakening in individuals energies before unknown, even to themselves. The religious controversies of this period changed society, as well as religion; indeed, it would be easy to prove, if this occasion were proper for it, that they changed society to a considerable extent, where they did not change the religion of the State. They changed man, himself, in his modes of thought, his consciousness of his own powers, and his desire of intellectual attainment.

The spirit of commercial and foreign adventure, therefore, on the one hand, which had gained so much strength and influence since the time of the discovery of America, and, on the other, the assertion and maintenance of religious liberty, having their source indeed in the Reformation, but continued, diversified, and continually strengthened by the subsequent divisions of sentiment and opinion among the reformers themselves, and this love of religious liberty drawing after it, or bringing along with it, as it always does, an ardent devotion to the principle of civil liberty also, were the powerful influences under which character was formed, and men trained for the great work of introducing English civilization, English law, and, what is more than all, Anglo-Saxon blood, into the wilderness of North America. Raleigh and his companions may be considered as the creatures, principally, of the first of these causes. Highspirited, full of the love of personal adventure, excited too, in some degree, by the hopes of sudden riches from the discovery of mines of the precious metals, and not unwilling to diversify the labors of settling a colony with occasional cruising against the Spaniards in the West Indian seas, they crossed and recrossed the ocean with a frequency which surprises us when we consider the state of navigation, and which evinces a most daring spirit.

The other cause peopled New England. The "May-flower" sought our shores under no high wrought spirit of commercial adventure, no love of gold, no mixture of purpose, warlike or hostile, to any human being. Like the dove from the ark, she had put forth only to find rest. Solemn supplications on the shore of the sea in Holland had invoked for her, at her departure, the blessings of Providence. The stars which guided her were the unobscured constellations of civil and religious liberty. Her deck was the altar of the living God. Fervent prayers from bended knees mingled, morning and evening, with the voices of ocean and the sighing of the wind in her shrouds. Every prosperous breeze, which, gently swelling her sails, helped the Pilgrims onward in their course, awoke new anthems of praise; and when the elements were wrought into fury, neither the tempest, tossing their fragile bark like a feather, nor the darkness and howling of the midnight storm, ever disturbed, in man or woman, the firm and settled purpose of their souls, to undergo all, and to do all, that the meekest patience, the boldest resolution, and the highest trust in God, could enable human beings to suffer or to perform.

Some differences may, doubtless, be traced at this day, between the descendants of the early colonists of Virginia and those of New England, owing to the different influences and different circumstances under which the respective settlements were made; but only enough to create a pleasing variety in the midst of a general family resemblance.

"―――― facies, non omnibus una,
Nec diversa tamen, qualem decet esse sorores."

But the habits, sentiments, and objects of both, soon became modified by local causes, growing out of their condition in the New World; and as this condition was essentially alike in both, and as both at once adopted the same general rules and principles of English jurisprudence, and became accustomed to the authority of representative bodies, these differences gradually diminished. They disappeared by the progress of time and the influence of intercourse. The necessity of some degree of union and coöperation to defend themselves against the savage tribes, tended to excite in them mutual respect and regard. They fought together in the wars against France. The great and common cause of the Revolution bound them to one another by new links of brotherhood; and finally, fortunately, happily and gloriously, the present constitution of government united them to form the great republic of the world, and bound up their interest and fortunes, till the whole earth sees that there is now for them, in present possession, as well as future hope, only "one country, one Constitution, and one destiny."

The colonization of the tropical region, and the whole of the southern parts of the continent, by Spain and Portugal, was conducted on other principles, under the influence of other motives, and followed by far different consequences. From the time of its discovery, the Spanish government pushed forward its settlements in America, not only with vigor, but with eagerness; so that long before the first permanent English settlement had been accomplished, in what is now the United States, Spain had conquered Mexico, Peru, and Chili, and stretched her power over nearly all the territory she ever acquired in this continent. The rapidity of these conquests is to be ascribed, in a great degree, to the eagerness, not to say the rapacity of those numerous bands of adventurers, who were stimulated by individual interests and private hopes, to subdue immense regions, and take possession of them in the name of the crown of Spain. The mines of gold and silver were the excitements to these efforts, and accordingly settlements were generally made, and Spanish authority established, on the immediate eve of the subjugation of territory, that the native population might be set to work by their new Spanish masters, in the mines.

From these facts, the love of gold — gold, not produced by industry, nor accumulated by commerce, but gold dug from its native bed in the bowels of the earth, and that earth ravished from its rightful possessors by every possible degree of enormity, cruelty, and crime, was long the governing passion in Spanish wars and Spanish settlements in America. Even Columbus himself did not wholly escape the influence of this base motive. In his early voyages we find him passing from island to island, inquiring everywhere for gold; as if God had opened the New World to the knowledge of the Old only to gratify a passion equally senseless and sordid; and to offer up millions of an unoffending race of men to the destruction of the sword, sharpened both by cruelty and rapacity. And yet Columbus was far above his age and country. Enthusiastic, indeed, but sober, religious, and magnanimous; born to great things and capable of high sentiments, as his noble discourse before Ferdinand and Isabella, as well as the whole history of his life, shows. Probably he sacrificed much to the known sentiments of others, and addressed to his followers motives likely to influence them. At the same time it is evident that he himself looked upon the world which he discovered as a world of wealth, all ready to be seized and enjoyed.

The conquerors and the European settlers of Spanish America were mainly military commanders and common soldiers. The monarchy of Spain was not transferred to this hemisphere, but it acted in it. as it acted at home, through its ordinary means, and its true representative, military force. The robbery and destruction of the native race was the achievement of standing armies, in the right of the king, and by his authority; fighting, in his name, for the aggrandizement of his power and the extension of his prerogatives; with military ideas under arbitrary maxims, a portion of that dreadful instrumentality by which a perfect despotism governs a people. As there was no liberty in Spain, how could liberty be transmitted to Spanish colonies?

The colonists of English America were of the people, and a people already free. They were of the middle, industrious, and already prosperous class, the inhabitants of commercial and manufacturing cities, among whom liberty first revived and respired, after a sleep of a thousand years in the bosom of the dark ages. Spain descended on the New World in the armed and terrible image of her monarchy and her soldiery; England approached it in the winning and popular garb of personal rights, public protection, and civil freedom. England transplanted liberty to America; Spain transplanted power. England, through the agency of private companies and the efforts of individuals, colonized this part of North America by industrious individuals, making their own way in the wilderness, defending themselves against the savages, recognizing their right to the soil, and with a general honest purpose of introducing knowledge, as well as Christianity, among them. Spain stooped on South America, like a falcon on its prey. Everything was force. Territories were acquired by fire and sword. Cities were destroyed by fire and sword. Hundreds of thousands of human beings fell by fire and sword. Even conversion to Christianity was attempted by fire and sword.

Behold, then, fellow-citizens, the difference resulting from the operation of the two principles! Here, to-day, on the summit of Bunker Hill, and at the foot of this monument, behold the difference! I would that the fifty thousand voices present could proclaim it, with a shout which should be heard over the globe. Our inheritance was of liberty, secured and regulated by law, and enlightened by religion and knowledge; that of South America was of power, stern, unrelenting, tyrannical, military power. And now look to the consequences of the two principles on the general and aggregate happiness of the human race. Behold the results, in all the regions conquered by Cortez and Pizarro, and the contrasted results here. I suppose the territory of the United States may amount to one-eighth, or one-tenth, of that colonized by Spain on this continent; and yet in all that vast region there are but between one and two millions of people of European color and European blood; while in the United States there are fourteen millions who rejoice in their descent from the people of the more northern part of Europe.

But we may follow the difference, in the original principle of colonization, and in its character and objects, still further. We must look to moral and intellectual results; we must consider consequences, not only as they show themselves in the greater or less multiplication of men, or the greater or less supply of their physical wants, but in their civilization, improvement, and happiness. We must inquire what progress has been made in the true science of liberty, in the knowledge of the great principles of self-government, and in the progress of man, as a social, moral, and religious being.

I would not willingly say anything on this occasion discourteous to the new governments, founded on the demolition of the power of the Spanish monarchy. They are yet on their trial, and I hope for a favorable result. But truth, sacred truth, and fidelity to the cause of civil liberty, compel me to say, that hitherto they have discovered quite too much of the spirit of that monarchy from which they separated themselves. Quite too frequent resort is made to military force; and quite too much of the substance of the people consumed in maintaining armies, not for defence against foreign aggression, but for enforcing obedience to domestic authority. Standing armies are the oppressive instruments for governing the people in the hands of hereditary and arbitrary monarchs. A military republic, a government founded on mock elections, and supported only by the sword, is a movement indeed, but a retrograde and disastrous movement, from the regular and old-fashioned monarchical systems.

If men would enjoy the blessings of republican government, they must govern themselves by reason, by mutual counsel, and consultation, by a sense and feeling of general interest, and by the acquiescence of the minority in the will of the majority, properly expressed; and above all, the military must be kept, according to the language of our Bill of Rights, in strict subordination to the civil authority. Wherever this lesson is not both learned and practised, there can be no political freedom. Absurd, preposterous is it — a scoff and a satire on free forms of constitutional·liberty, for frames of government to be prescribed by military leaders, and the right of suffrage to be exercised at the point of the sword.

Making all allowance for situation and climate, it cannot be doubted by intelligent minds that the difference now existing between North and South America is justly attributable, in a great degree, to political institutions in the Old World and in the New. And how broad that difference is! Suppose an assembly, in one of the valleys, or on the side of one of the mountains of the southern half of the hemisphere, to be held, this day, in the neighborhood of a large city;—what would be the scene presented? Yonder is a volcano, flaming and smoking, but shedding no light, moral or intellectual. At its foot is the mine, yielding, perhaps, sometimes, large gains to capital, but in which labor is destined to eternal and unrequited toil, and followed only by penury and beggary. The city is filled with armed men; not a free people, armed and coming forth voluntarily to rejoice in a public festivity; but hireling troops, supported by forced loans, excessive impositions on commerce, or taxes wrung from a half-fed, and a half-clothed population. For the great, there are palaces covered with gold; for the poor, there are hovels of the meanest sort. There is an ecclesiastical hierarchy, enjoying the wealth of princes; but there are no means of education to the people. Do public improvements favor intercourse between place and place? So far from this, the traveller cannot pass from town to town without danger, every mile, of robbery and assassination. I would not overcharge or exaggerate this picture; but its principal sketches are all too true.

And how does it contrast with the scene now actually before us? Look around upon these fields; they are verdant and beautiful, well cultivated, and at this moment loaded with the riches of the early harvest. The hands which till them are free owners of the soil, enjoying equal rights, and protected by law from oppression and tyranny. Look to the thousand vessels in our sight, filling the harbor, or covering the neighboring sea. They are the instruments of a profitable commerce, carried on by men who know that the profits of their hardy enterprise, when they make them, are their own; and this commerce is encouraged and regulated by wise laws, and defended, when need be, by the valor and patriotism of the country.

Look to that fair city, the abode of so much diffused wealth, so much general happiness and comfort, so much personal independence, and so much general knowledge, and not undistinguished, I may be permitted to add, for hospitality and social refinement. She fears no forced contributions, no siege or sacking from military leaders of rival factions. The hundred temples, in which her citizens worship God, are in no danger of sacrilege. The regular administration of the laws encounters no obstacle. The long processions of children and youth, which you see this day, issuing by thousands from her free schools, prove the care and anxiety with which a popular government provides for the education and morals of the people. Everywhere there is order; everywhere there is security. Everywhere the law reaches to the highest, and reaches to the lowest, to protect all in their rights, and to restrain all from wrong; and over all hovers liberty, that liberty which our fathers fought and fell for on this very spot, with her eye ever watchful, and her eagle wing ever wide outspread.

The colonies of Spain, from their origin to their end, were subject to the sovereign authority of the kingdom. Their government, as well as their commerce, was a strict home monopoly. If we add to this, the established usage of filling important posts in the administration of the colonies exclusively by natives of old Spain, thus cutting off forever all hopes of honorable preferment from every man born in the Western hemisphere, causes enough rise up before us at once to account fully for the subsequent history and character of these provinces. The Viceroys and Provincial Governors of Spain were never at home in their governments in America. They did not feel that they were of the people whom they governed. Their official character and employment have a good deal of resemblance to those of the pro-consuls of Rome in Asia, Sicily, and Gaul; but obviously no resemblance to those of Carver and Winthrop, and very little to those of the Governors of Virginia after that colony had established a popular House of Burgesses.

The English colonists in America, generally speaking, were men who were seeking new homes in a new world. They brought with them their families and all that was most dear to them. This was especially the case with the colonists of Plymouth and Massachusetts. Many of them were educated men, and all possessed their full share, according to their social condition, of the knowledge and attainments of that age. The distinctive characteristic of their settlement is the introduction of the civilization of Europe into a wilderness, without bringing with it the political institutions of Europe. The arts, sciences, and literature of England came over with the settlers. That great portion of the common law which regulates the social and personal relations and conduct of men came also. The jury came; the habeas corpus came; the testamentary power came; and the law of inheritance and descent came also, except that part of it which recognizes the rights of primogeniture, which either did not come at all, or soon gave way to the rule of equal partition of estates among children. But the monarchy did not come, nor the aristocracy, nor the church, as an estate of the realm. Political institutions were to be framed anew such as should be adapted to the state of things. But it could not be doubtful what should be the nature and character of these institutions. A general social equality prevailed among the settlers, and an equality of political rights seemed the natural, if not the necessary consequence.

After forty years of revolution, violence, and war, the people of France have placed at the head of the fundamental instrument of their government, as the great boon obtained by all their sufferings and sacrifices, the declaration, that all Frenchmen are equal before the law. What France has reached only by the expenditure of so much blood and treasure, and the exhibition of so much crime, the English colonists obtained by simply changing their place, carrying with them the intellectual and moral culture of Europe, and the personal and social relations to which they were accustomed, but leaving behind their political institutions. It has been said with much vivacity that the felicity of the American colonists consisted in their escape from the past. This is true so far as respects political establishments, but no further. They brought with them a full portion of all the riches of the past, in science, in art, in morals, religion, and literature. The Bible came with them. And it is not to be doubted that to the free and universal reading of the Bible, in that age, men were much indebted for right views of civil liberty. The Bible is a book of faith, and a book of doctrine, and a book of morals, and a book of religion, of especial revelation from God; but it is also a book which teaches man his own individual responsibility, his own dignity, and his equality with his fellow-man.

Bacon, and Locke, and Milton, and Shakspere, also came with the colonists. These colonists came to form new political systems, but all that belonged to cultivated man, to family, to neighborhood, to social relations, accompanied them. In the Doric phrase of one of our own historians, "they came to settle on bare creation"; but their settlement in the wilderness, nevertheless, was not a lodgement of nomade tribes, a mere resting-place of roaming savages. It was the beginning of a permanent community, the fixed residence of cultivated men. Not only was English literature read, but English, good English, was spoken and written, before the axe had made way to let in the sun upon the habitations and fields of Plymouth and Massachusetts. And whatever may be said to the contrary, a correct use of the English language is, at this day, more general throughout the United States than it is throughout England herself.

But another grand characteristic is, that, in the English colonies, political affairs were left to be managed by the colonists themselves. This is another fact wholly distinguishing them in character, as it has distinguished them in fortune, from the colonists of Spain. Here lies the foundation of that experience in self-government which has preserved order, and security, and regularity, amidst the play of popular institutions. Home government was the secret of the prosperity of the North American settlements. The more distinguished of the New England colonists, with a most remarkable sagacity, and a long-sighted reach into futurity, refused to come to America unless they could bring with them charters providing for the administration of their affairs in this country. They saw, from the first, the evils of being governed in the New World by counsels held in the Old. Acknowledging the general superiority of the crown, they still insisted on the right of passing local laws, and of local administration. And history teaches us the justice and the value of this determination in the example of Virginia. The early attempts to settle that colony failed, sometimes with the most melancholy and fatal consequences, from want of knowledge, care, and attention on the part of those who had the charge of their affairs in England; and it was only after the issuing of the third charter that its prosperity fairly commenced. The cause was, that by that third charter the people of Virginia (for by this time they deserve to be so called) were allowed to constitute and establish the first popular Representative Assembly which ever convened on this continent — the Virginia House of Burgesses.

The great elements, then, of the American system of government, originally introduced by the colonies, and which were early in operation, and ready to be developed, more and more, as the progress of events should justify or demand, were:

Escape from the existing political systems of Europe, including its religious hierarchies; but the continued possession and enjoyment of its science and arts, its literature, and its manners;

Home government, or the power of making in the colony the municipal laws which were to govern it;

Equality of Rights;

Representative Assemblies, or forms of government founded on popular elections.

Few topics are more inviting, or more fit for philosophical discussion, than the effect of institutions, founded upon these principles, on the happiness of mankind; or, in other words, the influence of the New World upon the Old.

Her obligations to Europe for science and art, laws, literature, and manners, America acknowledges, as she ought, with respect and gratitude. And the people of the United States, descendants of the English stock, grateful for the treasures of knowledge derived from their English ancestors, admit also, with thanks and filial regard, that among those ancestors, under the culture of

Hampden and Sydney, and other assiduous friends, that seed of popular liberty first germinated which on our soil has shot up to its full height, until its branches overshadow all the land.

But America has not failed to make returns. If she has not cancelled the obligation, or equalled it by others of like weight, she has, at least, made respectable advances towards equality. And she admits, that, standing in the midst of civilized nations, and in a civilized age — a nation among nations — there is a high part which she is expected to act, for the general advancement of human interests and human welfare.

American mines have filled the mints of Europe with the precious metals. The productions of the American soil and climate have poured out their abundance of luxuries for the tables of the rich, and of necessaries for the sustenance of the poor. Birds and animals of beauty and value have been added to the European stocks; and transplantations from the transcendant and unequalled riches of our forests have mingled themselves profusely with the elms, and ashes, and druidical oaks of England.

America has made contributions far more vast. Who can estimate the amount, or the value, of the augmentation of the commerce of the world that has resulted from America? Who can imagine to himself what would now be the shock to the Eastern continent if the Atlantic were no longer traversable, or if there were no longer American productions, or American markets?

But America exercises influences, or holds out examples, for the consideration of the Old World, of a much higher, because they are of a moral and political character.

America has furnished to Europe proof of the fact, that popular institutions, founded on equality and the principle of representation, are capable of maintaining governments — able to secure the rights of person, property, and reputation.

America has proved that it is practicable to elevate the mass of mankind — that portion which in Europe is called the laboring, or lower class; to raise them to self-respect, to make them competent to act a part in the great right, and great duty, of self-government; and this she has proved may be done by education and the diffusion of knowledge. She holds out an example, — a thousand times more enchanting than ever was presented before, — to those nine-tenths of the human race who are born without hereditary fortune or hereditary rank.

America has furnished to the world the character of Washington! And if our American institutions had done nothing else, that alone would have entitled them to the respect of mankind.

Washington! "First in war, first in peace, and first in the hearts of his countrymen!" Washington is all our own! The enthusiastic veneration and regard in which the people of the United States hold him, prove them to be worthy of such a countryman; while his reputation abroad reflects the highest honor on his country and its institutions. I would cheerfully put the question to-day to the intelligence of Europe and the world, What character of the century, upon the whole, stands out in the relief of history most pure, most respectable, most sublime? and I doubt not that, by a suffrage approaching to unanimity, the answer would be Washington!

The structure now standing before us, by its uprightness, its solidity, its durability, is no unfit emblem of his character. His public virtues and public principles were as firm as the earth on which it stands; his personal motives, as pure as the serene heaven in which its summit is lost. But, indeed, though a fit, it is an inadequate emblem. Towering high above the column which our hands have builded, beheld, not by the inhabitants of a single city or a single State, but by all the families of man, ascends the colossal grandeur of the character and life of Washington. In all the constituents of the one — in all the acts of the other — in all its titles to immortal love, admiration, and renown — it is an American production. It is the embodiment and vindication of our transatlantic liberty.

Born upon our soil — of parents also born upon it — never for a moment having had sight of the Old World — instructed, according to the modes of his time, only in the spare, plain, but wholesome elementary knowledge which our institutions provide for the children of the people; growing up beneath and penetrated by the genuine influences of American society; living from infancy to manhood, and age, amidst our expanding, but not luxurious, civilization; partaking in our great destiny of labor, our long contest with unreclaimed nature and uncivilized man; our agony of glory, the War of Independence; our great victory of peace, the formation of the Union, and the establishment of the Constitution — he is all — all our own! Washington is ours. That crowded and glorious life —

> "Where multitudes of virtues passed along,
> Each pressing foremost, in the mighty throng
> Ambitious to be seen, then making room
> For greater multitudes that were to come;"

that life was the life of an American citizen.

I claim him for America. In all the perils, in every darkened moment of the State, in the midst of the reproaches of enemies and the misgiving of friends, I turn to that transcendent name for courage and for consolation. To him who denies, or doubts, whether our fervid liberty can be combined with law, with order, with the security of property, with the pursuits and advancement of happiness; to him who denies that our institutions are capable of producing exaltation of soul, and the passion of true glory — to him who denies that we have contributed anything to the stock of great lessons and great examples — to all these I reply by pointing to Washington!

And now, friends and fellow-citizens, it is time to bring this discourse to a close.

We have indulged in gratifying recollections of the past, in the prosperity and pleasures of the present, and in high hopes of the future. But let us remember that we have duties and obligations to perform corresponding to the blessings which we enjoy. Let us remember the trust, the sacred trust, attaching to the rich inheritance which we have received from our fathers. Let us feel our personal responsibility, to the full extent of our power and influence, for the preservation of our institutions of civil and religious liberty. And let us remember that it is only religion, and morals, and knowledge, that can make men respectable and happy under any form of government. Let us hold fast the great truth, that communities are responsible, as well as individuals; that no government is respectable which is not just; that without unspotted purity of public faith, without sacred public principle, fidelity, and honor, no mere forms of government, no machinery of laws, can give dignity to political society. In our day and generation let us seek to raise and improve the moral sentiment, so that we may look, not for a degraded, but for an elevated and improved future. And when we, and our children, shall all have been consigned to the house appointed for all living, may love of country — and pride of country — glow with equal fervor among those to whom our names and our blood shall have descended! And then, when honored and decrepid age shall lean against the base of this monument, and troops of ingenuous youth shall be gathered round it, and when the one shall speak to the other of its objects, the purposes of its construction, and the great and glorious events with which it is connected — there shall rise, from every youthful breast, the ejaculation — "Thank God, I — I also — AM AN AMERICAN."

GREENOUGH'S DESIGN FOR CORNERS OF PLATFORM.

APPENDIX F.

GRANDMOTHER'S STORY OF BUNKER HILL BATTLE,

AS SHE SAW IT FROM THE BELFRY.[1]

By Dr. Oliver Wendell Holmes.

'Tis like stirring living embers when, at eighty, one remembers
All the achings and the quakings of " the times that tried men's souls;"
When I talk of *Whig* and *Tory*, when I tell the *R-bel* story,
To you the words are ashes, but to me they're burning coals.

I had heard the muskets' rattle of the April running battle;
Lord Percy's hunted soldiers, I can see their red coats still;
But a deadly chill comes o'er me, as the day looms up before me,
When a thousand men lay bleeding on the slopes of Bunker's Hill.

'Twas a peaceful summer's morning, when the first thing gave us warning
Was the booming of the cannon from the river and the shore:
" Child," says grandma, " what's the matter, what is all this noise and clatter?
Have those scalping Indian devils come to murder us once more?"

Poor old soul! my sides were shaking in the midst of all my quaking.
To hear her talk of Indians when the guns began to roar:
She had seen the burning village, and the slaughter and the pillage,
When the Mohawks killed her father with their bullets through his door.

---

[1] Copyright, 1875, by James R. Osgood & Co. Used by permission of, and by arrangement with, Messrs. Houghton, Mifflin & Co.

Then I said, " Now, dear old granny, don't you fret and worry any,
For I'll soon come back and tell you whether this is work or play;
There can't be mischief in it, so I won't be gone a minute " —
For a minute then I started. I was gone the livelong day.

No time for bodice-lacing or for looking-glass grimacing;
Down my hair went as I hurried, tumbling half-way to my heels;
God forbid your ever knowing, when there's blood around her flowing,
How the lonely, helpless daughter of a quiet household feels!

In the street I heard a thumping; and I knew it was the stumping
Of the Corporal, our old neighbor, on that wooden leg he wore,
With a knot of women round him, — it was lucky I had found him,
So I followed with the others, and the Corporal marched before.

They were making for the steeple, — the old soldier and his people;
The pigeons circled round us as we climbed the creaking stair,
Just across the narrow river — Oh, so close it made me shiver! —
Stood a fortress on the hill-top that but yesterday was bare.

Not slow our eyes to find it; well we knew who stood behind it,
Though the earthwork hid them from us, and the stubborn walls were
    dumb :
Here were sister, wife, and mother, looking wild upon each other,
And their lips were white with terror as they said, THE HOUR HAS COME!

The morning slowly wasted, not a morsel had we tasted,
And our heads were almost splitting with the cannons' deafening thrill,
When a figure tall and stately round the rampart strode sedately;
It was PRESCOTT, one since told me; he commanded on the hill.

Every woman's heart grew bigger when we saw his manly figure,
With the banyan buckled round it, standing up so straight and tall;
Like a gentleman of leisure who is strolling out for pleasure,
Through the storm of shells and cannon-shot he walked around the wall.

At eleven the streets were swarming, for the red-coats' ranks were
    forming;
At noon in marching order they were moving to the piers;
How the bayonets gleamed and glistened, as we looked far down, and
    listened
To the trampling and the drum-beat of the belted grenadiers!

At length the men have started, with a cheer (it seemed faint-hearted),
In their scarlet regimentals, with their knapsacks on their backs,
And the reddening, rippling water, as after a sea-fight's slaughter,
Round the barges gliding onward blushed like blood along their tracks.

So they crossed to the other border, and again they formed in order;
And the boats came back for soldiers, came for soldiers, soldiers still:
The time seemed everlasting to us women faint and fasting, —
At last they're moving, marching, marching proudly up the hill.

We can see the bright steel glancing all along the lines advancing —
Now the front rank fires a volley — they have thrown away their shot;
For behind their earthwork lying, all the balls above them flying,
Our people need not hurry; so they wait and answer not.

Then the Corporal, our old cripple (he would swear sometimes and
    tipple), —
He had heard the bullets whistle (in the old French war) before, —
Calls out in words of jeering, just as if they all were hearing, —
And his wooden leg thumps fiercely on the dusty belfry floor : —

"Oh! fire away, ye villains, and earn King George's shillin's,
But ye'll waste a ton of powder afore a 'rebel' falls:
You may bang the dirt and welcome, they're as safe as Dan'l Malcolm
Ten foot beneath the gravestone that you've splintered with your
    balls!"

In the hush of expectation, in the awe and trepidation
Of the dread approaching moment, we are well-nigh breathless all;
Though the rotten bars are failing on the rickety belfry railing,
We are crowding up against them like the waves against a wall.

Just a glimpse (the air is clearer), they are nearer, — nearer, — nearer,
When a flash — a curling smoke-wreath — then a crash — the steeple shakes —
The deadly truce is ended; the tempest's shroud is rended;
Like a morning mist it gathered, like a thunder-cloud it breaks!

O the sight our eyes discover as the blue-black smoke blows over!
The red-coats stretched in windrows as a mower rakes his hay;
Here a scarlet heap is lying, there a headlong crowd is flying
Like a billow that has broken and is shivered into spray.

Then we cried, "The troops are routed! they are beat — it can't be doubted!
God be thanked, the fight is over!" — Ah! the grim old soldier's smile!
"Tell us, tell us why you look so?" (we could hardly speak, we shook so), —
"Are they beaten? *Are* they beaten? ARE they beaten?" — "Wait a while."

O the trembling and the terror! for too soon we saw our error:
They are baffled, not defeated; we have driven them back in vain;
And the columns that were scattered, round the colors that were tattered,
Toward the sullen silent fortress turn their belted breasts again.

All at once, as we are gazing, lo! the roofs of Charlestown blazing!
They have fired the harmless village; in an hour it will be down!
The Lord in Heaven confound them, rain his fire and brimstone round them, —
The robbing, murdering red-coats that would burn a peaceful town!

They are marching, stern and solemn; we can see each massive column
As they near the naked earth-mound with the slanting walls so steep.
Have our soldiers got faint-hearted, and in noiseless haste departed?
Are they panic-struck and helpless? Are they palsied or asleep?

APPENDIX F.   249

Now! the walls they're almost under! scarce a rod the foes asunder!
Nor a firelock flashed against them! up the earthwork they will swarm!
But the words have scarce been spoken, when the ominous calm is
    broken,
And a bellowing crash has emptied all the vengeance of the storm!

So again, with murderous slaughter, pelted backwards to the water,
Fly Pigot's running heroes and the frightened braves of Howe;
And we shout, " At last they're done for, it's their barges they have
    run for:
They are beaten, beaten, beaten ; and the battle's over now!"

And we looked, poor timid creatures, on the rough old soldier's features,
Our lips afraid to question, but he knew what we would ask :
" Not sure," he said ; " keep quiet, — once more, I guess, they'll try
    it —
Here's damnation to the cut-throats!"——then he handed me his flask,

Saying, "Gal, you're looking shaky; have a drop of old Jamaiky;
I'm afeard there'll be more trouble afore the job is done ; "
So I took one scorching swallow ; dreadful faint I felt and hollow,
Standing there from early morning when the firing was begun.

All through those hours of trial I had watched a calm clock dial,
As the hands kept creeping, creeping, — they were creeping round to
    four,
When the old man said, " They're forming with their bagonets fixed for
    storming :
It's the death-grip that's a coming, — they will try the works once
    more."

With brazen trumpets blaring, the flames behind them glaring,
The deadly wall before them, in close array they come ;
Still onward, upward toiling, like a dragon's fold uncoiling, —
Like the rattlesnake's shrill warning the reverberating drum!

Over heaps all torn and gory — shall I tell the fearful story,
How they surged above the breastwork, as a sea breaks over a deck;
How, driven, yet scarce defeated, our worn-out men retreated,
With their powder-horns all emptied, like the swimmers from a wreck?

It has all been told and painted; as for me, they say I fainted,
And the wooden-legged old Corporal stumped with me down the stair:
When I woke from dreams affrighted the evening lamps were lighted, —
On the floor a youth was lying; his bleeding breast was bare.

And I heard through all the flurry, "Send for WARREN! hurry! hurry!
Tell him here's a soldier bleeding, and he'll come and dress his wound!"
Ah, we knew not till the morrow told its tale of death and sorrow,
How the starlight found him stiffened on the dark and bloody ground.

Who the youth was, what his name was, where the place from which
   he came was,
Who had brought him from the battle, and had left him at our door,
He could not speak to tell us; but 'twas one of our brave fellows,
As the homespun plainly showed us which the dying soldier wore.

For they all thought he was dying, as they gathered round him crying, —
And they said, "Oh, how they'll miss him!" and, "What *will* his
   mother do?"
Then his eyelids just unclosing like a child's that has been dozing,
He faintly murmured, "Mother!" —— and — I saw his eyes were blue.

— "Why, grandma, how you're winking!" — Ah, my child, it sets me
   thinking
Of a story not like this one. Well, he somehow lived along;
So we came to know each other, and I nursed him like a — mother,
Till at last he stood before me, tall, and rosy-cheeked, and strong.

And we sometimes walked together in the pleasant summer weather;
— "Please to tell us what his name was?" — Just your own, my little
   dear, —
There's his picture Copley painted: we became so well acquainted,
That, — in short, that's why I'm grandma, and you children all are
   here!

APPENDIX G.

As this book is especially devoted to the actions of the rank and file of our army, the following items may be of interest as showing the manual of arms in use at that period. Our Colonial troops were undoubtedly drilled upon the English pattern, or, if not, we are naturally interested to know the precision of drill attained by those regular troops with which our volunteers were confronted.

In 1743 there was printed here a book with the title, "An Abstract of Military Discipline; more particularly with Regard to the Manu*el* (sic) Exercise, Evolutions, and Firings of the FOOT, from Col. Bland. Boston, Printed by Rogers & Fowle, for D. Henchman in Cornhill, 1743. sm. 8vo., pp. 64." This was doubtless the text-book in use by our companies, training in every village. In the "London Magazine and Monthly Chronologer" for 1746, I find the following eight pages of illustrations of the Manual Exercise of the Foot-Guards, which is identical with Col. Bland's treatise as reprinted, except that the latter confessedly omits the bayonet exercise. This Manual indeed is of earlier date, as I find in "Notes and Queries," 2d S., vol. ix., pp. 76, 77, and 109, the "Exercise that was Introduced in Flanders, by Lieut. Gen. Ingoldsby, in 1706–7." The orders are almost identical with those used in 1740, and we thus are presented with a lively picture of the English soldier during the whole period from Marlborough's Wars to our Revolution.

There is indeed a possibility that our troops had, at least in part, been instructed under a simpler form. In 1768 there appeared in Boston a book thus entitled: "[The Manual Exercise] extracted from the Plan of Discipline, for the Norfolk Militia. Boston: New England: Printed by Richard Draper, Printer to His Excellency the Governor and the Honorable His Majesty's Council, 1768. Sold at his Printing-Office in Newbury-Street. Price, One Pistareen. small 8vo., pp. 104."

The MANUAL EXERCISE of the FOOT GUARDS.

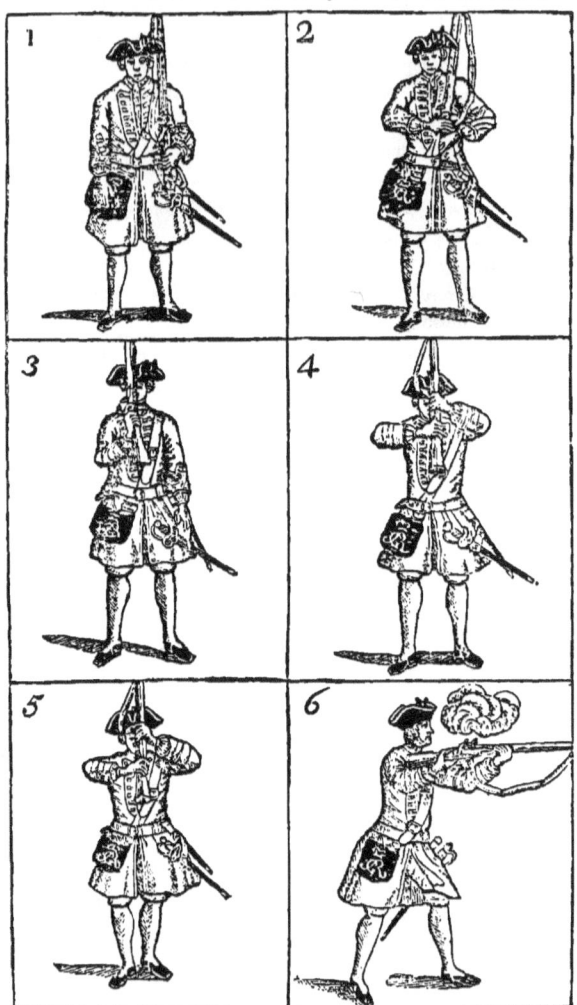

1 Take Care.   2 Join your Right-Hand to your Firelock.   3 Prife your Firelock.
4 Join your Left-Hand to your Firelock,   5 Cock your Firelock,   6 Prefent. Fire.

The MANUAL EXERCISE of the FOOT GUARDS.

7. Recover your Arms. *See Fig.* 12. Halfcock your Firelock. 8. Handle your Primer. 9. Prime, *the first Motion.* 10. Prime, *the last Motion.* 11. Shut your Pan. 12. Cast about to charge, *the first Motion.*

The Manual Exercise, &c.

13 Cast about to charge. 14 Handle your Cartridge. 15 Open your Cartridge
16 Charge with Cartridge. 17 Draw your Rammer, the first Motion. 18 Draw
your Rammer, the last Motion.

The MANUAL EXERCISE of the FOOT GUARDS.

19 Shorten your Rammer, *the firſt Motion.*   20 Shorten your Rammer.   21 Put them in the Barrel.   22 Ram down your Charge.   23 Recover your Rammer Shorten your Rammer. *See Fig.* 19.   24 Return your Rammer.

The MANUAL EXERCISE, &c.

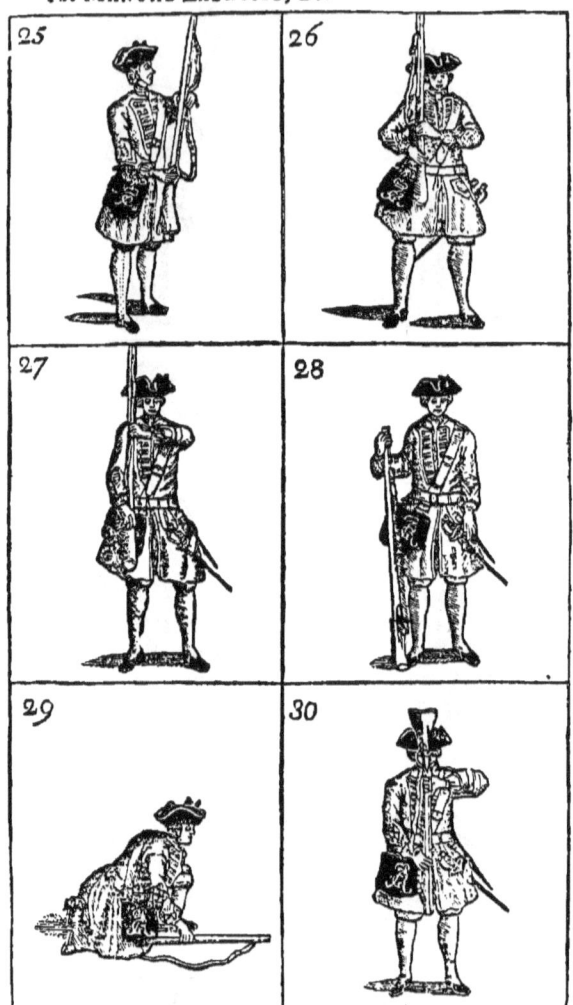

25. Caſt off your Firelock. *See Fig.* 13. Your right Hand under your Lock.
26. Poiſe. *See Fig.* 2. Shoulder. *See Fig.* 1. Reſt your Firelock. 27. Order your Firelock, *the firſt Motion.* 28. Order your Firelock, *the laſt Motion.* 29. Ground your Firelock. Take up your Firelock. *See Fig.* 28. 30. Reſt. *See Fig.* 26. Club your Firelock, *the firſt Motion.*

The MANUAL EXERCISE of the FOOT-GUARDS.

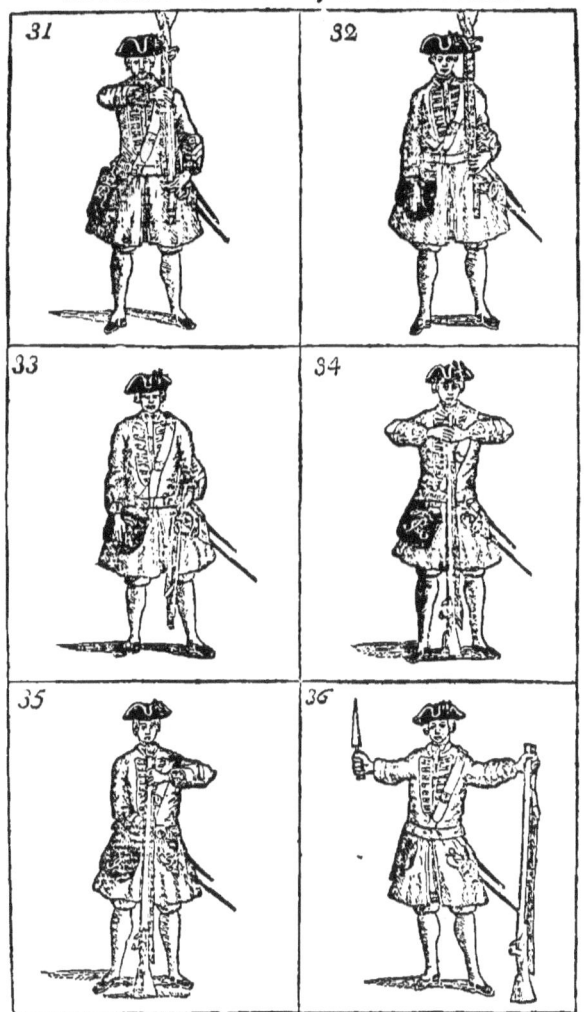

31. Club your Firelock, *the third Motion.* 32. Club your Firelock, *the laſt Motion.*
33. Reſt. *See Fig.* 26. Secure your Firelock. 34. Shoulder. *See Fig.* 1. Poiſe.
See Fig. 3. Reſt on your Arms. 35. Draw your Bayonet, *the firſt Motion.* 36. Draw
your Bayonet.

The Manual Exercise, &c.

37 Fix your Bayonet.   38 Rest your Bayonet.   39 Charge your Bayonet
Breast-high, *the second Motion.*   40 Charge your Bayonet Breast-high.   41 Push
your Bayonet.   42 Recover your Bayonet.

The MANUAL EXERCISE of the FOOT GUARDS.

43 Reft your Bayonet on your Left Arm.   44 Reft, *see Fig.* 26.   Shoulder, *see Fig.* 1.   Prefent your Arms.   45 To the Right 4 Times.   46 To the Right about.   47 To the Left as you were, *see Fig.* 44.   To the Left 4 Times.   48 To the Left about, *see Fig.* 46.   To the Right as you were, *see Fig.* 44.   Poife, *see Fig.* 3.   Reft on your Arms, *see Fig.* 34.   Unfix your Bayonet.   Return your Bayonet, *see Fig.* 35.   Poife, *see Fig.* 3.   Shoulder, *see Fig.* 1.

(259)

It appears that in August, 1774, the Worcester county Convention voted "that the Norfolk exercise be adopted" (Journal, p. 639); and again "to request the Provincial Congress to establish the Norfolk exercise with such alterations as they shall think proper, instead of the exercise of 1764." (Journal, p. 646.) The First Provincial Congress (Journal, p. 41) had on Oct. 28, 1774, resolved "That it be recommended to the inhabitants of this province, that in order to their perfecting themselves in the military art, they proceed in the method ordered by his majesty in the year 1764, it being, in the opinion of this Congress, best calculated for appearance and defence." Nov. 25, the Worcester petition was received and referred; Dec. 9, a special committee was directed to consider it, and also "a plan of military exercise proposed by Capt. Timothy Pickering." Dec. 8, the committee reported, "the report was read and accepted," but what it was, is not stated. (Journal, pp. 41, 48, 50, 67, 74.)

To return to the manual possibly in use in 1775. The Norfolk system was in use in the county of Norfolk, England. The Boston reprint of 1768 has the following preface: "The following Exercise originally designed for the Norfolk Militia, being found to be more concise and easy, and thereby better adapted to Militia than any other; I do hereby direct and order that it be used by the Officers of all the Regiments of Foot within this Province, in training the Soldiers under their several Commands. Fra. Barnard. Boston, May 2, 1768."

This Manual is: —

1. Rest ⎫
2. Order ⎪
3. Ground ⎪
4. Take up ⎬ Your Firelocks.
5. Rest   ⎪
6. Shoulder ⎪
7. Club   ⎪
8. Shoulder ⎪
9. Secure ⎭
10. Shoulder.
11. Fix your Bayonets.
12. Shoulder.
13. { Carry your Firelocks on your right arms.
14. Shoulder.
15. Present your Arms.
16. Face to the Right.
17. To the Right.
18. To the Right about.
19. Face to the Left.

20. To the Left.
21. To the Left about.
22. Charge your Bayonets.
23. Recover your Arms.
24. Prime and Load.
25. Shoulder.
26. As Front Rank, make Ready.
27. Present.
28. Fire.
29. Shoulder.
30. As Center Rank, make Ready.
31. Present.
32. Fire.
33. Shoulder.
34. As Rear Rank, make Ready.

35. Present.
36. Fire.
37. Shoulder.
38. Rear Ranks, close to the Front, March.
39. Make Ready.
40. Present.
41. Fire.
42. Charge your Bayonets.
43. Recover your Arms.
44. Rear Ranks, take your former Distance.
45. March.
46. Halt, Front.
47. Shut your Pans.
48. Shoulder.
49. Return your Bayonets.
50. Shoulder.

The Continental Army was finally drilled under the Manual introduced by Baron Steuben. It was prescribed by Congress March 29, 1779, and one of the early editions of the Regulations was printed in 1793 at Boston "printed and sold by John W. Folsom, Union street, sold also by John Norman, Newbury street." It contains 8 plates. Another edition was issued in 1794 at Boston, for David West, No. 36 Marlborough St., and John West, No. 75 Cornhill. Doolittle engraved the plates. It contains also the United States Militia Act of May 8, 1792, the Massachusetts Act of June 22, 1793, and the Articles of War of Oct. 24, 1786. The Massachusetts Act, § 28, declared the United States rules and regulations should be observed by the militia, and that every commissioned officer should "immediately provide himself with a book containing those rules."

In 1802, William Norman, Book and Chart Seller, published at Boston a new edition, containing "nine copper-plates, including a plate exhibiting the various motions of the Manual Exercise." Probably the new plates were engraved by John Norman.

This extra plate, as it gives a lively picture of the so-called Continental costume, as well as the Manual, is here reproduced.

In 1807, William Pelham, of Boston, printed a new edition with Norman's plates, "the whole published under the inspection of the Adjutant-General of Massachusetts." In the same year Backus & Whiting, of Albany, issued an edition, perhaps not the first, of the Regulations, with different engravings. I am informed by high authority, that portions of Steuben's rules still stand unchanged in the present U.S. Manual.

That a great change took place later on is evident from "A General System of British Tactics and Military Arrangement" &c., published by T. Egerton in London, in 1809, and prepared by Capt. J. H. Whitmore. The Manual Exercise is thus set forth —

Secure Arms.	Carry Arms.
Shoulder Arms.	Make Ready.
Order Arms.	Present.
Fix Bayonets.	Fire.
Shoulder Arms.	Load.
Present Arms.	Handle cartridge.
Shoulder Arms.	Prime.
Port Arms.	About.
Charge Bayonets.	Draw ramrods.
Shoulder Arms.	Ram down cartridge.
Advance Arms.	Return ramrods.
Shoulder Arms.	Shoulder Arms.
Support Arms.	

We pass from this detail, to the actual Articles of War under which our troops were enlisted, and by which they were governed at the time of the battle of Bunker Hill. Feb. 9, 1774, the Provincial Congress appointed Col. Palmer, Col. Cushing and Mr. [Nathan] Cushing of Scituate, a committee "to prepare all such rules and regulations, for the officers and men of the constitutional army which may be raised in this province, as shall be necessary for the good order thereof." April 5th, their report was read and passed and is set forth in the Journal, pp. 120–129. It was also printed in a pamphlet shape and is here reprinted.

II. Co‑

‑tridge

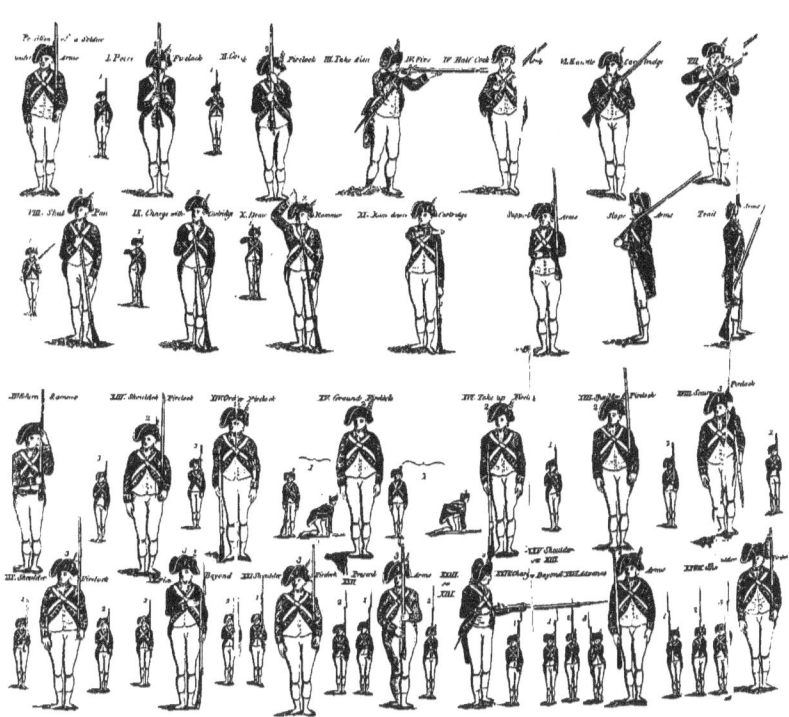

RULES AND REGULATIONS
FOR THE
MASSACHUSETTS ARMY.

PUBLISHED BY ORDER.

SALEM:
PRINTED BY SAMUEL AND EBENEZER HALL.
1775.

IN PROVINCIAL CONGRESS,
Concord, April 5th, 1775.

WHEREAS the Lust of Power, which of old oppressed, persecuted and exiled our pious and virtuous Ancestors, from their fair Possessions in Britain, now pursues, with tenfold Severity, us, their guiltless Children, who are unjustly and wickedly charged with Licentiousness, Sedition, Treason and Rebellion; and being deeply impressed with a Sense of the almost incredible Fatigues and Hardships our venerable Progenitors encountered, who fled from Oppression for the sake of civil and religious Liberty for themselves and their Offspring, and began a Settlement here, on bare Creation, at their own Expence; and having seriously considered the duty we owe to GOD, to the Memory of such invincible Worthies, to the King, to Great-Britain, our Country, ourselves and Posterity, do think it an indispensable Duty, by all lawful Ways and Means in our Power, to recover, maintain, defend and preserve, the free exercise of all those civil and religious Rights and Liberties for which many of our Fore-Fathers fought, — bled — and died; and to hand them down entire for the free Enjoyment of the latest Posterity: And whereas the keeping of a standing Army in any of these Colonies in Times of Peace, without the Consent of the Legislature of that Colony in which such an Army is kept, is against Law: And whereas such an Army, with a large naval Force, is now placed in the Harbour of Boston, for the purpose of subjecting us to the Power of the British Parliament: And whereas we are frequently told by the Tools of Administration, Dupes to ministerial Usurpation, that Great-Britain will not, in any Degree, relax in her Measures, until we acknowledge her " Right to make Laws binding upon us in all Cases whatsoever;" and that if we *refuse to be Slaves, if we persist in our Denial of her Claim, the Dispute must be decided by Arms, in which, 'tis said by our Enemies, — "We shall "have no Chance, being undisciplined, Cowards, disobedient, impatient "of Command, and possessed of that Spirit of levelling which admits of "no Order, Subordination, Rule or Government:" — And whereas, from the ministerial Army and Fleet now at Boston, the large Reinforcement of Troops expected, the late circular Letters to the Governors upon the Continent, the general Tenor of Intelligence from Great-Britain, and the hostile Preparations making here, as also from the Threats and frequent Insults of our Enemies in the capital Town, we have Reason to apprehend that the sudden Destruction of this Colony is in Contemplation, if not determined upon:*

And whereas the great Law of Self-preservation may suddenly require our raising and keeping an Army of Observation and Defence, in order to prevent, or repel, any farther Attempts to enforce the late cruel and oppressive Acts of the British Parliament, which are evidently designed to subject us and the whole Continent to the most ignominious Slavery: And whereas, in Case of raising and keeping such an Army, it will be necessary that the Officers and Soldiers in the same be fully acquainted with their Duty, and that the Articles, Rules and Regulations thereof be made as plain as possible; and having great confidence in the Honour and publick Virtue of the Inhabitants of this Colony, that they will readily obey the Officers chosen by themselves, and will cheerfully do their Duty, when known, without any such severe Articles and Rules (except in capital Cases) and cruel Punishments as are usually practised in standing Armies, and will submit to all such Rules and Regulations as are founded in Reason, Honour and Virtue:

It is therefore RESOLVED, That the following Articles, Rules and Regulations for the Army, that may be raised for the Defence and Security of our Lives, Liberties and Estates, be, and hereby are earnestly recommended. to be strictly adhered to by all Officers, Soldiers and others concerned, as they regard their own Honour and the publick Good.

ARTICLE 1. All Officers and Soldiers, not having just impediment, shall diligently frequent Divine Service and Sermon in the Places appointed for the assembling of the Regiment, Troop or Company to which they belong; and such as wilfully absent themselves, or being present, behave indecently or irreverently, shall, if commissioned Officers, be brought before a regimental Court-Martial, there to be publicly and severely reprimanded by the President; if non-commissioned Officers, or Soldiers. every Person so offending shall for his first Offence forfeit One Shilling to be deducted out of his Wages; — for the second Offence he shall not only forfeit One Shilling, but be confined, not exceeding twenty-four Hours; and for every like Offence shall suffer and pay in like Manner, which Money, so forfeited, shall be applied to the Use of the sick Soldiers of the Troop or Company to which the Offender belongs.

ART. 2. Whatsoever non-commissioned Officer or Soldier shall use any unlawful Oath or Execration, shall incur the Penalties expressed in the first Article; and if a commissioned Officer be thus guilty of profane Cursing or Swearing, he shall forfeit and pay for each and every such Offence the Sum of Four Shillings, lawful Money.

ART. 3. Any Officer or Soldier, who shall behave himself with Contempt or Disrespect towards the General or Generals, or Commanders in Chief of the Massachusetts Forces, or shall speak Words tending to his or their Hurt or Dishonour, shall be punished according to the Nature of his Offence, by the Judgment of a general Court-Martial.

ART. 4. Any Officer or Soldier, who shall begin, excite, cause or join in any Mutiny or Sedition, in the Regiment, Troop or Company to which he belongs, or in any other Regiment, Troop or Company of the Massachusetts Forces, either by Land or Sea, or in any Party, Post, Detachment, or Guard, on any Pretence whatsoever, shall suffer such Punishment as by a general Court-Martial shall be ordered.

ART. 5. Any Officer, non-commissioned Officer, or Soldier, who being present at any Mutiny, or Sedition, does not use his utmost Endeavours to suppress the same, or coming to the Knowledge of any Mutiny, or intended Mutiny, does not, without Delay, give Information thereof to the commanding Officer, shall be punished by Order of a general Court-Martial according to the Nature of his Offence.

ART. 6. Any Officer or Soldier, who shall strike his superior Officer, or draw or offer to draw, or shall lift up any Weapon, or offer any Violence against him, being in the Execution of his Office, on any Pretence whatsoever, or shall disobey any lawful Commands of his superior Officer, shall suffer such Punishment as shall, according to the Nature of his Offence, be ordered by the Sentence of a general Court-Martial.

ART. 7. Any non-commissioned Officer or Soldier, who shall desert, or without Leave of his commanding Officer, absent himself from the Troop or Company to which he belongs, or from any Detachment of the same, shall, upon being convicted thereof, be punished according to the Nature of his Offence, at the Discretion of a general Court-Martial.

ART. 8. Whatsoever Officer or Soldier shall be convicted of having advised or persuaded any other Officer or Soldier to desert, shall suffer such Punishment as shall be ordered by the Sentence of a general Court-Martial.

ART. 9. All Officers, of what Condition soever, shall have Power to part and Quell all Quarrels, Frays, and Disorders, though the Persons concerned should belong to another Regiment, Troop or Company; and either order Officers to be arrested, or non-commissioned Officers or Soldiers to be confined and imprisoned, till their proper superior Officers shall be acquainted therewith; and whoever shall refuse to obey such Officer (though of an inferior Rank) or shall draw his Sword upon him, shall be punished at the Discretion of a general Court-Martial.

ART. 10. No Officer or Soldier shall use any reproachful or provoking Speeches or Gestures to another; nor shall presume to send a Challenge to any Person to fight a Duel: And whoever shall knowingly and willingly suffer any Person whatsoever to go forth to fight a Duel; or shall second, promote, or carry any Challenge, shall be deemed as a Principal: And whatsoever Officer or Soldier shall upbraid another for refusing a Challenge, shall also be considered as a Challenger: And all such offenders, in any of these or such like Cases, shall be punished at the Discretion of a general Court-Martial.

ART. 11. Every Officer commanding in Quarters, or on a March, shall keep good Order, and, to the utmost of his Power, redress all such Abuses, or Disorders, which may be committed by any Officer or Soldier under his command; if upon any Complaint made to him of Officers or Soldiers beating, or otherwise ill-treating any Person, or of committing any Kind of Riot, to the disquieting of the Inhabitants of this Continent; he the said Commander, who shall refuse or omit to see Justice done on the Offender or Offenders, and Reparation made to the Party or Parties injured, as far as the Offenders Wages shall enable him or them, shall, upon due Proof thereof, be punished as Ordered by a general Court-Martial, in such Manner as if he himself had committed the Crimes or Disorders complained of.

ART. 12. If any Officer should think himself to be wronged by his Colonel or the commanding Officer of the Regiment, and shall, upon due Application made to him, be refused to be redressed, he may complain to the General or Commander in Chief of the Massachusetts Forces, in order to obtain Justice, who is hereby required to examine into said Complaint, and see that Justice be done.

ART. 13. If any inferior Officer, or Soldier, shall think himself wronged by his Captain or other Officer commanding the troop or Company to which he belongs, he is to complain thereof to the commanding Officer of the Regiment, who is hereby required to summon a regimental Court-Martial, for the doing Justice to the Complainant; from which regimental Court-Martial, either Party may, if he thinks himself still aggrieved, appeal to a general Court-Martial; but if, upon a second

APPENDIX G. 267

Hearing, the Appeal shall appear to be vexatious and groundless, the Person so appealing shall be punished at the Discretion of the general Court-Martial.

ART. 14. Whatsoever non-commissioned Officer, or Soldier, shall be convicted, at a regimental Court-Martial, of having sold, or designedly, or through neglect, wasted the Ammunition, Arms, or Provisions, or other Military Stores, delivered out to him, to be employed in the Service of this Colony, shall, if an officer, be reduced to a private Centinel; and if a private Soldier, shall suffer such Punishment as shall be ordered by a regimental Court-Martial.

ART. 15. All non-commissioned Officers and Soldiers, who shall be found one Mile from Camp, without Leave in writing from their commanding Officer, shall suffer such Punishment as shall be inflicted on him or them by the Sentence of a regimental Court-Martial.

ART. 16. No Officer or Soldier shall lie out of his Quarters or Camp without Leave from the commanding Officer of the Regiment, upon Penalty of being punished according to the Nature of his Offence, by Order of a regimental Court-Martial.

ART. 17. Every non-commissioned Officer and Soldier shall retire to his Quarters, or Tent, at the beating of the Retreat; in Default of which, he shall be punished according to the Nature of his Offence, by Order of the commanding Officer.

ART. 18. No Officer, non-commissioned Officer, or Soldier, shall fail of repairing, at the Time fixed, to the Place of Parade or Exercise, or other Rendezvous appointed by the commanding Officer, if not prevented by Sickness, or some other evident Necessity; or shall go from the said Place of Rendezvous, or from his Guard, without Leave from his commanding Officer, before he shall be regularly dismissed or relieved, on Penalty of being punished according to the Nature of his Offence, by the Sentence of a regimental Court-Martial.

ART. 19. Whatsoever commissioned Officer shall be found drunk on his Guard, Party or other Duty, under Arms, shall be cashiered for it; any non-commissioned Officer or Soldier, so offending, shall suffer such Punishment as shall be ordered by the Sentence of a regimental Court-Martial.

ART. 20. Whatsoever Centinel shall be found sleeping upon his Post, or shall leave it before he shall be regularly relieved, shall suffer such Punishment as shall be ordered by the Sentence of a general Court-Martial.

ART. 21. Any Person belonging to the Massachusetts Army, who by discharging of Fire-Arms, beating of Drums, or by any other Means whatsover, shall occasion false Alarms, in Camp or Quarters, shall suffer such Punishment as shall be ordered by the Sentence of a general Court-Martial.

ART. 22. Any Officer or Soldier, who shall without urgent Necessity, or without Leave of his superior Officer, quit his Platoon or Division, shall be punished according to the Nature of his Offence, by the Sentence of a regimental Court-Martial.

ART. 23. No Officer or Soldier shall do Violence, or offer any insult, or abuse, to any Person who shall bring Provisions, or other Necessaries, to the Camp or Quarters of the Massachusetts Army; any Officer or Soldier, so offending, shall, upon Complaint being made to the commanding Officer, suffer such Punishment as shall be ordered by a regimental Court-Martial.

ART. 24. Whatsoever Officer or Soldier shall shamefully abandon any Post committed to his Charge, or shall speak Words inducing others to do the like, in Time of an Engagement, shall suffer Death immediately.

ART. 25. Any Person belonging to the Massachusetts Army, who shall make known the Watch-word to any Person who is not intitled to receive it, according to the Rules and Discipline of War, or who shall presume to give a Parole, or Watch-word different from what he received, shall suffer Death, or such other Punishment as shall be ordered by the Sentence of a general Court-Martial.

ART. 26. Whosoever, belonging to the Massachusetts Army, shall relieve the Enemy with Money, Victuals or Ammunition, or shall knowingly harbour or protect an Enemy, shall suffer such Punishment as by a general Court-Martial shall be ordered.

ART. 27. Whosoever, belonging to the Massachusetts Army, shall be convicted of holding Correspondence with, or of giving Intelligence to the Enemy, either directly or indirectly, shall suffer such Punishment as by a general Court-Martial shall be ordered.

ART. 28. All public Stores taken in the Enemy's Camp or Magazines, whether of Artillery, Ammunition, Clothing or Provisions, shall be secured for the Use of the Massachusetts Colony.

ART. 29. If any Officer or Soldier shall leave his Post or Colours, in Time of an Engagement, to go in Search of Plunder, he shall, upon being convicted thereof before a general Court-Martial, suffer such Punishment as by said Court-Martial shall be ordered.

ART. 30. If any Commander of any Post, Intrenchment or Fortress, shall be *compelled*, by the Officers or Soldiers under his Command, to give it up to the Enemy, or to abandon it, the commissioned Officer, non-commissioned Officers or Soldiers who shall be convicted of having so offended, shall suffer Death, or such other Punishment as may be inflicted upon them by the Sentence of a general Court-Martial.

ART. 31. All Suttlers and Retailers to a Camp, and all Persons whatsoever, serving with the Massachusetts Army, in the Field, though not inlisted Soldiers, are to be subject to the Articles, Rules and Regulations of the Massachusetts Army.

ART. 32. No general Court-Martial shall consist of a less Number than thirteen, none of which shall be under the Degree of a commissioned Officer; and the President shall be a Field Officer: And the President of each and every Court-Martial, whether general or regimental, shall have Power to administer an Oath to every Witness, in order to the Trial of Offenders. And the Members of all Courts-Martial shall be duly sworn by the President; and the next in Rank on the Court-Martial shall administer the Oath to the President.

ART. 33. The Members, both of general and regimental Courts-Martial, shall, when belonging to different Corps, take the same Rank which they held in the Army; but when Courts-Martial shall be composed of Officers of one Corps, they shall take their Ranks according to their Commissions by which they are mustered in the said Corps.

ART. 34. All the Members of a Court-Martial, are to behave with Calmness, Decency and Impartiality; and in the giving of their Votes, are to begin with the youngest or lowest in Commission.

ART. 35. No Field Officer shall be tried by any Person under the Degree of a Captain; nor shall any Proceedings or Trials be carried on, excepting between the Hours of eight in the Morning, and three in the Afternoon, excepting in Cases which require an immediate Example.

ART. 36. The Commissioned Officers of every regiment may, by the Appointment of their Colonel or Commanding Officer, hold regimental Courts-Martial for the enquiring into such Disputes or criminal Matters as may come before them, and for the inflicting corporal Punishments for small Offences, and shall give Judgment by the Majority of Voices; but no Sentence shall be executed till the commanding Officer (not being a Member of the Court-Martial) shall have confirmed the same.

ART. 37. No regimental Court-Martial shall consist of less than five Officers, excepting in Cases where that Number cannot be conveniently assembled, when three may be sufficient; who are likewise to determine upon the Sentence by the Majority of Voices; which Sentence is to be confirmed by the commanding Officer, not being a Member of the Court-Martial.

ART. 38. Every Officer, commanding in any Fort, Castle, or Barrack, or elsewhere, where the Corps under his Command consists of Detachments from different Regiments, or of independent Companies, may assemble Courts-Martial for the Trial of Offenders in the same Manner as if they were regimental, whose Sentence is not to be executed till it shall be confirmed by the said commanding Officer.

ART. 39. No Person whosoever shall use menacing Words, Signs or Gestures in the Presence of a Court-Martial then setting, or shall cause any Disorder or Riot, so as to disturb their Proceedings, on the Penalty of being Punished at the Discretion of the said Court-Martial.

ART. 40. To the End that Offenders may be brought to Justice; whenever any Officer or Soldier shall commit a Crime deserving Punishment, he shall by his commanding Officer, if an Officer, be put in Arrest; if a non-commissioned Officer or Soldier, be imprisoned till he shall be either tried by a Court-Martial, or shall be lawfully discharged by proper Authority.

ART. 41. No Officer or Soldier who shall be put in Arrest, or Imprisonment, shall continue in his Confinement more than eight Days, or till such Time as a Court-Martial can be conveniently assembled.

ART. 42. No Officer commanding a Guard, or Provost-Marshal, shall refuse to receive or keep any Prisoner committed to his Charge, by an Officer belonging to the Massachusetts Forces; which Officer shall at the same Time deliver an Account in Writing, signed by himself, of the Crime with which the said Prisoner is charged.

ART 43. No Officer commanding a Guard, or Provost-Marshal, shall presume to release any Prisoner committed to his Charge, without proper Authority for so doing; nor shall he suffer any Prisoner to escape, on the Penalty of being punished for it, by the Sentence of a general Court-Martial.

ART. 44. Every Officer or a Provost-Marshal, to whose Charge Prisoners shall be committed, is hereby required, within twenty-four Hours after such Commitment, or as soon as he shall be relieved from his Guard, to give in Writing to the Colonel of the Regiment to whom the Prisoner belongs (where the Prisoner is confined upon the Guard belonging to the said Regiment, and that his Offence only relates to the Neglect of Duty in his own Corps) or to the Commander in Chief, their Names, their Crimes, and the Names of the Officers who commanded them, on the Penalty of being punished for his Disobedience or Neglect, at the Discretion of a general Court-Martial.

ART. 45. And if any Officer under Arrest shall leave his Confinement before he is set at Liberty by the Officer who confined him, or by a superior Power, he shall be cashiered for it.

ART. 46. Whatsoever commissioned Officer shall be convicted before a general Court-Martial, of behaving in a scandalous, infamous Manner, such as is unbecoming the Character of an Officer and a Gentleman, shall be discharged from the Service.

ART. 47. All Officers, Conductors, Gunners, Matrosses, Drivers, or any other Persons whatsoever, receiving Pay or Hire, in the Service of the Massachusetts Artillery, shall be governed by the aforesaid Rules and Articles, and shall be subject to be tried by Courts-Martial, in like manner with the Officers and Soldiers of the Massachusetts Troops.

ART. 48. For Differences arising amongst themselves, or in Matters relating solely to their own Corps, the Courts-Martial may be comprised of their own Officers; but where a Number sufficient of such Officers cannot be assembled, or in Matters wherein other Corps are interested, the Officers of Artillery shall sit in Courts-Martial with the Officers of the other Corps.

ART. 49. All Crimes not capital, and all Disorders and Neglects which Officers and Soldiers may be guilty of, to the Prejudice of good Order and Military Discipline, though not mentioned in the Articles of War, are to be taken Cognizance of by a general or regimental Court-Martial, according to the Nature and Degree of the Offence, and be punished at their Discretion.

ART. 50. No Courts-Martial shall order any Offender to be whipped, or receive, more than thirty-nine Stripes for any one Offence.

ART. 51. The Field Officers of each and every Regiment are to appoint some suitable Person belonging to such Regiment, to receive all such Fines as may arise within the same, for any Breach of any of the foregoing Articles, and shall direct the same to be carefully and properly applied to the Relief of such sick, wounded, or necessitous Soldiers, as belong to such Regiments; and such Person shall account with such Officer for all Fines received, and the Application thereof.

ART. 52. All Members setting in Courts-Martial shall be sworn by the President of said Courts, which President shall himself be sworn by the Officer in said Court next in Rank: — The Oath to be administered previous to their proceeding to the Trial of any Offender, in Form following, viz.

"*You A B swear that you will well and truly try, and impartially determine the Cause of the Prisoner now to be tried, according to the Rules for regulating the Massachusetts Army. So help you God.*"

ART. 53. All Persons called to give Evidence, in any Case, before a Court-Martial, who shall refuse to give Evidence, shall be punished for such Refusal, at the Discretion of such Court-Martial: The Oath to be administered in the Form following, viz.

"*You swear the Evidence you shall give in the Case now in hearing, shall be the Truth, the whole Truth, and nothing but the Truth. So help you God.*"

Signed by Order of the Provincial Congress,
John Hancock, President.

A true Extract from the Minutes,
Benjamin Lincoln, Secretary.

We have already seen that the Second Provincial Congress on April 23rd 1775, voted that an army of 30,000 men be raised, and that Massachusetts raise 13,600 as her share. April 26, 1775. (Journal, p. 152) voted that the companies in each regiment be reduced from 100 men to 59, including three officers, one captain, two subalterns; and that each regiment be reduced to ten of these companies.

Oct. 27, 1774, Congress chose three general officers; viz., Jedediah Preble, Artemas Ward and Seth Pomeroy. Feb. 9, 1775, they chose the same and added John Thomas and William Heath. Feb. 15th, they added John Whitcomb. Gen. Preble, owing to age and infirmities, declined the command, and the position devolved upon Gen. Ward, who acted in this capacity April 20th, 1775 and thereafter, although not commissioned as General and Commander-in-chief of the Massachusetts forces till May 19th, 1775.

June 14, 1775. (Journal, p. 333) John Whitcomb was chosen "first major-general of the Massachusetts Army," and Joseph Warren "second major-general of the Massachusetts Army."

"The Second Continental Congress assembled at Philadelphia May 10th, 1775, adopted, on the motion of John Adams, the army besieging Boston, and voted to raise ten companies of riflemen in Pennsylvania, Maryland & Virginia. This was the origin of the far-famed continental army" (Frothingham, p. 214). Four major-generals were appointed, Ward, Lee, Schuyler and Putnam; and eight brigadier-generals, Pomeroy, Montgomery, Wooster, Heath, Spencer, Thomas, Sullivan and Green; with Gates as adjutant-general. Washington was chosen commander-in-chief, June 15th, 1775, and assumed command in Cambridge, July 3rd.

It will be thus seen that strictly speaking the troops who fought at Bunker Hill were part of the Continental Army. The Committee of Safety in their official account of the battle, dated July 25th, 1775, term our troops "the New England army," and this form has been inscribed on our Tablets, as pointing out the correct, popular idea, that our troops acted on that day in behalf of their respective provinces, not being aware of the action taken three days before at Philadelphia. It will be noticed that our Articles of War were

APPENDIX G.

for the Massachusetts Army, and that Warren's rank was major-general in that army.

I cannot close this account of our troops more appropriately than by the following quotation from a letter of Elbridge Gerry, dated Oct. 9, 1775, and cited by Frothingham (p. 265), as it shows the pre-eminent position which Massachusetts claims in the first armed resistance to British authority.

"Let it be remembered that the first attack was made on this colony; that we had to keep a regular force, without the support of regular government; that we had to support in the field from 12 to 14,000 men, when the whole forces voted by the other New England governments amounted to 8,560 only. That New Hampshire found it impracticable to support its own troops at so short a notice, and was for a considerable time supplied with provisions from this province. That after we had ransacked the seaports, and obtained all that was not wanted for their support, and had stopped two cargoes of flour owned in Boston, it was found that all the pork and grain in the government would not more than supply the inhabitants and the army until the new crops came in; and that there was no way left, unassisted as we were by the continent or any other colony, — for we never had a barrel of continental flour to supply the army, — but to write a circular letter to every town in the counties of Worcester, Hampshire and Berkshire, desiring them in the most pressing terms to send in provisions, and engaging that the inhabitants should be allowed the customary price in their respective towns, and the teamsters the usual rate for carting. But for this measure, the forces of this colony and New Hampshire must have been dispersed."

Finally, let me recite here the glowing words of Alexander H. Everett, at the Celebration of June 17, 1836.

"Yes, fellow-citizens and friends! when our neighboring metropolis and her sister cities shall have had their day of power, prosperity and glory, and passed away; when Boston, New York and Philadelphia shall have been what Rome, Athens, Memphis and Babylon at their proudest period never were, and shall have sunk again, in conformity with the immutable law that regulates all human things, into the state of ruin in which those celebrated seats of empire are now; when of all the achievements of art and wealth that now surround us, or may hereafter adorn this neighborhood, the hand of Time shall have swept away everything excepting that simple granite obelisk, which will probably outlast all the structures it is destined to overlook; even then, at that remote period, the friends of liberty and virtue will come up from the bosom of distant lands, peopled by nations as yet without a name, over intervening oceans and continents, — from the shores perhaps of Australasia, Felix Boothia, or wherever else the genius of civilization may have fixed his temporary abode, — to pay their vows on Bunker Hill."

www.ingramcontent.com/pod-product-compliance
Lightning Source LLC
Chambersburg PA
CBHW031903220426
43663CB00006B/746